MEXICAN COSTUME

MEXICAN

COSTUME

CHLOË SAYER

A Colonnade Book

Published by British Museum Publications

Colonnade Books
are published by British Museum Publications Ltd
and are offered as contributions to the enjoyment, study
and understanding of art, archaeology and history

The same publishers also produce the official
publications of the British Museum

© 1985 Chloë Sayer

Published by British Museum Publications Ltd
46 Bloomsbury Street, London WC1B 3QQ

British Library Cataloguing in Publication Data
Sayer, Chloë
    Mexican costume.
    1. Costume — Mexico — History
    I. Title
391'.00972   GT625

ISBN 0-7141-8031-9

Designed by Harry Green

Set in Monophoto Photina
and printed in Great Britain by
Jolly & Barber Ltd, Rugby, Warwickshire

Page 1 Pottery figurine of a woman from Teotihuacán
with a wrap-around skirt. Museo Nacional de
Antropología, Mexico.

Pages 2–3 Lithograph from *Mexico y sus alredores*,
1855–6, showing Indians carrying their wares from
Tacubaya to Chapultepec.

Contents

Acknowledgements

I should like to thank the Museum of Mankind, the Pitt Rivers Museum and the Victoria and Albert Museum for help during my research. Elizabeth Carmichael went through the text with great care and thoroughness, and made many valuable suggestions. Patricia Anawalt, Fructuoso Irigoyen and Campbell W. Pennington have generously offered information. The Natural History Museum and Royal Botanic Gardens, Kew, have answered several queries.

I am indebted to David Lavender for unstinting help with photography, and to Ava Vargas for the use of his photographs. I should also like to thank Elia Gutiérrez and Lucila and Rafael Múzquiz for their encouragement, and Ruth D. Lechuga for her help and advice over many years. I should like to dedicate this book to the memory of the late Marcos Ortiz, whose photographs also appear.

In addition, the author and publishers are grateful to the following institutions and individuals for permission to reproduce photographs and line drawings:

Photographs
Archivo Histórico Fotográfico (INAH), Pachuca 116, 117, 197, 219; British Library 52 (both), 53 (both), 96–7, 101, 113 (bottom), 114; Trustees of the British Museum 12–13, 25, 27, 32, 49, 50, 71, 76–7, 98 (bottom), 112–13 (top), 137, 180, 215, 224–5; Colegios de Tepotzotlán 89; Raúl Kamffer 105; David Lavender 18, 47, 54, 55, 56, 57, 63, 64, 67, 72, 73, 86, 87, 100, 103, 115 (both), 125, 128, 147, 149 (top), 150, 152, 154–5, 158, 170, 173, 179, 187, 191, 213, 222, 227; Museo Nacional de Antropología, México 19, 21, 23, 34 (both), 36, 38, 40, 42, 44, 70, 72; Museo Nacional de Historia, Chapultepec Castle, México 92; Marcos Ortiz 8, 58, 59, 60 (both), 131 (top), 142 (bottom), 153, 161, 172, 174, 175, 177 (right), 178, 188, 195 (top), 205, 207, 220; Parham Park, W. Sussex, courtesy of Mrs P. A. Tritton (photographs D. W. Gardiner) 51, 107; Pitt Rivers Museum, University of Oxford (photographs Elsie McDougall) 141 (top), 182; Christian Rasmussen 226; Southwest Museum, Los Angeles 14; Ava Vargas 145, 167, 168, 201, 206–7; Victoria and Albert Museum, London 74–5, 82, 84, 85, 88, 94.

Line drawings
Designs from Pre-Columbian Mexico, Jorge Enciso, Dover Publications, Inc., 1971 20; *Pre-Hispanic Mexican Stamp Designs*, Frederick Field, Dover Publications, Inc., 1974 46; *The Sculptures of El Tajín, Veracruz, Mexico*, Michael Edwin Kampen, University of Florida Press, 1972 23; David Lavender 17, 232; Pitt Rivers Museum, University of Oxford, Elsie McDougall 182; *The Ancient Maya*, 3rd edn, Sylvanus Griswold Morley, rev. by George W. Brainerd © 1946, 1947 and 1956, Stanford University Press and the Board of Trustees of the Leland Stanford Junior University 28, 31, 37.

Photographs and drawings on the following pages are the author's copyright: 21 (top), 62, 118–19, 120–1, 127, 131 (bottom), 141 (bottom), 142 (top), 144, 149 (bottom), 162, 163, 164, 165, 166, 169, 171, 176, 177 (left), 192–3, 195 (bottom), 208, 211, 212, 214, 229, 231, 233, 234.

Chronology

PRE-CONQUEST MEXICO

PERIODS:	EARLY PRE-CLASSIC 1500 BC–1000 BC	MIDDLE PRE-CLASSIC 1000 BC–300 BC	LATE PRE-CLASSIC 300 BC–AD 300	EARLY CLASSIC AD 300–AD 600	LATE CLASSIC AD 600–AD 900	EARLY POST-CLASSIC AD 900–AD 1200	LATE POST-CLASSIC AD 1200–AD 1519
CENTRAL HIGHLANDS	Tehuacán Valley potsherd with textile imprint 1500–900 BC	Tehuacán Valley woven textile fragment 900–200 BC		Teotihuacán civilisation: influence spreads through Middle America		Toltec rule and the creation of Tula, abandoned c.1168	Aztec enter the Valley of Mexico c.1247. Growth of the Aztec empire 1426–1519
		Farming settlements at Tlatilco, Zacatenco, Cuicuilco and Copilco c.1500 BC–AD 100				Xochicalco founded c.800	
GULF COAST		Olmec civilisation at La Venta and other sites c.1000–400 BC. Olmec influence spreads across Middle America			Peak activity at the Classic Veracruz site of El Tajín		
				Production of figurines at Remojadas			
OAXACA			Monte Albán, phase I	Monte Albán, phase II	Monte Albán enlarged by the Zapotec	Monte Albán occupied by the Mixtec	
MAYA AREA				Maya civilisation at its height: sites at Palenque, Bonampak and Yaxchilán; shift northwards to the Yucatán Peninsula		Arrival of Toltec 987 Importance of Chichén Itzá and Mayapán. Maya civilisation in decline	

The Archaic period, not shown here, preceded the Early Pre-Classic period.

POST-CONQUEST MEXICO

1519 Arrival of Cortés	1864 Maximilian becomes Emperor of Mexico
1521 Fall of the Aztec empire	1867 Maximilian executed. Juárez re-elected as President
1528–1535 Mexico ruled by royal *Audiencia*	1876–1911 Presidency of Porfirio Díaz
1535 Arrival of Mendoza, Mexico's first viceroy	1910–1920 Mexican Revolution
1767 Jesuits expelled	1917 New constitution drafted
1810 Hidalgo executed	1920 Obregón becomes President
1821 The *Plan de Iguala* proclaims Mexico's independence from Spain	1921–1940 Reformist period
1824 Creation of federal republic	1929 Creation of the PRI (Partido Revolucionario Institucional)
1845 Texas joins USA	
1847 US forces invade Mexico City	1938 Oil fields, mines and natural resources declared property of the nation
1848 Mexico sells northern territories by treaty to USA	
1857 Benito Juárez becomes President. Separation of Church and State	1948 Creation of the INI (Instituto Nacional Indigenista)
1862 French forces invade demanding payment of debts	

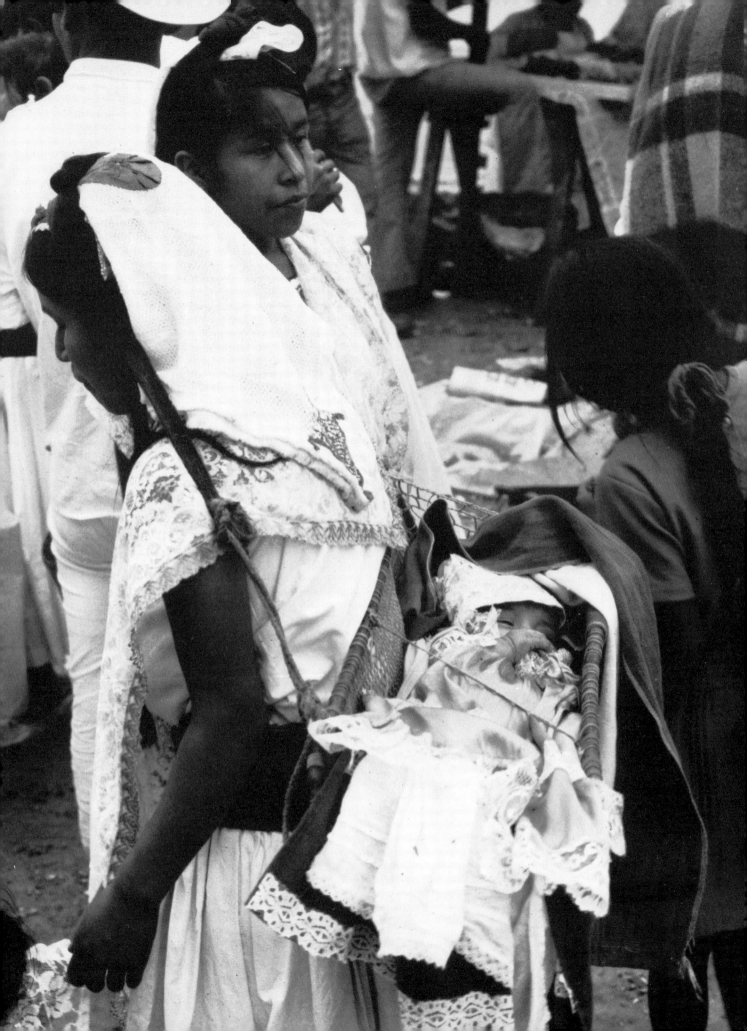

Introduction

Contemporary Indian dress frequently combines ancient and modern elements. This Nahua woman from Cuetzalán, Puebla, wears a *quechquémitl*, or pre-Conquest torso-garment, of factory lace. On her head she wears a second *quechquémitl*: gauze-woven from shop-bought thread on a backstrap loom, it features an appliquéd rosette. The baby is carried by tump-line in a netted basket with a wooden frame.

In ancient Mexico costume differences not only set the rich and powerful apart from the poor; they also indicated the wearer's cultural group and place of origin. Today there are still over fifty different Indian peoples living in Mexico, many of whom have kept to a particular style of dress, with variations to distinguish each village within a community. This sort of traditionalism has become increasingly rare in most areas of the world, as is shown by the widespread adoption of business suits, T-shirts and blue jeans. It is hardly surprising, therefore, that when tourists from Europe and the USA visit the remoter parts of Mexico they are impressed by the sight of Indian villagers wearing elaborately woven or embroidered clothing in their everyday lives.

Mexico's widely varying geography has contributed greatly to the sense of independence felt by many such peoples. It has also fostered an extensive range of dress styles, which have evolved to suit environmental and climatic conditions. A land of contrasts, Mexico is made up of fertile valleys, tropical lowland forests, arid deserts, high mountain peaks and deep canyons which together cover about 761,600 square miles. In the north her widest extremity forms a border with the USA, while to the south-east lie Guatemala and Belize. Two long coastlines are formed by the Pacific Ocean in the west and by the Gulf of Mexico with the Caribbean Sea in the east. Vegetation and climate depend upon altitude, for in the interior land rises to heights of more than two miles along the ranges of the Sierra Madre.

Set in a valley on the *altiplano*, or central plateau, lies the Mexican capital. Built where the ancient Aztec city of Tenochtitlan once stood, it is now one of the largest and most modern cities in the world. With a fast-growing population that already exceeds sixteen million, Mexico City is the political, cultural and economic hub of the nation. Further north lie other large cities, such as Guadalajara and Monterrey, which also house large populations and where industry thrives in support of the national economy. In all these urban landscapes shop-window dummies display up-to-the-minute fashions which differ little from those seen in London or New York.

Nevertheless, despite the lure of towns and cities, over half Mexico's 76.8 million inhabitants still live in rural areas and work the land. Highways and networks of smaller roads are being built each year to connect different parts of the country, but the ruggedness of the landscape remains a major obstacle to modernisation. Even today there are regions which have barely been mapped out. Many communities, which lie no more than ten or twenty miles apart as the crow flies, are cut off from one another by almost impassable peaks and crevasses. This is why it is possible to conceive of Mexico as a split nation. A villager who comes down from the Guerrero mountains to sell handicrafts in a sophisticated coastal resort such as Acapulco often feels like a foreigner in the midst of his own countrymen. Similarly, Mexicans from the cities, once they leave the tarmac of the highways, can feel like strangers in the remoter areas of their country. Between Mexico's modern towns and her many isolated villages lies a gulf not only of miles but often of years.

It has proved hard to obtain reliable census figures in such rugged and inaccessible regions, but present estimates put Mexico's indigenous population at around six million. Costume, language, dance and craft techniques all serve to unite members of different groups, and to link present generations with their ancestors. Time cannot stand still, however, even among those most resistant to change: there are plans for building new roads which will penetrate further into the interior; radio and television are spreading year by year; and the development of oil-wells is affecting the way of life in large areas along the Bay of Campeche and in the states of Tabasco and Chiapas.

For many Indian peoples the pressure for change is likely to prove stronger over the next decade than in the four and a half centuries which have elapsed since the Spanish Conquest. Research has indicated that when Indians are in a state of transition, and are being absorbed into the national culture, costume is often one of the first aspects of

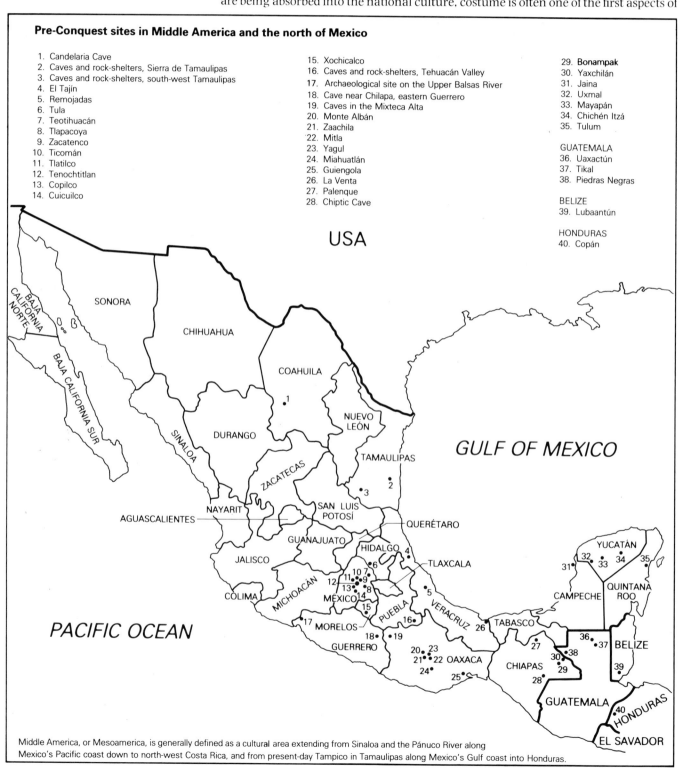

Pre-Conquest sites in Middle America and the north of Mexico

1. Candelaria Cave
2. Caves and rock-shelters, Sierra de Tamaulipas
3. Caves and rock-shelters, south-west Tamaulipas
4. El Tajín
5. Remojadas
6. Tula
7. Teotihuacán
8. Tlapacoya
9. Zacatenco
10. Ticomán
11. Tlatilco
12. Tenochtitlan
13. Copilco
14. Cuicuilco

15. Xochicalco
16. Caves and rock-shelters, Tehuacán Valley
17. Archaeological site on the Upper Balsas River
18. Cave near Chilapa, eastern Guerrero
19. Caves in the Mixteca Alta
20. Monte Albán
21. Zaachila
22. Mitla
23. Yagul
24. Miahuatlán
25. Guiengola
26. La Venta
27. Palenque
28. Chiptic Cave

29. **Bonampak**
30. Yaxchilán
31. Jaina
32. Uxmal
33. Mayapán
34. Chichén Itzá
35. Tulum

GUATEMALA
36. Uaxactún
37. Tikal
38. Piedras Negras

BELIZE
39. Lubaantún

HONDURAS
40. Copán

USA

GULF OF MEXICO

PACIFIC OCEAN

Middle America, or Mesoamerica, is generally defined as a cultural area extending from Sinaloa and the Pánuco River along Mexico's Pacific coast down to north-west Costa Rica, and from present-day Tampico in Tamaulipas along Mexico's Gulf coast into Honduras.

their own indigenous culture to disappear. In this book I have attempted to describe some of the many textile skills and styles of dress still to be found in Mexico, before factory fabrics and shop-bought clothing replace the rich and varied legacy inherited from New and Old World civilisations.

Textile centres and Indian villages in contemporary Mexico

SONORA
1. Quitovac (Papago)
2. Punta Chueca (Seri)
3. Yecora (Pima)
4. Bacavachi (Mayo)

CHIHUAHUA
5. Norogachic (Tarahumara)
6. Nabogame (Northern Tepehuan)

COAHUILA
7. Saltillo

ZACATECAS
8. Zacatecas

NAYARIT
9. Jesus María (Cora)

JALISCO
10. San Andrés Cohamiata (Huichol)
11. Tuxpan (Nahua)

SAN LUIS POTOSÍ
12. Santa María del Río
13. Cuatlamayán (Nahua)
14. Tancanhuitz (Huastec)
15. Tamaletón (Huastec)

GUANAJUATO
16. San Miguel Allende

QUERÉTARO
17. Tolimán (Otomí)
18. Vizarrón (Otomí)
19. Querétaro

HIDALGO
20. Pisaflores (Tepehua)
21. Huejutla de Reyes
22. Huautla (Nahua)
23. Zimapán (Otomí)
24. Ixmiquilpan, Mezquital Valley (Otomí)
25. Huehuetla (Tepehua)
26. Tenango de Doria (Otomí)
27. Acaxochitlán
28. Santa Ana Hueytlalpan (Otomí)

VERÁCRUZ
29. Tantoyuca (Huastec)
30. Chicontepec (Nahua)
31. Sasaltitla (Nahua)
32. Papantla (Totonac)
33. Amatlán de los Reyes (Nahua)
34. Cosoleacaque (Nahua)
35. Sayula (Popoluca)

PUEBLA
36. Mecapalapa (Totonac, Tepehua)
37. Pantepec (Totonac, Tepehua)
38. Atla (Nahua)
39. San Pablito (Otomí)
40. Huilacapixtla (Nahua)
41. Huauchinango (Nahua)
42. Coacuila (Nahua)
43. Puebla de los Angeles
44. Atlixco (Nahua)
45. Tepemaxalco (Nahua)
46. Los Reyes Metzontla (Popoloca)
47. San José Miahuatlán (Nahua)
48. San Sebastián Zinacatepec (Nahua)
49. Altepexi (Nahua)
50. Zoatecpan (Nahua)
51. Hueyapan (Nahua)
52. Cuetzalán (Nahua)

TLAXCALA
53. Ixtenco (Otomí)
54. San Bernardino Contla

MORELOS
55. Hueyapan (Nahua)
56. Tetelcingo (Nahua)

MEXICO
57. Chapa de Mota (Otomí)
58. Chinconcuac
59. San Miguel Ameyalco (Otomí)
60. Tenancingo
61. Toluca
62. Coatepec Harinas
63. Santiago Temoyaya (Otomí)
64. San Francisco de la Loma (Mazahua)

MICHOACÁN
65. Patamban (Tarascan)
66. Ocumicho (Tarascan)
67. Angahuan (Tarascan)
68. Aranza (Tarascan)
69. Cuanajo (Tarascan)
70. Pátzcuaro (Tarascan)

GUERRERO
71. San Miguel Totolapan (Cuitlatec)
72. Zitlala (Nahua)
73. Acatlán (Nahua)
74. San Miguel Metlatonoc (Mixtec)
75. Xochistlahuaca (Amuzgo)

OAXACA
76. Jamiltepec (Mixtec)
77. Pinotepa Nacional (Mixtec)
78. San Pedro Jicayán (Mixtec)
79. Pinotepa de Don Luis (Mixtec)
80. San Pedro Amuzgos (Amuzgo)
81. Ixtayutla (Tacuate)
82. Santa María Zacatepec (Tacuate)
83. San Andrés Chicahuaxtla (Trique)
84. San Mateo Peñasco (Mixtec)
85. San Sebastián Peñoles (Mixtec)
86. Teotongo (Chocho)
87. Huautla de Jiménez (Mazatec)
88. San Andrés Teotilalpan (Cuicatec)
89. San Felipe Usila (Chinantec)
90. Valle Nacional (Chinantec)
91. Mixistlán (Mixe)
92. Yalalag (Zapotec)
93. Santo Tomás Jalieza (Zapotec)
94. San Antonino Ocotlán (Zapotec)
95. Oaxaca
96. Tehuantepec (Zapotec)
97. Juchitán (Zapotec)
98. Huamelula (Chontal)
99. San Mateo del Mar (Huave)
100. Tuxtla Gutiérrez (Zoque)
101. Comitán
102. Venustiano Carranza (Tzotzil)
103. San Cristóbal de las Casas
104. San Juan Chamula (Tzotzil)
105. Magdalenas (Tzotzil)
106. Tenejapa (Tzeltal)
107. Santo Tomás Oxchuc (Tzeltal)
108. Las Margaritas (Tojolabal)
109. Lacanjá (Lacandón)
110. Najá (Lacandón)

YUCATÁN
111. Xocen (Maya)

Many of the places described here as Indian are also inhabited by *mestizos*.

Extended view of a Classic-period Maya
polychrome vessel from Nebaj,
Guatemala, showing a chief receiving
offerings. Museum of Mankind, London.

PART I

COSTUME BEFORE
THE CONQUEST

1 Central Mexico, the Gulf Coast and the Maya

Classic Veracruz figurine of painted clay from El Tajín showing a mother with her child. She wears necklaces, ear-plugs, an elaborate head-dress and a rounded *quechquémitl* over a wrap-around skirt. Southwest Museum, Los Angeles.

Unfortunately for the study of early Mexican costume, adverse climatic conditions have meant that few pre-Hispanic textiles have survived. The organic composition of cloth makes it a highly perishable substance, vulnerable to bacteria and fungus. Excesses of heat and damp, in conjunction with acid or alkaline soils, have tended in most regions to accelerate the process of decay; yet, despite these hazards, some vestiges have been recovered, and their very rarity makes these finds among the most exciting in the field of archaeology. Two factors have contributed principally to their preservation – the dry caves, often used as burial sites, that sheltered them, and the presence in many cases of copper artefacts such as bells. The corrosive properties of copper, acting as a sterilising agent, served over the centuries to stave off mould and bacteria. A major source for textile remains, however, has proved to be the sacred well at Chichén Itzá, used by the ancient Maya for sacrifice and for making offerings to the gods. Carbonised fragments of cloth have been brought up from its depths, where thick mud had encased and preserved them.

With a very small number of noteworthy exceptions the examples so far excavated are only fragments which give little indication as to the size, shape or function of the original garment. However, even these, when carefully analysed, can give some insight into the fibres, dyes and weaving techniques that were used. The offerings and grave-goods that accompany these textile remains also play an important part, for they help archaeologists to establish dates and to chart the advance of weaving skills in Mexico.

Unfortunately, cloth specimens have not always been accorded this same importance. In the past archaeologists have tended to discard textile fragments and have concentrated on more durable and better-preserved aspects of past cultures. The first means employed by early Indian peoples to represent the human being was the modelling in clay of tiny figurines, some only a few inches high. Thousands of these have survived to give us an idea of the costume – or its lack – which was current over 3,000 years ago. As styles of dress evolved, so too did the art of sculpture, culminating in elaborate stone carvings both in relief and in the round. Although many are highly stylised, with little emphasis on detail, some are remarkably naturalistic and suggest not only the garments worn but even the design motifs of the fabric.

Large numbers of these pottery and stone figures were originally painted, but in most cases the colouring has almost totally disappeared. Polychrome vessels, however, give us an idea of the range of colours employed. Mural paintings show still more clearly the use of colour and the evolution in styles of dress for the later periods. Excavations and chance discovery have revealed mural paintings of great splendour, many done in true fresco. As with sculpture or painted vessels the human figure is often stylised, but large-scale representation allows for greater attention to detail.

The task of reconstructing the costumes of ancient Mexico is further advanced by a small number of codices, or pictorial manuscripts, the principal examples known to date being either Maya, Mixtec or Aztec. Painted on deerskin, bark paper, or more rarely agave paper, most were folded concertina-fashion and dealt with such subjects as astrology, history, genealogy, mythology, prophesy and ritual. Costumed figures were outlined in black, usually against a gesso background, and shown in profile according to the conventions of the period; dress and decorations were, however, often drawn frontally. Gods, priests, rulers and warriors in colourful regalia are among the characters portrayed (see p. 50).

In addition to these visual resources there are many references to costume and textile skills in Spanish records of the Colonial period. Administrative reports, termed *Relaciones geográficas*, were compiled in response to a questionnaire formulated in 1577 by order of Philip II. Question 15 gave rise to much valuable information, for it related to the life of the Indians and asked for a description of 'their former and present manner of dressing'. Clerics and soldiers such as Fray Diego Durán, Bishop Diego de Landa and Bernal Díaz del Castillo also wrote about prevailing customs and beliefs around the time of the Conquest. The most thorough study of indigenous life was undoubtably that of Fray Bernardino de Sahagún. With the help of learned Indian informants he compiled a major work in Náhuatl (the Aztec language) with copious illustrations. Originally entitled *Historia general de las cosas de Nueva España*, or 'General history of the things of New Spain', it has become known as the Codex Florentino after the city where it is now preserved.

These chroniclers were writing as observers of an alien culture, and it is their freshness of vision that makes their accounts so vivid and evocative, as they passionately decry the 'savage' and pagan customs of the Mexican Indians, only to give way a few lines later to praise and amazement at the achievements of these peoples of the New World. Although there remain many areas for speculation, these historical reports offer modern scholars a wealth of information compared with the purely archaeological data for earlier periods.

It is widely accepted that the first immigrants to the New World arrived from Asia across the Bering Straits some 20,000 to 40,000 years ago, crossing from Siberia to Alaska. Gradually they fanned out across North, Central and South America, and over long periods of time separate cultures developed without any proven outside influence until the arrival of the Spaniards in the sixteenth century. These first Americans were nomads, hunting animals and gathering wild plants for food. Even after the Conquest there were still groups of semi-nomadic Indians in northern Mexico; their clothing, according to Spanish descriptions quoted by William B. Griffen, consisted largely of animal skins and their ornaments of shells, feathers and bones.

Some time between 7000 and 5000 BC incipient forms of agriculture were evident, culminating in the domestication of wild maize plants, and from about 1500 BC small farming communities began to develop, ensured of a regular supply of food. Much valuable information about the evolution of craft techniques during both the Archaic and the Pre-Classic periods (see Chronology, p. 7) has been gained from excavations carried out by Richard S. MacNeish in the dry caves of the Tehuacán Valley in southeastern Puebla. These rock-shelters were in a state of continuous occupation from before 6500 BC until the Conquest. Among the artefacts left by seasonally nomadic hunters were scrapers for cleaning skins and needles of polished bone or antler. Other pre-ceramic finds, dated to between 6500 and 4800 BC, include the remains of basketry, cordage, twining and netting.

The importance of these last two skills is confirmed by textile specimens from sites in northern Mexico. Worked without a loom, netting relies on a single element which is looped or knotted in a variety of ways to create often large areas of fabric with an open-meshed or compact appearance. By using coloured strands occupants of the Candelaria Cave in Coahuila were able to construct patterns of great intricacy and refinement. Twining, unlike netting, requires two elements; these are interlaced by hand, hence the term 'finger weaving' which is also applied to this technique. Examples from Tehuacán and other sites include sandals, pieces of matting and textile fragments, but achievements seem never to have equalled the famous and richly

Right (top) Twining. Two or more weft threads are twisted around each other to enclose one or more warp threads. There are many variations on this procedure which can be used to produce baskets as well as cloth. The drawing shows weft-twining with a half-twist.

Right (middle and bottom) Netting. Successive rows of pliable yarn are (*middle*) knotted or (*bottom*) looped into the preceding row to create close- or open-meshed fabric. Contemporary shoulder-bags are often netted with the aid of a frame.

Far right (top and bottom) Mat-making. This technique, also used in basketry, requires two elements to cross at right angles and may have led to loom-weaving. The lower example is checker-woven on an over-one-under-one principle, while the other is twill-woven to create diagonal patterning.

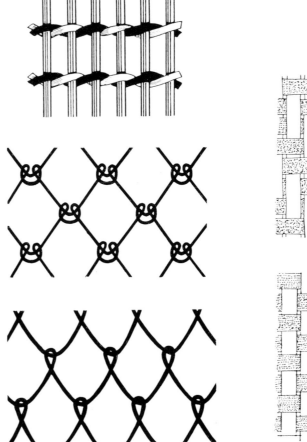

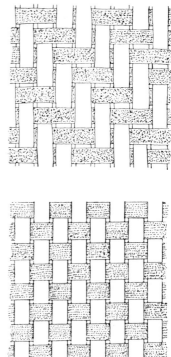

patterned Chilkat blankets which were still finger-woven until recent times on the north-west coast of the USA.

The development of both skills was closely linked with the preparation of fibres. Instead of the short lengths of often inflexible materials used for basketry, long and pliant yarns were needed, and their existence made loom-weaving possible. Various theories have been put forward suggesting that the use of the loom was introduced into Mexico from South America, but this is by no means certain, and it seems equally likely that weaving evolved independently, inspired by mat-making and similar basketry methods. At Tehuacán a potsherd bearing a textile imprint has been dated to between 1500 and 900 BC, and the oldest textile fragment to between 900 and 200 BC, while in south-western Tamaulipas loom-weaving is represented by an even earlier example from between 1800 and 1400 BC.

The technical problems of weaving have been resolved in many different ways throughout the world, resulting in a wide variety of looms. To save time and energy most advanced cultures have devised systems for supporting the warp in such a way that the threads are divided into two sets. During weaving these are raised alternately, forming a shed, or opening, for the weft to pass through. In central, southern and parts of northern Mexico this purpose was served by the *telar de cintura*, or backstrap loom, which is still employed in countless Indian villages today (see Appendix 1). The apparatus is simple, with no rigid framework, and each web generally represents a

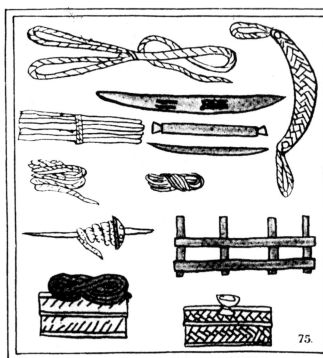

The Codex Florentino offers valuable information about pre-Conquest weaving methods. *Left* The backstrap loom. Warp threads are stretched between two horizontal bars: one is tied to a tree or post; the other is attached by a strap to the weaver who controls the tension of the warps with her body. *Right* Spinning and weaving implements, still used by contemporary weavers (see Appendix 1).

separate warping operation. Before setting up her loom, the weaver must first wind her yarn into a figure of eight to create a cross which will ultimately form the shed. Next she must decide how many selvages her cloth is to have. By winding the warp threads directly round both loom bars, she limits herself to a textile with side selvages only. If she requires four-selvage cloth, however, then the warp skeins should be held by cords which encircle the end bars. Well-preserved textile specimens show that pre-Conquest weavers created webs with two, four and even, albeit rarely, three selvages. With textiles of the first and last type uncut warps provided looped fringes, while severed warps were knotted to prevent unravelling.

Extremely long webs of cloth can be woven on a backstrap loom, but the width is determined by the weaver's armspan. If she requires a broader width than she can achieve with a single web, then two or more may be seamed together. The weaving process proceeds away from the weaver, who winds her newly completed cloth on to a rolling stick. A tenter is used to control the width of most webs: often made from a hollow reed, it is stretched across the underside of the weaving and held in place by thorns. It is common practice, when starting a four-selvage web, to complete a short section at one end called a heading. The loom is then reversed and the weaving begun again at the opposite end. This custom not only regulates the width of cloth by securing the spacing of the warps but also prevents them from tangling. When the weaving is nearly completed, the space which remains between the heading and the main section becomes too small to receive the batten or a narrower substitute, and weavers often employ a comb to push back the weft threads. Examples of weaving combs found in archaeological excavations suggest that this practice is extremely ancient.

Although the backstrap loom was widely employed throughout Middle America, some northern communities evolved a loom of a different type. Still in use today, it is

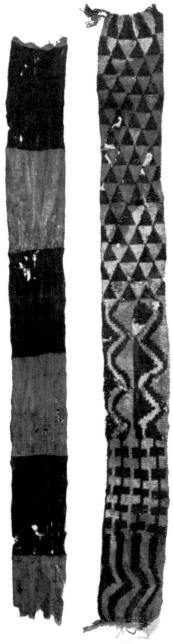

Two narrow strips of cloth, probably headbands, from Candelaria Cave, Coahuila, made by the *Laguneros*, or lagoon-dwellers, and dated to between AD 1000 and 1600. *Right* knotless netting, worked with two-ply, z-twisted *lechuguilla*. Undyed strands were combined with dark brown strands to create complex designs. L. 50¾ in (129 cm). *Left* plain-woven, probably on a backstrap loom, from yucca. The alternating undyed, rust and dark brown areas were achieved by end-to-end warp locking (see Appendix 2). L. 48 in (122 cm). Museo Nacional de Antropología, Mexico.

horizontal and stationary, and consists of two beams lashed to two logs or four posts near ground level (see p. 145). The warp threads, which eventually form a continuous web, are severed, leaving the cloth with side selvages and a fringe at each end. References to this type of loom occur in early Spanish records, and it has been suggested by Lila O'Neale that pre-Hispanic textile remains from Chihuahua were woven in this way, because their unusual width puts them beyond the span of the backstrap loom. Unfortunately, most textile finds are too fragmentary to allow for this type of speculation.

Mexico's varied geography and climate foster a wide variety of trees, shrubs and plants, many of which provided early communities with strong and flexible fibres for weaving. These fall into three categories, the first comprising leaf fibres from monocotyledonous plants. Generally termed 'hard', these fibres are for the most part long, white and smooth. The Mexican agave, popularly called *maguey*, flourishes in semi-desert regions and includes some 200 species. *Agave sisalana* produces sisal, while the fibres from *Agave lecheguilla* and *Agave zapupe* are sometimes referred to as *lechuguilla* and *zapupe*. Often, however, agave fibres are simply known as *ixtle*, *pita* or *henequén*, irrespective of species. In northern zones yarns were also derived from the leaves of *Yucca carnerosana* and *Yucca treculeana*, and from *Samuela carnerosana*, popularly known as *palma ixtle*.

In the second category were the resilient bast filaments obtained from the fibrous inner barks of dicotyledonous plants. Many species grow only in certain areas, so their use would have been confined to local communities. Examples of cloth woven from *Apocynum cannabinum* have been excavated in Chihuahua, while the use of *Urtica caracasana* was described soon after the Conquest by Francisco Hernández in his *Historia de las plantas de Nueva España*. Referred to by him as a type of stinging nettle, it was known by the Aztec as *tzitzicatzli*, which in modern spelling gives *chichicastle*.

Seed-pod fibres make up the third category. There are various species capable of producing downy fibres, but none are as long and serviceable as cotton. It is generally accepted that American cotton, or *Gossypium hirsutum*, is indigenous to the Old World, together with the toffee-brown strain referred to as *Gossypium mexicanum*. Fragments of a white cotton boll excavated at Tehuacán have been dated to around 5800 BC, and cotton was used to weave the earliest cloth specimen found at the site. Several later weavings feature non-cotton yarns, but in parts of the north where the climate was ill-suited to cotton inhabitants derived their yarns solely from leaf and bast fibres. Rare examples of cotton cloth found at northern sites were almost certainly obtained through trade.

Dry conditions in the Candelaria Cave, Coahuila, have preserved not just netted textiles of *lechuguilla* but also loom-weavings made from yucca, and it is surprising to note that their firm and even yarns were probably hand-twisted. This method, current at other northern sites, was achieved by rolling the fibres on the leg. To the south twine for netting was also hand-twisted – as it still is today in some Indian villages – but cotton was spun with the aid of a spindle. It is clear that even in early times weavers knew how to vary the texture of cloth by s- or z-twisting their yarns, and by alternating loosely spun with tightly spun yarns. These were used singly and doubly, but three- and four-ply yarns were sometimes preferred for added strength when seaming webs together.

The advancement of textile skills on the *altiplano* may be guessed at from costume details displayed by a multitude of clay figurines found at farming settlements such as

Mixtec spinner from the Codex
Vindobonensis. A contemporary spinner
appears on p. 131.

Tlatilco, Zacatenco, Cuicuilco and Copilco. The span of occupation at these sites ran
from approximately 1500 BC to AD 100. Figurines of the earliest periods are mostly
female and portray an almost total lack of clothing. They concentrate instead on necklaces, amulets and ear-plugs, and show a wide variety of head-dresses and coiffures.
Faces, bodies and hair are often adorned with red and yellow paint, while certain
forms of patterning suggest tattooing.

The gradual evolution of costume in the region is reflected in the range of slightly
later figurines representing both sexes. Women were portrayed first with *cache-sexes*
(colloquially 'gee-strings'), some featuring side cords of beads, and later with skirts.
The shortest examples resembled simple hip-bands, but knee- and ankle-length styles
were frequently shown. So too were flared skirts; apparently worn by both men and
women who may represent dancers, they were often accompanied by long and voluminous bloomers with a dimpled appearance, suggesting the use of seed-pods or
butterfly cocoons. These would have provided a rattling accompaniment to the dance,
as is the case in parts of northern Mexico today.

Male attire consisted more usually, however, of a head-dress and loincloth: often
this last garment was just a narrow band knotted in various ways, but two-part
loincloths were also shown with one band serving as a sash and the other passing
between the legs. Sometimes too wider bands were arranged to look like shorts. By the
Late Pre-Classic period some men had adopted a hip-length sleeveless jacket, thought
by some modern investigators to be an open-fronted *xicolli*, while women had
developed a closed shoulder-cape termed a *quechquémitl*. Another garment which seems
to have appeared around this time was a female tunic, represented with open sides.
Although it would be described today as a *huipil*, it was known to the Aztec as a *huipilli*.

There is no way of knowing what methods and materials were initially used by
Valley-settlers to fabricate their clothing. The presence of deer-bone needles and awls
for making holes points to the use of skins, and excavations at Tlapacoya have produced a piece of hide from the Late Pre-Classic era. It is also possible that netting and
twining were practised. Non-woven garments of various periods excavated in other
areas include a semicircular netted 'kilt' and the remains of a twined robe from
Tamaulipas, as well as netted headbands from Coahuila, and these skills may have
been put to similar use on the *altiplano*. The existence of weaving is confirmed, however, by the discovery of cloth at Zacatenco: dated to around 1000 BC or earlier, it
was woven from cotton yarn in one direction, and from yucca or perhaps *Samuela
carnerosana* in the other. At the neighbouring site of Ticomán a grey substance has
been found which could, it is thought, be the remains of decomposed feathers used in
the construction or decoration of a textile.

Not all village cultures progressed at the same rate, however. The refinement of
pottery and other finds at Tlatilco suggests an unusually high level of advancement,
and this may have been the result of contact with Olmec civilisation. The Olmec
people inhabited the tropical Gulf Coast lowlands of what is today southern Veracruz
and Tabasco between approximately 1000 and 400 BC. They set the pattern for the
subsequent great civilisations of Classic-period Mexico in the construction of large
ceremonial centres with temple-pyramids, ball-courts and other major architectural
features. Particularly notable were their monumental stone carvings and exquisite
lapidary work in jade. The origins of Olmec civilisation are obscure, but they seem to
have been the first people to employ a calendrical system and to develop the use of
hieroglyphic writing. In Olmec art there are rare portrayals of women with knee-

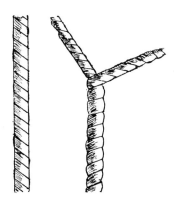

Yarn may be tightly or loosely spun. Fibres are twisted to the right or left. *Left* z-twisted yarn; *centre* s-twisted yarn (the central bar of the letter suggests the spiral of the thread); *right* two-ply yarn.

Pottery figurine of a woman from Teotihuacán with a wrap-around skirt. *Quechquémitl* frequently exhibited a curved appearance. Painted markings suggest that garments were patterned. Museo Nacional de Antropología, Mexico.

length skirts and ear-plugs. Men, when clothed, apparently wore loincloths, wide collars, pectorals, ear-plugs, armbands and tightly fitting helmets. Badly weathered relief carvings show towering head-dresses and hint tantalisingly at additional male garments such as short kilts, but it is hard to make out the details with clarity. It is widely believed that all later cultures in Middle America rest on an Olmec base, yet there is no way of evaluating their influence in costume and the textile arts.

Throughout Mexico between approximately AD 300 and 900 there occurred a cultural florescence, usually referred to by archaeologists as the Classic period. This era saw the rise of sharp divisions in society and the consolidation of an élite ruling class, together with increasing specialisation by artisans. Within this 600-year period there were great developments in architecture and the other arts, and in the use of calendrical and writing systems. Portrayed in sculpture and pottery is an elaborate pantheon with many deities representing natural forces and phenomena, showing that religious ideas too had evolved from the simpler practices of earlier times. The achievements of the age were magnificently represented at Teotihuacán, in the Valley of Mexico. Here Mexico's first truly urban civilisation flourished, incorporating terraced pyramids, plazas and so-called palaces. Colourful mural paintings, elaborately sculpted façades, stone carvings, clay figurines and fine pottery vessels reveal a high degree of artistry. It has been suggested by Michael D. Coe that their creators, the artisans, may have inhabited a tangled complex of rooms and alleyways in a particular part of the city of Tlamimilolpa. Textile-workers could have lived here too, for costume was clearly a preoccupation with Teotihuacán's rulers, who almost certainly used clothing and adornment as a way of reflecting status.

The mural paintings provide valuable information about male dress. At its simplest it consisted of a loincloth with a single end hanging down behind, but some examples show the ends falling to front and back. Also portrayed were male aprons, worn with a sash, and hip-cloths. A further range of garments included kilts, capes and voluminous tunics which may have been closed *xicolli*. The sleeveless jacket, or open-fronted *xicolli*, was also represented. Most of the personages depicted were dignitaries, priests and warriors, and it seems likely that these costume elements reflected their position in society. Although the stylisation of the murals occasionally makes it difficult to identify all the details of dress, many garments appear to be decoratively finished with fringes and feathers. Head-dresses were varied, often emulating animals and birds, and exhibiting a profusion of exotic plumes. High-backed sandals were frequently shown, together with necklaces, bracelets and ear-plugs, to which dangling adornments were sometimes added. Female dress is best illustrated by a quantity of figurines featuring wrap-around skirts and closed shoulder-capes, or *quechquémitl*, worn with necklaces, ear-plugs and head-dresses of often imposing dimensions. Only a few traces of paint remain, but it is probable that women dressed as colourfully as men, and that weavers had acquired a knowledge of dyeing methods.

It was customary at Teotihuacán to cremate the dead, and archaeologists have recovered several fragments of cloth from burials. Their charred state precludes the study of colouring and decorative techniques, but analysis has revealed the use of bast fibres and cotton. According to the investigator Elizabeth Strömberg, cotton remains from Tlamimilolpa give 'the impression of a highly developed art of spinning and weaving', with one specimen attaining a 'gossamer thinness', and another ribbed example displaying an 'irreproachable evenness'. Most Pre-Classic finds had been plain-woven on an over-one-under-one principle, but archaeological sites of the Classic era have yielded proof of additional weaving styles. One piece of cloth from Tlamimilolpa is thought to represent tapestry weaving with interlocking wefts, although the threads could also be interpreted as end-to-end locking warps (see Appendix 2). No doubt attaches to the presence of compound twill, however.

Woven remains from other sites cast still more light on the evolution of loom techniques in Mexico. Excavations in La Perra Cave have produced two two-and-two twilled cloths, proving that the technique was already current by 300 BC in the Sierra de Tamaulipas, while textile specimens from the Tehuacán Valley confirm the existence of basket and semi-basket weaves in the region after 200 BC. Both methods are variants on plain weaving, and are less elaborate than twill, so it seems likely that they were also employed at Teotihuacán. Additional information is supplied by one of two mummy blankets from Tehuacán. Virtually intact and dated to between 200 BC and AD 700, the outer blanket displays warp stripes in several colours; prepared during warping, this pattern indicates the use of pre-dyed yarns. Along one loop-fringed end weft-cording has been employed: this procedure, which serves to create ridges in the cloth, depends on the insertion of several weft strands through a single shed. To compensate for the lack of an end-selvage the weaver has also provided the blanket with a twined end-border while it was on the loom.

Non-woven finds from both Tehuacán and Tlamimilolpa include numerous examples of cloth made from the beaten inner bark of wild fig trees of the genus *Ficus.* Specimens from the second site are charred fragments, but from Tehuacán come a variety of narrow strips, a black-dyed cloth, a large 'blanket', several miniature sandals and also bark-beaters. Irmgard W. Johnson states that 'the beaten fibres have a thin meshlike quality, somewhat like cheesecloth or mosquito netting, which could only mean that they were used as cloth and not as paper'. It seems certain that bark cloth had a ceremonial importance, and that it was used to make offerings to the gods, but it may also have provided articles of clothing or adornment. Although, according to Carmen Cook de Leonard, no samples of leather have been reported for the Classic period, it was probably employed at Teotihuacán for sandals and head-dresses.

Separate regions in Mexico appear to have been linked by trade routes since early times, and this exchange of produce promoted the spread of ideas and technical advances. Teotihuacán's influence affected the whole of Middle America and was widely felt on the hot and humid Gulf Coast, yet the art style of that area remained highly distinctive. At Remojadas and neighbouring sites in central Veracruz potters fashioned a multitude of male and female figurines which illustrate costume of the region. Women were shown mainly wearing wrap-around skirts and *quechquémitl* (see p. 14), although the *huipil* was also represented. Garments suggest not only plain weaving but also elaborate forms of patterning. Hair was often dressed with ribbons or decorated headbands, and jewellery consisted of bracelets, ear- and lip-plugs, and necklaces of jade, pearls or shell. Male figurines exhibit long loincloths, turbans and a profusion of ornaments, while figures of both sexes have bodies and faces painted with red and black markings. Artificial deformation of the skull is evident, as is the practice of filing teeth into sharp points and other forms considered decorative. (In some parts of Middle America teeth were not only filed, but also inlaid with plugs of jade or other precious substances.)

On the Gulf Coast plain, at the ceremonial centre of El Tajín, a number of relief carvings in stone show male figures arrayed in a more elaborate style. Many are badly weather-beaten, but detailed line-drawings by Michael Edwin Kampen reveal a variety

Remojadas-style pottery figurine of a 'laughing' man in a loincloth with traces of face and body painting. In central Veracruz teeth were often filed and heads flattened – an effect probably achieved by tying boards, front and back, to infants' skulls. Museo Nacional de Antropología, Mexico.

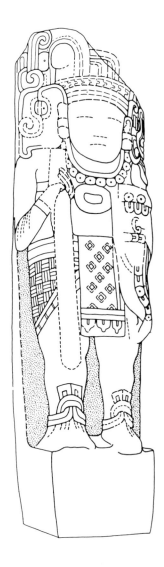

Stone carving from El Tajín showing a man wearing a loincloth with lozenge motifs, sandals and a plumed head-dress. His patterned hip-cloth was probably achieved by folding a square web diagonally and knotting it in front under the tab of the loincloth. Drawing by Michael Edwin Kampen.

of garments: these include loincloths, sashes, thick waistbands, hip-cloths and kilts which are often richly patterned and decoratively edged. Head-dresses range from tight-fitting caps to headbands supporting a mass of plumes. Many characters represent players in the ceremonial ball game, while others impersonate birds and animals. Only a few figures wear sandals, but a large number have necklaces and round or bar-shaped ear-plugs.

Activity at El Tajín reached its peak towards the end of the Classic period – perhaps even slightly later – but generally speaking central Mexico had fallen into a state of

Lintel 24 from Yaxchilán, dedicated
AD 709. A richly dressed figure kneels
before the ruler 'Shield Jaguar' and
draws sacrificial blood by passing a rope
with thorns through the tongue.
H. 43 in (109 cm). Museum of Mankind,
London.

confusion by the end of the ninth century, with marauding tribes vying for supremacy. The unifying force of Teotihuacán had long since disappeared, leaving a vacuum in its wake. Only one important centre grew up during this time of unrest – Xochicalco in Morelos, often described as a bridge linking the Classic with the Post-Classic era.

The new age brought with it a new mode of organised life and was characterised by a strong emphasis on militarism. Peoples of this period embarked on the worship of fierce, warlike gods, and with these cults came the spread of human sacrifice. Metallurgy also made its appearance around this time, probably introduced into Mexico via Central America from the Andean region. The first metal objects were almost entirely of copper and consisted largely of ornaments such as small bells cast by the lost-wax method. Although these have helped to preserve a number of textiles from this Post-Classic period, however, no cloth remains have as yet been found for the highly influential civilisation of the Toltec, who built up a huge empire and established themselves as a dominant force in central Mexico during the tenth and eleventh centuries.

For the Aztec, who were subsequently to claim the Toltec as ancestors, their very name became synonymous with artistry and skill. Their rule was regarded as a golden age, and a profusion of talents was attributed to them. With the overthrow of the Toltec came the destruction of Tula, their principal site, but from a few surviving stone carvings we can tell something of their garments, which may have been inspired by Gulf Coast styles. As Patricia Anawalt notes in a paper entitled 'The Ethnic History of the Toltecs as Reflected in their Clothing', male dress included sashes, loincloths, hip-cloths, triangular aprons, short kilts, feathered capes and quilted tunics for warriors. Pointed male *quechquémitl* too were occasionally shown, almost certainly in a ceremonial context. Head-dresses were varied, sandals were high-backed, and adornments included leg and armbands, ear-plugs, button-like beads in one or both nostrils or, alternatively, nose-bars worn through the septum. Female attire included wrap-around skirts, or *enredos*, and rounded shoulder-capes which may have been *quechquémitl*.

With the collapse of the Toltec empire a new era of unrest set in throughout central Mexico. In the south and south-east, however, other civilisations had risen to prominence. Of these the most brilliant was that of the Maya: justly celebrated as mathematicians and astronomers, they devised complex calendar systems of extraordinary accuracy and developed means of recording their calculations with hieroglyphic inscriptions. They also excelled as architects, muralists, potters and sculptors.

In view of these remarkable achievements it is hardly surprising that their weavings and dress should have been among the most splendid and varied in Middle America. When considering Maya costume, however, it should be remembered that the Maya were not a single, unified nation; there never was a centralised empire, with one ruler and one language. Maya civilisation seems instead to have been based on a loose federation of city states which together covered over 117,000 square miles – an area as immense as it was varied. Pine-clad mountain ranges that rise to a height of nearly 13,000 ft (3,965 m), fertile valleys, tropical rain-forests and dry limestone plains were all included within their territories. These stretched across what are now the Mexican states of Tabasco, Chiapas, Campeche and Quintana Roo, taking in the Yucatán Peninsula and reaching out across Belize and Guatemala into the western parts of Honduras and El Salvador.

Maya culture not only evolved in geographically contrasting areas with widely

differing climates, however; it also involved large shifts of population and developed over many centuries. By the time of their final overthrow at the hands of Spanish forces, the Maya had endured as a cultural entity for at least 2,500 years. Although their origins remain a mystery, it seems possible that the early Maya either shared in or were influenced by the great Olmec culture. By the Pre-Classic period small proto-Maya communities had begun to grow up, often in the more mountainous southern regions. As dependence on agriculture increased, craft skills developed, and archaeological finds have included remnants of basketry, matting and woven textiles, as well as a number of pottery figurines. Sadly these are mostly broken and incomplete.

The Classic era, which began around AD 300, is generally considered to have lasted until approximately AD 900. In the depths of the forests great ceremonial centres grew up – for example, at Tikal in Guatemala, at Copán in Honduras, and at Palenque, Bonampak and Yaxchilán in Chiapas. The Maya of this period were great sculptors, often embellishing their buildings with hieroglyphic texts and exquisite carvings in low relief. Frescoes afforded another type of ornament, and the discovery in 1946 of Bonampak, which is the Maya word for 'painted walls', has provided tremendous insight into Maya life and costume. Further information may be gained from the polychrome paintings which decorate much Maya pottery, or from carved and engraved jades which often show richly costumed figures.

Towards the end of the Classic period the rain-forest sites were abandoned, and the development of Maya culture shifted north to the Yucatán Peninsula. There a magnificent centre was already flourishing at Uxmal, the façades of its buildings richly ornamented with geometric motifs in stone mosaic. The sacred island of Jaina, just off Campeche, served as a necropolis for the Maya who lived along the coast. This site has yielded to archaeologists and looters alike a large number of highly sophisticated and lifelike pottery figurines which are a prime source for the study of Maya costume. Also belonging to the Late Classic period are a cache of broken, mould-made figurines found in 1976 at El Lagartero near the Guatemalan border in the Chiapas highlands. Similarities between the two series indicate that certain clothing styles were common to the inhabitants of the southern and northern zones.

Throughout their long evolution the Maya had never been isolated from the rest of Mexico. The excavation of pottery remains has proved that trading links existed between the Maya and the Mexican highlanders, in particular with the inhabitants of Teotihuacán, but contact with other peoples never affected the essence of Maya culture. The start of the Post-Classic period was marked, however, by the invasion of Yucatán by Toltec warriors. The new militaristic order was reflected in the architecture of Chichén Itzá, which came to dominate the Peninsula, while representations of the human figure showed Toltec features and Toltec styles of dress. Eventually Chichén Itzá was displaced by Mayapán as the ruling centre, and Toltec influence faded away. The Maya were once again in control, and remained so until the Spanish Conquest, but rival rulers engaged in almost constant warfare. As a result architecture and the other arts never recovered from the decline which they had entered at the finish of the Classic era.

Enough remained of Maya culture, though, for Bishop Diego de Landa to write in the sixteenth century in his *Relación de las cosas de Yucatán*: 'Before the Spaniards had conquered that country, the natives lived together in a very civilised fashion. . .'. His account of Maya culture combines censure with hard-won praise and presents a detailed picture of Maya life based on data collected from Indian informants. It also

Maya polychrome vessel with glyph panels (for extended view see pp. 12–13). Male figures wear loincloths, fringed hip-cloths, ornaments for the ear, wrist and neck, and voluminous head-dresses. Museum of Mankind, London.

includes a number of references to costume and to personal adornment. The clay figurines from Jaina serve to illustrate these references which go some way towards supplementing the lack of carved and sculpted human figures on the Peninsula, for the already mentioned Toltec-style figures can hardly be taken to represent Maya costume. Invaluable though the writings of Landa and his contemporaries may be, however, they can never fully compensate for the mass destruction of codices which he ordained. Only three have survived, all from the Post-Classic period.

Codices, mural paintings, carvings and sculpture, painted pottery and clay figurines, when taken with the writings of the Spanish chroniclers, all point to the richness of Maya costume, which varied according to time, place and the customs of different peoples within the Maya family. By the Classic era a wide range of garments had evolved, and these were worn by the nobility with a profusion of adornments. Archaeologists have unearthed jade beads, pendants, ear-plugs and other ornaments in large numbers, but actual textile remains have proved extremely scarce. Detailed representations suggest that cloth was often highly decorative, incorporating a wealth of complex patterning with a wide spectrum of colours, and appearances are borne out by fragments from the Post-Classic era which owe their preservation to unusual environmental conditions. In Chiapas, for example, samples of cloth survived in dry caves and in one instance in a sealed jar, while at Mayapán the presence of copper artefacts helped to preserve another series of textile remains. By far the richest source of weavings, however, has proved to be the *Cenote*, or Well of Sacrifice, at Chichén Itzá. Approximately 600 fragments, none measuring more than a few inches in any dimension, have been brought up from the depths and analysed.

Although in a few cases hard fibres (probably sisal) were used, the majority of all textile specimens were woven from cotton. We have Landa's written evidence that cotton was in plentiful supply throughout the northern zone: 'Cotton is gathered in wonderful quantity and grows in all parts of the land and there are two kinds of it. One they sow every year and its little tree does not last more than that year and is very small. The stalk of the other lasts five or six years and bears its fruit every year which are pods like walnuts with a green shell, which opens in four parts in due time and contains cotton.' Both species of native cotton described here were known by the Maya as *taman*. *K'an xik* was the term used for the light coffee-brown variety, and textile fragments from Mayapán which were woven with this species have retained their original tawny colour.

Spinning and weaving techniques were much as in other parts of Mexico. Pottery spindle whorls are all that remain of ancient Maya implements, but the backstrap loom is depicted in various sources. In his *Relación* Landa conjured up convivial domestic scenes when he wrote: 'They [the women of the Peninsula] have the habit of helping each other in spinning and weaving, and they repay each other for these kinds of work as their husbands do work on their lands. And on these occasions they always have their witty speeches in joking and telling good stories and occasionally a little gossip.' Similar scenes are common in countless Indian villages today.

It is important to remember that pre-Hispanic garments were not cut or tailored in the European fashion but assembled from squares or rectangles of cloth as it came from the loom. Their elegance and decorative appeal derived largely, therefore, from the texture and patterning of the cloth itself, and archaeological specimens confirm that weaving reached a high degree of refinement among the ancient Maya. Techniques include plain, basket and semi-basket weaving, and feature warp and weft stripes as well as checks (see Appendix 2). Tapestry weaving is represented by a number of fragments, and although the *kelim* style predominates, alternative weft-interlocking devices are also shown.

Other loom procedures include weft-wrap openwork and gauze. Such techniques are difficult to identify with any certainty in frescoes, codices or carvings, because although criss-cross designs on clothing suggest the texture of these weaves, they could equally well portray netting – a craft practised by the ancient Maya and depicted in the Codex Dresden. Also illustrated by textile specimens are twill and the super-structural devices of brocading and looped-weft, or pile weaving, while the construction of a weft-fringe, twined separately and sewn on to the selvage of the cloth, closely recalls a similar example from the Tehuacán Valley. All the procedures mentioned so far were present at Chichén Itzá, where yarns were mostly one- or two-ply and z-twisted. From Mayapán, however, comes a rare specimen of double-weaving, and it seems likely that Maya weavers may have practised further skills for which we have no corroborative evidence. This may also be true of embroidery, which is represented by textile remains from the great *Cenote*, apparently worked with a form of running stitch.

The fragmentary nature of specimens means that in most cases the overall patterning has been lost, but discernible elements consist mainly of crosses, diamonds and frets similar to many of the relief motifs on the façades at Uxmal. Figurative carvings of the Classic period provide additional information, however. These are often incised to portray details of textile decoration as at Yaxchilán, where many of the stone lintels show geometric markings of great intricacy which suggest brocading. In modern Chiapas, where many weavers specialise in this technique, garments still incorporate lozenges and stepped frets reminiscent of ancient tradition. A further link with the past occurs in Venustiano Carranza, where contemporary brocaded birds recall a

Representations of Maya textiles from Classic monuments (*top row*) and Post-Classic wall paintings and pottery (*bottom row*). Designs may have been woven on the loom, embroidered, painted freehand or achieved through *batik* or *plangi*. Drawing by Sylvanus Morley.

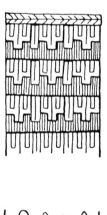
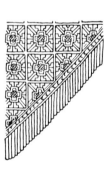

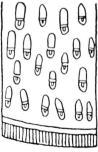

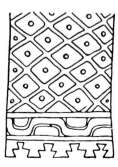

Maya cloth fragment with similar decoration which is currently on view in the Museo Nacional de Antropología e Historia.

Given the complexity of Maya patterning, it seems likely that weavers generally dyed the individual yarns rather than the finished fabric. Textile specimens recovered from the *Cenote* are completely carbonised, with no trace of colour left in the cloth, but according to Landa the Maya of Yucatán used 'colours of many different kinds made from the dyes of certain trees and flowers'. If Landa is to be believed, however, such dyes were not colour-fast, 'since the Indians have not known how to perfect them with gums, which give them the medium which they need so that they shall not fade'. Organic colourants employed by the Maya probably included indigo, logwood, annatto seeds and many of the other sources described in Chapter 5, while a range of earths and clays could have given additional shades. Cochineal was one of two important dyes from the animal world and, despite Landa's disparaging remark regarding Indian colourants, it found great favour in Europe during the Colonial period. The other much prized dye was obtained along the Pacific coast from shellfish – *Purpura patula pansa*, a species related to the Mediterranean mollusc which gave the famous 'royal purple of Tyre'.

It is probable that shellfish-dyed yarn was used to weave the middle section of a three-web cotton textile fragment from the Chiptic Cave, Chiapas. Preserved in a sealed jar, this remarkable find also illustrates two unusual ways of patterning cloth, both carried out after weaving. The top section (one of only two examples for this technique in Mexico) displays designs in red, blue, turquoise, black and light brown, and proves that patterns were sometimes painted freehand on to cloth. The bottom section is rarer still, for it constitutes the only example of *batik* ever found in Mexico. The curving lines that make up the design were probably traced with tree resin or beeswax; brown colouring was then applied to the cloth while the reserved areas remained naturally white. It may well be that the Maya also practised *ikat* and *plangi* – two other methods of resist-dyeing which occur in contemporary Mexico – but although archaeological remains confirm the existence of *ikat* for northern Peru, no pre-Conquest Mexican examples have as yet been found for either technique.

The ancient Maya had many other proven methods for decorating cloth, however. Sadly nothing has survived to illustrate the fragile and delicate art of feather-working, but Spanish reports refer to it and record the high value which was placed on the plumage of exotic birds, in particular the *quetzal*. According to Landa, the Maya sometimes raised birds 'for their own pleasure, and for the feathers from which to make their fine clothes'. Downy feathers were often incorporated into the fringes of cotton fabrics, or used for weaving and embroidery. 'They raise a certain kind of large white mallard ducks, which I think came to them from Peru, for the plumage', wrote Landa, 'and so often pluck their breasts, and they want that plumage for the embroidery of their garments.' Fray Bernardino de Sahagún, writing of the Aztec, described the craft of the feather-worker in detail. One method consisted in 'fastening the feathers to the background with paste', while a second required the additional aid of 'thread and cord' (see p. 67). The Maya presumably used feathers in the same way to adorn the shields and capes of warriors: often shown in bas-reliefs, they also appear on repoussé gold discs recovered from the *Cenote* at Chichén Itzá. The Maya may, in addition, have made rigid capes by mounting feathers on a wickerwork base.

Many garments incorporated not only feathers but also shells, copper bells and other small adornments. At Tikal a relief carving from the Early Classic period constitutes the earliest-known example of an elaborate clothing technique: later portrayed at other sites, it consisted in threading tubular beads, possibly of jade, to form male skirts and capes. It is not possible to judge from these representations whether a textile backing was used, however.

Animal skins were greatly prized by the Maya, who sometimes made them into clothing. According to Landa, 'Some . . . such as the lords and captains . . . went to war, clothed with feathers and skins of tigers and lions if they owned them'. The animals mistakenly referred to as tigers and lions were probably jaguars and pumas, and scenes from the Bonampak murals show warriors of the Classic period arrayed in skins. Small fragments of tanned hide from the *Cenote* show that the Maya also made use of leather, presumably for sandals and shields. According to Landa, skins were cured with tree bark. Bark of another type, when beaten, provided the Maya with cloth: rich in fibres, it was used for codices as well as clothing, and may have pre-dated weaving in the region.

Woven textiles, dyestuffs, feathers and other materials all served as articles for barter for, as Landa wrote of the Peninsula Maya, 'the occupation to which they had the greatest inclination was trade'. Routes often stretched extremely long distances, as is shown by gold and copper artefacts in the *Cenote* from as far away as Colombia, Panama and the Valley of Mexico. The Maya of the coast did much of their trade by sea – a fact which led to the first encounter between Europeans and Mexican Indians in AD 1502, when Columbus met with Maya trading canoes off the island of Guanaja near Honduras. The merchandise was extremely varied and included, according to Peter Martyr d'Anghera, 'bells, razors, knives . . . and chiefly draperies and different articles of spun cotton in brilliant colours'. On land barter was facilitated by well-kept roads linking the different city states of the Yucatán Peninsula. Markets played an important part in the life of the Maya for, in Landa's words, 'at their markets they traded in everything which was in that country'. Landa and his contemporaries were describing what remained of Yucatec culture, but trade must have been even more intense during the Classic period, and it is to be presumed that the constant exchange of produce was accompanied by some interchange of weaving patterns and styles of dress.

As in central Mexico, costume did not reach its full range before the Classic era. Information for the Pre-Classic period is provided by incomplete figurines which exhibit little clothing, with the occasional exception of skirt-like garments, small caps or turbans, and articles of jewellery such as ear-plugs or necklaces. With the growth of major ceremonial centres and the rise of a ruling and priestly class, however, costume entered an era of great vitality and splendour. We know that Aztec laws restricted certain styles of dress to rigid social groupings, and it seems likely that similar rulings existed among the Maya. At Bonampak there is a mural which shows prisoners with slaves or servants wearing simple loincloths, while the Jaina figurines may be thought to represent a cross-section of society. In virtually all other instances, however, costumed figures portray warriors, priests, rulers and other members of a privileged social order. Only in the sixteenth century did Landa and his contemporaries describe clothing styles for the rank and file, and it is clear that although many of the garments worn by the peasantry were basically the same as those of the élite, theirs never attained the wealth of ornamentation associated with the nobility.

Of all male garments the most widely worn was the *ex* or breechclout. Depicted on painted pottery, in codices, murals and sculpture, it was described by Landa as follows: 'Their clothing was a band of the width of the hand, which served them for drawers and breeches. They wound it several times round the waist, so that one end fell in front and one end fell behind, and these ends the women made with a great deal of care and with feather-work.' According to the *Relación* of Valladolid, 'many Indians went nude with only the loincloth'. In carvings of the Classic period the *ex* is sometimes covered by an overhanging 'apron'. Various examples reach as low as the ankles while apparently carrying an abundance of additional ornaments, and it seems likely that a stronger backing than cotton cloth may occasionally have been needed.

Despite Landa's comment, quoted above, it is clear from rare representations that the Maya did fashion breeches, albeit for ceremonial wear only. More usual, however,

Representations of Maya loincloths from monuments of the Classic period. Styles of embellishment varied considerably among the nobility. Such examples suggest complex weaves, intricate fringes, feather-work and the addition of ornaments and carvings. Drawing by Sylvanus Morley.

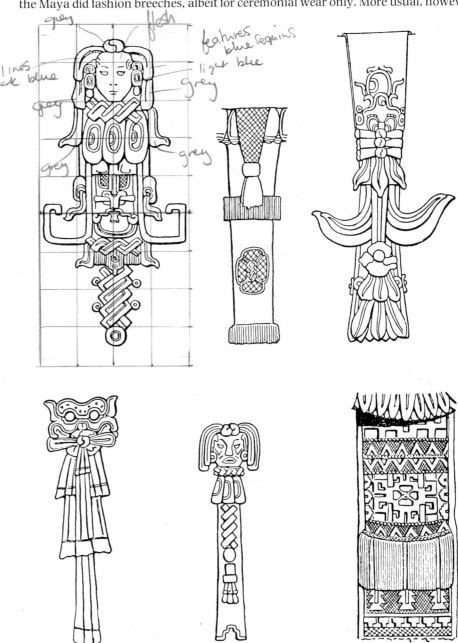

Lintel 16 from Yaxchilán. The standing figure wears high-backed sandals, a magnificently plumed head-dress and a wealth of adornments. Other costume elements include a loincloth, a belt, a tight-fitting tunic with discs, a stole-like garment and a short kilt. These last two items may have been quilted. Museum of Mankind, London.

was the portrayal of skirts which appear at a number of sites. Worn over loincloths right up until the Conquest, these garments present many variations. One costume element, frequently shown in carvings, murals and codices, was wrapped round the hips: variously interpreted as a back-skirt or hip-cloth, it hung down behind but was short in front. Kilts which barely reach mid-thigh are worn by warriors in one of the Bonampak murals, while lintel 26 at Yaxchilán features a beaded style. Stela II from the same site shows a fringed knee-length skirt which is often repeated elsewhere, but the Maya also used a rare garment which seemingly finished in a point at the front; a further variation with the triangular edge to the side occurs in a mural at Bonampak.

In many of these instances skirts are seen to be wrapped like a woman's *enredo* about the wearer, and the same is true of the male ankle-length skirts which appear in the Codex Dresden and on several Jaina figurines. Like their shorter counterparts, long skirts were generally made from cloth. At Tulum and Palenque, however, representations suggest heavy beads, while at Bonampak priests or dignitaries wear long skirts of jaguar skin painted red on the inside. Apparently these garments could be combined, for a male figure in the Bonampak murals is shown wearing a short wrap-around skirt over a second, much longer, one. Floating panels constitute another striking variation within the skirt category: depicted in the Codex Dresden are priests with narrow lengths of cloth suspended from the waist, while a magnificently attired figurine from Jaina exhibits a similar garment.

The sashes needed to secure skirts and occasionally loincloths were often very ornate. The Bonampak murals, which have the advantage of colour, show red, blue, black and white sashes with long ends, while belts portrayed in stone sculpture of the Classic period are frequently adorned with large carved heads, probably of jade, and hung with heavy pendants. Very splendid examples may, like 'aprons', have required a strong backing to support the weight of such ornamentation.

The cloak, or *pati*, was worn like the breechclout by men of all ranks and displayed corresponding degrees of adornment. 'They [the Maya of the Peninsula] wore large square *mantas* [cloaks] and they tied them over their shoulders', wrote Landa, who also noted that they slept 'covering themselves with their *mantas* of cotton'. The simple garment of the common man became a magnificent mantle when worn by the nobility. Richly decorated examples, sometimes fastened at the front with ornamental brooches, appear in sculpture and murals of the Classic period, often enveloping their high-ranking wearers from shoulder to ankle. Although woven cloth is most generally suggested, some representations show jaguar skins or, as already mentioned, beading or feathers. Not all cloaks are portrayed as large and square; many are little more than shoulder-capes, while others appear shorter at the front than the back. Mysteriously, some garments clearly present rounded edges. These may best be seen in three-dimensional representations from Jaina. Adding further variety to this costume category are front cloaks, of the type shown on a polychrome jar from Uaxactún in Guatemala.

It is evident from rare and tantalising representations that other articles of dress were used by Maya men at different times in different places. Lintels 16 and 26 from Yaxchilán both show a tight-fitting, sleeveless tunic to the waist, with barely discernible textile patterning and two vertical rows of discs for added adornment. The Bonampak murals also exhibit closed shirts, some made of jaguar skin and belted at the waist. Another interesting garment portrayed at Jaina and Piedras Negras resembles a long chasuble which hangs loosely from the shoulders. In addition the

Late Classic pottery figurines from Jaina. *Left* Male dignitary wearing a blue-painted coat, or open-fronted *xicolli*, and a wide-brimmed hat with flower. The Maya may have accentuated the appearance of the nose with a bridge-like addition. *Right* Male dignitary wearing a chasuble-like robe. Both figures probably represent priests. Museo Nacional de Antropología, Mexico.

ancient Maya had front-opening jackets and coats, as is shown by figurines from Jaina and El Lagartero. According to the *Relación* of Valladolid, 'All the Indians of these provinces . . . went clothed; the lords in certain *xicoles* of cotton and feathers woven into a kind of many coloured jacket of two flaps'. Visual sources hint at still further styles of dress: these include extremely wide bead collars which cover the shoulders in the manner of a short cape, and twisted lengths of cloth, seen on bas-reliefs at Palenque, which hang down the backs of wearers.

Regardless of place or period, virtually no ceremonial costume was complete without a head-dress. As Joy Mahler remarks, the variety is such that an attempt at classification could amount to a description of each one individually. For sheer splendour it would be hard to rival the Bonampak murals: in one scene dancers display immense green head-dresses made from the iridescent plumes of the *quetzal* bird; in another warriors exhibit towering structures which take the shape of jaguars and alligators. Frames of wicker or wood were probably used as supports for the wealth of plumes, jade carvings, animal skins and other components favoured by the Maya, but additional sources show a rather different range of head-coverings. These include cloth turbans and voluminous mushroom-shaped caps, while figurines from Jaina indicate that inhabitants of the Peninsula occasionally wore hats.

Sandals are rarely shown in the codices, yet they appear frequently on bas-reliefs; according to Landa, the Yucatec Maya 'wore sandals of hemp or of the dry untanned skin of the deer'. As with other articles of dress, the simple and unadorned sandals of the common man were replete with ornamentation when worn by members of the privileged class. One type of sandal which is frequently represented features a high ankle support of the kind seen at Teotihuacán; this style is still current in certain communities of the Chiapas highlands.

Many contemporary Maya keep small possessions and loose change in little bags, and Landa was referring to a similar custom when he wrote of 'small purses of net' which served during visits to market to hold cocoa beans, stone beads or red shells. All three were employed as money and could be used to buy the articles of jewellery with which the Maya liked to adorn themselves. It seems from sixteenth-century accounts that the lower classes wore nose and ear ornaments, generally fashioned from bone, shell, stone or wood. The range of jewellery displayed by the nobility was, of course, far wider and more lavish: visual sources repeatedly show wrist- and knee-bands, anklets and brooches, together with a variety of necklaces including pectorals, pendants and wide collars. To make these adornments jewellers used shells, feathers, jade, obsidian, amber, bone, jaguar teeth and claws, as well as alligator teeth. Gold and copper artefacts from the *Cenote* also prove that in later times these metals were hammered and decorated with *repoussé* technique. In order to accommodate the flaring ear-plugs which are so frequently shown ear lobes were pierced and stretched. Another custom involved the piercing of the septum to receive nose ornaments. Post-Classic representations from Chichén Itzá show nostril buttons, but this is thought by Alfred M. Tozzer to be a Toltec tradition introduced from central Mexico.

It is clear that each echelon of life in Maya society was distinguished by emblems of dress and adornment. The size of a head-dress or the length of a skirt were probably representations of authority and status which we are unable to interpret fully today. In addition to the range of generalised male garments already discussed, however, specialist occupations evidently possessed their own styles of clothing. One particularly large and important group was made up of warriors whose awe-inspiring head-dresses emulated animals, birds and alligators. This custom is illustrated not just by the Bonampak murals but also by a number of lowland figurines with zoomorphic helmets totally encasing the face. We know from Bernal Díaz del Castillo that Maya warriors wore 'armour made of cotton reaching to the knees', while according to Landa, 'They [the Yucatec Maya] . . . made short jackets of quilted cotton and of coarse salt, quilted in two thicknesses or quiltings; and these were very strong'. This statement is usually interpreted to mean that the cotton was soaked in brine, but Tozzer believes that Landa has confused the Maya word for 'salt' with the word for 'twisted cord'. Apparent examples of quilting hang like stoles from the necks of various figures from Jaina and Palenque and seem to recur in lintels at Yaxchilán. Were they, as Robert and Barbara Rands have suggested, forms of flexible armour?

Other specialist occupations included that of ball-player. To judge by several

Late Classic pottery figurine from Jaina showing a weaver. Her mysterious torso-garment, possibly a *quechquémitl*, is longer at the back than the front. A bird is perched on the post which supports her backstrap loom. H. 6½ in (16.5 cm). Museo Nacional de Antropología, Mexico.

figures participants in the Maya ball game wore wide protective belts and knee-pads. Like the ball game, dance and music were looked upon as religious observances to be performed on ceremonial occasions and never for mere spectacle. The Bonampak murals show a group of skirted musicians, bare above the waist, with long sashes and massive head-dresses. As for the costumes of dancers, these were both lavish and varied. One magnificently arrayed group at Bonampak display towering head-dresses of *quetzal* plumes. Attached to their belts are splendid flaring wings which appear to be fringed or feathered.

The scarcity of costume portrayals at Post-Classic sites makes it hard to gauge how much Classic splendour remained after the Toltec invasion. Carved warriors at Chichén Itzá are almost perfect replicas of the gigantic stone columns from Tula and prove the power of Toltec influence; yet the writings of Landa show that something at least of the ancient magnificence still lingered at the time of the Conquest. A staunch Catholic with a horror of all things pagan, he was nevertheless moved by the sight of a Maya priest to record this evocative description:

He came forth clothed in a jacket of red feathers, embroidered with other coloured feathers, and from the ends of it hung other long feathers, and he wore a sort of *coroza* [head-dress] on his head of the same feathers; and under the jacket many cotton ribbons hanging down to the ground like tails. And in his hand he carried an *aspergillum*, made of a short stick finely worked, and for the hairs or bristles of the hyssop there were certain tails of serpents which are like rattlesnakes. And he showed exactly the same gravity as the Pope shows in crowning an Emperor; and it was a remarkable thing to see how much nobility all this dress gave to them.

There are commonly fewer representations of women than of men, suggesting that their role was largely confined to the domestic sphere. Mothers taught their daughters to cook, to keep house, and, very importantly, to spin and to weave under the protection of the goddess Ixchel. A high value was attached to fine textiles, and women wove not only to clothe themselves and their families but also to supply the tribute which the ruling classes levied from the community. Textiles were additionally used to discharge legal penalties or fines on the Peninsula, and bartered by traders for the luxury produce of other regions. Textiles also had a religious and ceremonial significance: the weavings recovered from the sacred well at Chichén Itzá were presumably cast into the waters as gifts to the gods. According to Landa, women on the Peninsula were 'very devout and pious, and also practised many acts of devotion before their idols, bringing incense before them and offering them presents of cotton stuffs . . .'. Elsewhere Landa noted that this cloth was often used to wrap the idols, and in the Chiapas highlands this custom has not been lost, for in many communities the Catholic saints are dressed in diminutive and beautifully woven garments.

To judge from the various representations which do exist women's dress consisted principally of a *pic*, or wrap-around skirt, and a *huipil*; the Codex Dresden also shows hip-cloths. Skirt decorations in the codices sometimes include a serrated lower edge and a horizontal border, while Lubaantún figurines from Belize often feature a broad and richly patterned band down the front of skirts. Although there is a figurine from Jaina which displays only a *pic* and sash, and although women and goddesses occasionally appear topless in the codices, most portrayals exhibit elegant *huipiles*. These were evidently subject to variation in width and length, just as they are today. One Jaina figurine is even shown with two *huipiles*, the second almost completely covering the first.

The writings of Spanish chroniclers contain several references to female costume, none of them particularly clear. Landa was favourably struck by the modesty shown by Maya women inhabiting the coast and the provinces of Bacalar and Campeche, 'for, besides the covering which they wore from the waist down, they covered their breasts, tying a folded *manta* [web of cotton cloth] underneath their armpits. All the others did not wear more than one garment like a long and wide sack, opened on both sides, and drawn in as far as the hips, where they fastened it together, with the same width as before'. This last garment, presumably a *huipil*, was similarly described by other writers. The *Relación* of Valladolid referred in addition to 'a cotton handkerchief': worn over the head, it was 'open like a short cowl, which also served to cover their breasts'. It has been suggested by Sylvanus Morley that this modesty cloth may have been a forerunner of the *rebozo*, or rectangular shawl, which evolved in Colonial times. The Bonampak murals do, however, offer a glimpse of a *huipil*-clad figure with

Ixchel, goddess of weaving, pregnancy, floods and perhaps also of the moon, from the Codex Dresden (AD 1200–1350). She wears a wrap-around skirt with a notched lower border and a fringed hip-cloth.

Late Classic pottery figurine from Jaina showing a woman wearing a wrap-around skirt under a lozenge-patterned *huipil*. Longer at the back than the front, it has a serrated edge and retains traces of blue paint, as does her head-dress. H. 7½ in (19 cm). Museo Nacional de Antropología, Mexico.

what Joy Mahler takes to be a red stole over her arms, and this may be more nearly related to the contemporary garment

Classic and Post-Classic portrayals of women hint tantalisingly at other mysterious garments. Lubaantún figurines, for example, show immensely broad, patterned bands which seemingly secure skirts at the waist and stop just below the breasts, while frescoes at Tulum portray female figures with what appear to be pointed *quechquémitl*. Also puzzling are the apparently curved torso-garments which feature on a number of Jaina figurines. Characterised by their extremely wide neck openings, these cape-like representations also suggest *quechquémitl*, yet are frequently longer at the back than the front; short versions are occasionally shown over a *huipil*. If both garments are indeed *quechquémitl*, then it seems possible that they were introduced into the peninsular region by Toltec invaders. The rounded edges of cape-like examples, together with those distinguishing certain male cloaks, are cause for much speculation among investigators. Did Maya weavers finish off the web of cloth in a curve while it was still on the loom as some Otomí weavers do today? Or did they cut and hem garments, contrary to the widely held belief that Indians never tailored their clothing?

In his *Relación* Landa referred to 'an old woman, clothed in a dress of feathers', and it seems likely that female costume may have incorporated other techniques such as tubular beading. Realistic portrayals of patterned cloth point to tapestry, brocade and gauze weaves, while the recurrent dots which feature on figurines from Lubaantún suggest tie-dyeing. At its most elaborate women's clothing was surely as decorative as men's. Sandals were not shown and probably were seldom used, but the Jaina figurines confirm that women, like men, occasionally wore large hats. As for jewellery, necklaces are much in evidence. According to Landa, Maya women 'pierced their ears in order to put in earrings like their husbands'. They also 'pierced their noses through the cartilage, which divides the nostrils in the middle, in order to put in the hole a stone of amber, and they considered this an adornment'.

A wealth of additional details given by Landa and his fellow chroniclers testify to the considerable care which was lavished on the appearance of both sexes. Women 'had a custom of filing their teeth leaving them like the teeth of a saw', and several skulls, both male and female, have been found with filed and inlaid teeth. Landa also described how mothers sought to make their children cross-eyed 'as a mark of beauty', and how they flattened babies' heads soon after birth, giving them the broad, high foreheads featured in so many carvings and murals. This was done, Fray Juan de Torquemada was told, because the custom 'gives us a noble air, and our heads are thus better adapted to carry loads'. Some representations, mostly of the Toltec period, do show beards, but chroniclers noted that facial hair was generally disliked on the Peninsula. We are told by Francisco Cervantes de Salazar that men 'were accustomed to pluck it out with some things like pincers', and by Landa that 'their mothers burned their faces in their childhood with hot cloths, so as to keep the beard from growing'.

Hair-styles were often elaborate. In Landa's time men apparently 'wore their hair long like women and on the top they burned a space like a great tonsure, and thus the hair grew long below, while that of the top of the head was left short. And they braided it and made a wreath of it around their heads leaving the queue like tassels'. Women 'wore their hair very long, they made of it, and still make of it a very elegant head-dress, with the hair divided into two parts and they plaited their hair for another kind of coiffure. . . . They dress the hair of little girls, until they reach a certain size, in four or two horns, which are very becoming to them'.

Late Classic pottery figurine from Jaina showing a male dignitary wearing a profusion of ornaments, two-thonged sandals and a head-dress with plumes and flowers. His ankle-length kilt is covered by floating panels alternately painted blue; facial markings suggest scarification. Museo Nacional de Antropología, Mexico.

Both sexes were given to washing and bathing frequently, 'without any modesty', according to Antonio de Herrera y Tordesillas. Men were 'great lovers of perfumes, and for this they used bouquets of flowers and odiferous herbs . . .', wrote Landa, who noted also that women anointed themselves 'with a certain red ointment like their husbands, and those who could afford it added to it a certain preparation of a gum, odiferous and very sticky . . . and the odour lasted many days without being lost, according to how good the anointing was'.

As if clothing did not provide enough decoration, the Maya also favoured tattooing and body-painting – two customs which highly displeased their conquerors, but which were practised throughout vast areas of Mexico. Men 'tattooed their bodies, and the more they do this, the more brave and valiant are they considered, as tattooing is accompanied with great suffering', wrote Landa, adding elsewhere that women 'tattooed their bodies from the waist up, except their breasts for nursing, with more delicate and beautiful designs than the men'. The perfumed ointment gave their skin a reddish tinge, but men employed a range of stronger colours. Francisco de Cárdenas Valencia, in his *Relación* of 1639 for the province of Yucatán, gave a description of Maya warriors whose bodies were entirely 'daubed with earth of many colours so that they appear as most ferocious devils'. In peacetime red was the usual colour for both the body and face, 'and although it was very unbecoming to them, yet they thought it very pleasing', observed Landa. According to this same authority, black paint related to periods of fasting, or was used to show that a young man was as yet unmarried. Both colours were associated with warriors, but blue was the prerogative of priests.

The symbolic value of colours was central to Maya customs and beliefs. According to Sylvanus Morley, blue was associated with sacrifice. Black, as the colour of obsidian, represented weapons and war, while red stood for blood. Yellow was the colour of ripe corn, and therefore symbolised food. Colours were also linked to the cardinal points. Red corresponded to the east, white to the north, black to the west, yellow to the south, and green to the *axis mundi* which was the central pole that pierced the several layers of the universe.

In the same way that different colours reflected the cosmic beliefs of the Maya, so too did all other aspects of their dress and personal appearance. Victor Von Hagen has attributed the luxuriance of Maya art, together with their lavish adornment of the human body, to *horror vacui*, or 'a horror of empty space', yet it is clear that their love of adornment was never motivated solely by aesthetic principles. The glyphs on a pendant or the patterning of a weave had a symbolic value which we are unable to interpret fully, but which undoubtedly represented far more than an exercise in personal vanity. While the Maya achieved a splendour in their dress which perhaps surpassed even our conjectures, the luxuriance displayed by the privileged was irrevocably governed by a rigorous discipline.

2 Oaxaca, Guerrero and the Aztec Empire

To the west of the Maya zone lies the state of Oaxaca. This is a region of misty mountain peaks and narrow valleys, but near the centre of the state three large valleys converge to form what is known as the Valley of Oaxaca. A warm climate and a plentiful rainfall make this an extremely fertile area, and archaeologists believe that man has lived here since very early times. Around 700 BC the first distinctive civilisation emerged. At major sites such as Monte Albán there is evidence of some contact with the Olmec world in this early phase, and in subsequent periods evidence of other cultural intrusions. By AD 500 the ceremonial centre at Monte Albán had been much enlarged and had entered its third and most significant phase under the Zapotec. The Zapotec excelled not only as architects but also as potters, and excavations have yielded large numbers of costumed figurines and elaborately modelled funerary urns showing gods or priests wearing god-masks.

Around AD 900 the Zapotec abandoned Monte Albán, which was occupied by the warlike Mixtec who are thought to have entered the Valley from northern Oaxaca and southern Puebla. Other Zapotec settlements also came under Mixtec domination. One of these was Mitla, where high-relief façades of stone mosaic testify to the artistry of the invaders. Mixtec lapidaries and metalsmiths were famed throughout the Mexican world, but much of their supreme artistry was lost when the Spanish *conquistadores* melted down their fine gold ornaments for bullion. However, occasional archaeological discoveries, such as that of Tomb 7 at Monte Albán, have revealed a wealth of funerary offerings. This burial, excavated in 1932 by Alfonso Caso, included exquisite carvings, examples of turquoise mosaics and a profusion of jewellery fashioned from jade, shells, jet and amber, as well as silver and gold, which were worked with a variety of techniques to create armlets, earrings, bells, lip-plugs, necklaces, breast-plates, pendants and a golden crown with a plume of gold. These finds give some idea of the magnificent adornments which were worn by the Mixtec élite, while beautifully painted codices provide valuable information about the different garments which prevailed in the region (see p. 50).

It is clear from these various sources that both the Zapotec and the Mixtec used clothing, head-dresses, insignia, body and facial painting, tattooing, coiffures and certain colours to indicate status within social, religious or military hierarchies. Particular styles, garments and types of cloth were apparently reserved for the nobility, who dressed with great splendour. Male clothing seems always to have included the *maxtlatl*, or loincloth; examples in the codices have long ends which hang down behind and in front of the wearer. Over the loincloth a short and rounded hip-cloth is often represented, although some male figures exhibit kilts to mid-thigh. From Miahuatlán, however, comes a Mixtec vessel showing a standing relief figure wearing a triangular apron over a loincloth with a wide knee-length front tab.

The *xicolli* was much worn by the Mixtec élite, and it appears frequently in the codices. According to Patricia Anawalt, this garment was not worn by Mixtec warriors as military attire but only by aristocratic males whose *xicolli* were predominantly red, and by priests whose *xicolli* usually featured black and white designs. Also shown in the codices are long cloth robes and torso-garments made from the skins of animals. In a few instances high-ranking personages wear back- or chest-capes which appear to be fringed or feather-trimmed. Although warriors did not go to battle in *xicolli*, they did use *ichcahuipilli*, or tunics of quilted cotton cloth, to protect them from spears and arrows.

As with the Maya, there was an astounding variety of head-dresses. Associated with the many gods of the Mixtec pantheon, they ranged from headbands and flowing clusters or crests of feathers to extravagant helmets fashioned in the likenesses of birds and animals. Eagles and jaguars were often represented, for they symbolised the two most important warrior orders. To complete the resemblance men were sometimes totally encased in profusely feathered garments and in jaguar skins or cloth decorated to suggest animal markings. In many cases only the wearer's hands, feet and face were visible. The ritual impersonation of sacred animals and birds was also customary among the Zapotec, as may be seen from their funerary urns, for many of the figures which adorn them display zoomorphic head-dresses of great splendour.

In the codices figures of noble rank are frequently arrayed in high-backed sandals and bedecked with armlets, legbands, ear-plugs – many with long, dangling decorations – nose ornaments worn through the septum, and wide necklaces hung with adornments. Warriors were rewarded for bravery in battle by being allowed to wear jewels and fine mantles, and the investiture of rulers was symbolised by the perforation of the nose to receive the royal turquoise nose-plug. Additional decoration was provided by edging the garments of the élite with shells and small round bells of gold or copper.

Male hair-styles were varied: some figures are shown with their long hair hanging loosely while the front section is cut to form a fringe; warriors, however, often appear with their hair in a tuft on the top of the head and an accompaniment of feathers and ribbons. The codices also offer a guide to the colours and designs with which the Mixtec painted themselves. Priests blackened their bodies to indicate that they were in the service of the gods and painted their faces with the emblems of these deities. At times warriors also painted themselves black, since military service was looked upon as dedication to the gods, while symbolic face-patterning related to status and to honours won in battle. Tattooing too was practised in Oaxaca, as is shown by several Zapotec pottery figures incised with curling designs and elaborate scroll-work. Cranial deformation and the filing and encrusting of teeth were also undertaken by Oaxacan peoples in their pursuit of human beauty.

From the codices it is clear that high-ranking Mixtec women, like men, enjoyed considerable personal adornment: face painting appears comparatively rarely, but there are examples of its use; jewellery includes ear-plugs, armbands, rich necklaces and large jade nose ornaments. In many cases noblewomen are shown wearing sandals and panaches of plumes or, more rarely, zoomorphic head-dresses representing jaguars and other creatures. Hair-styles are often very decorative: sometimes the tresses hang down loosely, while the front section is cut into a heavy fringe; alternatively, the hair may be twined around itself on the top of the head, or wrapped with coloured cords to create a turban-like effect. This last style, which was also current among Zapotec women, has been retained to this day in the Zapotec village of Yalalag (see p. 219).

Two garments still widely used in Oaxaca are the *enredo*, or wrap-around skirt, which is held in place by a waist-sash, and the *huipil*. Both types of clothing are illustrated by Mixtec pottery figurines and codices. More frequently shown than the *huipil* was the *quechquémitl*, however, which is no longer worn in Oaxaca. There were two styles: one was rounded and hung down over the arms (see p. 50); the second was triangular. Both types were represented by Zapotec potters, but it is clear from the codices that they were sometimes worn together by Mixtec women of high rank. Occasionally, as in the Codex Selden, the *quechquémitl* was shown over a *huipil*. Rounded capes seem also to have been worn.

Pottery figure on a Zapotec funerary urn showing a woman with sandals, a rounded *quechquémitl*, a wrap-around skirt and a *rodete*, or head-dress of cords. The Mixtec spinner on p. 20 wears a similar costume. Museo Nacional de Antropología, Mexico.

The role of the triangular *quechquémitl* as a symbol of power and status is reflected in the codices, where name-glyphs accompany Mixtec noblewomen such as 2 House 'Jewelled *Quechquémitl*' and 3 Tiger 'War *Quechquémitl*'. It is possible that women played a very important part in ancient Mixtec society, for they are shown not only as rulers and priestesses but also as warriors. According to Doris Heyden, the triangular *quechquémitl* may have been awarded to indicate military prowess. In one scene Lady 6 Monkey is shown taking a prisoner on the battlefield: she wears a skirt and short rounded cape, and carries a shield and spear; beside her the scribe has drawn her name-glyph and a triangular *quechquémitl* decorated with chevron patterning to symbolise war.

Finely woven textiles were obviously much prized, and garments such as the *xicolli* or the *quechquémitl* were used as offerings for male and female deities. Fray Francisco de Burgoa, in his *Geográfica descripción*, wrote that *mantas* (cloaks) were given in tribute and as sacrificial offerings; he also noted that they were made of fine thread and beautifully decorated. As with other pre-Conquest cultures, the textile techniques of Mixtec and Zapotec weavers are largely a matter for speculation, but the codices contain a wide range of designs. The *xicolli* of the priests, worked in black and white, are particularly striking: textile motifs include crosses, dots, stepped frets, cross-hatch patterning, convoluted scroll-work and stylised flowers with four or more petals. Women's garments were dyed various colours, and their *enredos* occasionally exhibit cross-hatching and diamond patterning, or horizontal bands near the hemline incorporating dots and concentric circles. Many of these designs were almost certainly brocaded into the cloth, but others may have been worked in tapestry weave (see Appendix 2). It also seems likely that a number of motifs were embroidered. Copper needles, excavated at Monte Albán, suggest that it was possible to achieve relatively fine stitching. Some designs look as if they may have been painted freehand on to cloth, in much the same way that red stripes were apparently painted on to the ritual costumes of bark paper shown in the codices. Clay stamps, found in large numbers, might also have been used to imprint designs.

Conjectures of this kind seem destined to remain largely unconfirmed, but a few fragments of cotton cloth have been found in the region. From Zaachila and Guiengola come examples of plain weaving, while excavations at Yagul have yielded evidence of semi-basket and one-and-three twill. In addition, miniature garments of cotton have been discovered in the dry caves of the Mixteca Alta. Probably intended as votive offerings, they have survived in their entirety and include two plain-woven *huipiles* with weft-cording and *kelim*-slot neck openings. One is distinguished by red smudges. A slightly larger *huipil* features a twined weft-fringe, as do two diminutive plain-woven *quechquémitl*. These garments were accompanied by several webs of cotton cloth: interestingly, one three-selvage example has a loop-fringed edge reinforced by twining. Also found were two pieces of bark cloth, one with orange-brown smudges, and the other painted with black lines. Excavations have not provided examples of agave cloth, but its use is confirmed by *Relaciones* which mention Zapotec skirts of cotton and *maguey* fibre, and Mixtec *mantas* of cotton and *henequén*.

To the west of the lands occupied by the Mixtec and the Zapotec lies the state of Guerrero. Here, in a dry basin of the Upper Balsas River, various important archaeological sites have been found, built by peoples of whom we know very little. To judge by several fragments of cloth which have been excavated this was a region where the textile arts flourished. Plain, basket, semi-basket, brocade and double weaving, to-

Scene from the Codex Zouche-Nuttall. The Mixtec priestess 10 Deer wears a triangular *quechquémitl* over a cape.

Motifs made with pottery stamps from Guerrero. Stamps may have been used in ancient Mexico to pattern textiles. *Top* stepped fret, or *xicalcoliuhqui*; *bottom* hocker, or frog-like motif.

gether with embroidery, are among the many techniques represented. The artistry of local weavers is further demonstrated, however, by three unusually large pieces of rust-coloured cloth which clearly belonged to the same garment. Because they were found by tomb-robbers in an earthenware pot, the precise location of the site is unknown, but it is thought to have been one of the caves near Chilapa in eastern Guerrero. Irmgard W. Johnson has written a detailed study of this invaluable textile, which was probably a *huipil* although, according to Alfonso Caso, it could also have been a nobleman's red *xicolli*. Carbon-dated to between AD 1210 and 1370, it originally comprised two webs joined by stitching and measured 32 in (82 cm) across. The length cannot be determined, but one of the three fragments features a decorative band of many colours which was sewn like a border along the garment's lower edge.

The cotton was spun with skill. All the warp and most of the weft threads were z-twisted and used singly, but in certain densely patterned areas wefts were s-twisted and two-ply. It is clear that the weaver also chose to vary the texture of her cloth by alternating loosely spun with tightly spun thread. The garment's delicate designs were achieved with a combination of loom techniques: plain weave alternates with semi-basket weave as well as with simple gauze weave, which in turn is combined with a type of complex gauze to create lacy areas with the texture of fine net; another decorative device involves weft brocading on a background of plain weave. Such combinations are current even today in parts of Guerrero and Oaxaca. Especially interesting, however, is the use of fill-in wefts in the shoulder area: to give the garment a slightly shaped appearance the weaver has introduced additional weft threads from the side of the neck opening; these were interwoven for varying distances, then brought back on themselves. As a result the inner edge of the web was substantially longer than the outer.

Because such large pieces of cloth have survived, it is possible to appreciate the overall arrangement of motifs. These consist largely of angular spirals and stepped frets, which were not merely repeated by the weaver but re-worked and re-shaped with great dexterity. Hocker designs were also popular in ancient Mexico; set inside trapezoidal spaces by the weaver, they exhibit characteristic trapezoidal heads and rhomboid bodies. Motifs such as these undoubtedly held a deep significance, and the hocker has often been interpreted as a fertility symbol. Two-headed hockers, which appear on several pottery vessels from Guerrero, are also shown, and it has been suggested by José Luis Franco that these may represent the union between male and female.

This rare garment offers additional information about dyeing techniques. Chemical analysis has revealed that iron oxide was responsible for the pinkish-red of the cloth. In densely woven areas where threads are tightly packed the colour is uneven, however, and it seems likely that the garment was either immersed in dye after completion or painted. The threads for the decorative band were dyed before weaving; blue, one of the five colours used, was probably derived from indigo.

A further feature is the presence of *tochomitl*, or fur from the soft underbelly of rabbits and hares. Once spun, the downy strands were s-twisted with cotton thread to give strong two-ply yarn which was used to weave large areas of the garment. The resulting cloth must once have been thick and velvety, but the passage of time has caused much of the fur to disintegrate, and it was identified only after careful examination. According to the writings of the Spanish chroniclers, *tochomitl* was widely traded and used by numerous Indian peoples, who not only wove it into their cloth but also embroidered it on to their garments. Fray Toribio de Benavente, known as Motolinía, praised its ability to dye to rich hues, its lasting colours and its silk-like sheen, while Francisco Clavijero noted that fur was used to make 'extremely soft cloth which men of rank wore in winter'. *Tochomitl* was supplanted after the Conquest by sheep's wool, but the Chilapa weaving constitutes a unique reminder of a once-important technique.

Despite the weaver's obvious skill, however, it is evident that the textile arts attained a far greater range and complexity than even this magnificent garment suggests. By the time of the Conquest the long process of evolution in the costume field had culminated in a splendour and diversity which we can only guess at from the admiring descriptions of the chroniclers. Included in the report which Hernán Cortés sent to the king of Spain is an account of gifts received from the Aztec emperor Moctezuma. These included 'many and varied pieces of jewellery of gold and silver, also plumage, with as many as five or six thousand textiles of cotton, all very rich, and woven and wrought in a variety of ways. Besides these, Moctezuma gave me a large quantity of his own textiles which, considering they were cotton and not silk, were such that there could not be fashioned or woven anything similar in the whole world for the variety and naturalness of the colours and for the handiwork. Amongst these were very splendid garments for men and women, bed clothing with which even that made from silk could not be compared . . . and sundry other things that for their quantity and quality I cannot describe to your Majesty'.

Spanish records provide much valuable information about Aztec textiles and styles of dress, but Cortés and his fellow observers were describing a civilisation at its height. Early Aztec history remains obscure, but according to their own legend they were the descendants of nomadic peoples from the north known as Chichimeca, or 'barbarians'.

Scene from the Codex Florentino showing successful warriors being awarded clothing. In Aztec society dress reflected the status of the wearer; although the loincloth and the *tilmatli*, or cloak, were worn by men of all ranks, materials and designs were strictly regulated.

Opposite Tribute levied by the Aztec from towns listed on the left included mantles, loincloths, *huipiles*, skirts and limb-encasing warrior costumes with head-dresses and shields. Codex Mendoza.

Illustrations of these accounts show men in the very simplest dress appropriate to their lives as hunters and gatherers. We are told by Sahagún that during their early wanderings the Aztec 'used only mantles and loincloths of *ixtle* [agave fibre]'. Their search for a new land ended when they reached the Valley of Mexico where they saw the sign for which divine guidance had prepared them: a giant eagle perched on a prickly pear cactus with a serpent in its beak. Having once taken possession of the region, the Aztec began to extend their territories. By 1519 they had established an empire that reached from the Gulf Coast to the Pacific, and stretched northwards as far as the desert and southwards into the mountains of Oaxaca. Within their borders were an estimated 15 million people, most of whom were not Aztec.

Despite their military supremacy, however, the Aztec showed little interest in imposing the forms of their own civilisation upon conquered peoples. Their empire never became a unified nation or even a confederation of states. It rested instead on an economic base, and allegiance was defined in terms of a complex tribute system. By levying regular taxes the Aztec ruling classes were able to assure themselves of an inexhaustible supply of luxury items from hot and cold regions. At the time of the Spanish Conquest the Aztec empire included 38 tributary provinces. The Codex Mendoza comprises an extensive pictorial record of contributions of clothing and jewellery (see p. 49). According to Jacques Soustelle, the province of Xilotepec (today Jilotepec in the state of Mexico) paid a yearly tax of 800 loads of women's clothes (16,000 articles in total), 816 loads of men's loincloths, 800 loads of embroidered skirts, 3,216 loads of *quachtli* (woven cloths), 2 suits for warriors with their head-dresses and shields, maize, and from 1 to 4 live eagles.

Such tributary wealth astonished Spanish observers, and the writings of Fray Diego Durán confirm the quality of produce, which included 'sumptuous cloaks for lords, differently woven and worked, so rich and decorative that some were edged with colours and plumage', and 'clothing for women . . . as cunning and handsome as it is possible to make'. Raw materials too were in demand. Aztec weavers relied on massive imports of cotton from the tropical coastal regions and hot, humid valleys where it grew in abundance. Also levied were large quantities of bark paper, or *amatl*, fibres such as *ixtle*, dyestuffs such as cochineal, and feathers. The tribute rolls cite 24,000 bunches of parrots' feathers as the tax payable by the town of Tochtepec alone.

Foreign trade constituted an additional source of luxury goods. The *pochteca* were a hereditary class of professional merchants who controlled all long-distance trading ventures. One important route led to the port of Xicalango in the territory of the Chontal Maya, who dominated sea-trade round the coasts of Yucatán, and here the *pochteca* were able to acquire jade, tropical plumage and jaguar skins brought by canoe from the Maya hinterland. Even hostile regions were penetrated by a special class of merchant known as 'the disguised ones' who, by adopting the clothing and the language of a region, could pass for natives.

Exotic merchandise and local produce were sold in the great market-place at Tlatelolco. 'There are daily assembled more than 60,000 souls, engaged in buying and selling', wrote Cortés. His companion-at-arms, Bernal Díaz del Castillo, has left an evocative description:

Let us begin with the dealers in gold, silver and precious stones, feathers, cloaks, and embroidered goods. . . . Next there were those who sold coarser cloth, and cotton goods and fabrics made of twisted thread. . . . There were those who sold *henequén* cloth and ropes and sandals they wear on their feet, which are made from the same plant. . . . In another part were the skins

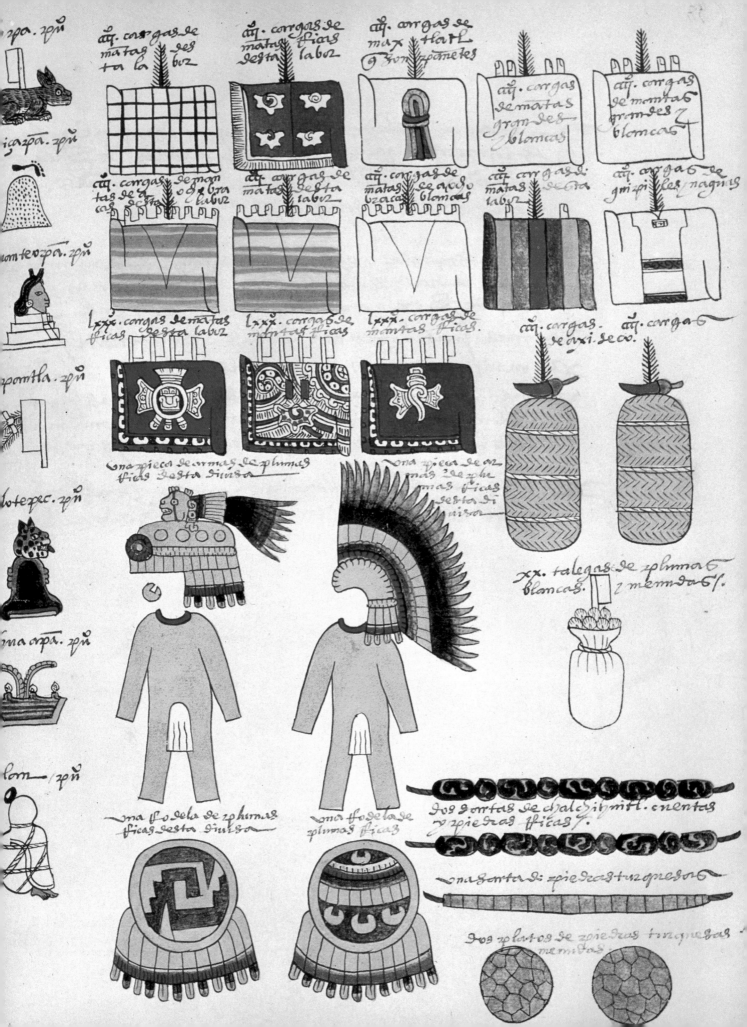

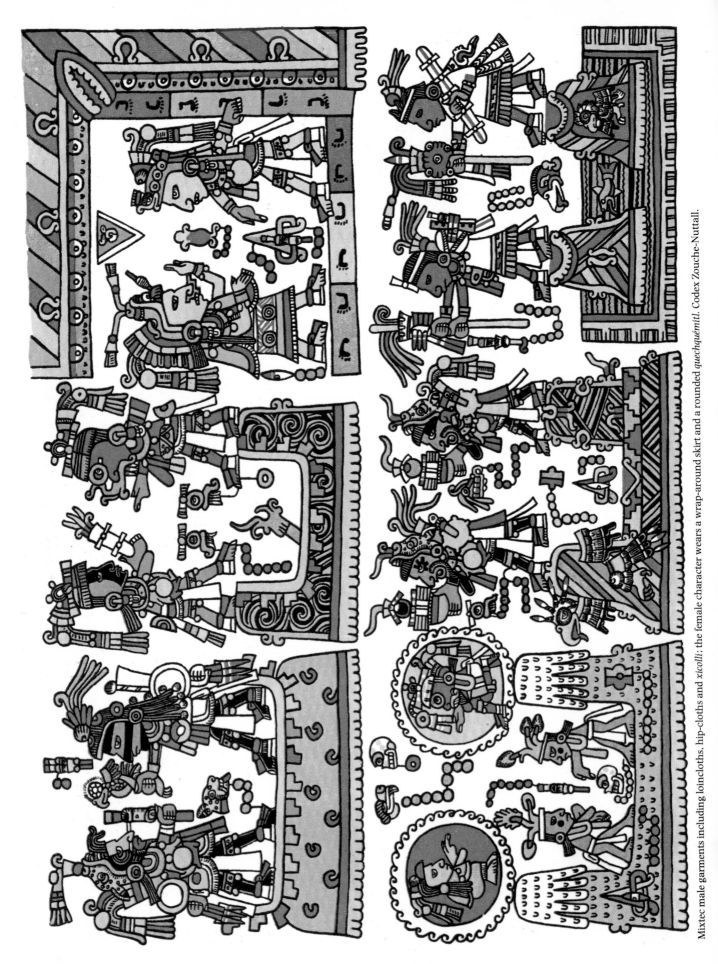

Mixtec male garments including loincloths, hip-cloths and *xicolli*; the female character wears a wrap-around skirt and a rounded *quechquémitl*. Codex Zouche-Nuttall.

End section of a silk-embroidered linen *rebozo* from the mid-18th century depicting life in Mexico City. w. 28¼ in (27 cm); L. 87 in (242 cm). Parham Park.

Lithographs by Carlos Nebel, published in 1836: (*top*) *tortilla*-makers in southern Puebla. The woman grinding maize is probably mulatto; her companions are Indian; (*bottom*) *huipil*-clad Indian women from mountain villages of the south-east. One wears a half-gourd on her head.

Lithographs by Carlos Nebel, published in 1836: (*top*) *hacienda* owner, wearing a *manga* and gaiters, rides with his daughter, servant and administrator; (*bottom*) village *poblanas* smoke and talk with a *sarape*-clad horseman.

Plate from *The Republic of Mexico in 1876*: (*from top to bottom*) '1. Amusgo Indians. S.W. region of Oaxaca. 2. Zapoteca and Tehuantepec Indians in ordinary and holiday dress. 3. Yucatecos. Mestizos in ordinary and holiday dress. Maya country Indian.'

LIT. V. DEBRAY Y Cª

Treadle-loomed, tapestry-woven Saltillo *sarapes* with cotton warp and wool weft. Dyes are natural and include cochineal and indigo. Museum of Mankind.

Right One-web example from last half of 19th century with added fringe and areas of *ombré* dyeing. w. 44 in (111.5 cm); L. 78 in (198 cm).
Below Two-web example from first half of 19th century. w. 62 in (157 cm); L. 94 in (238.5 cm).

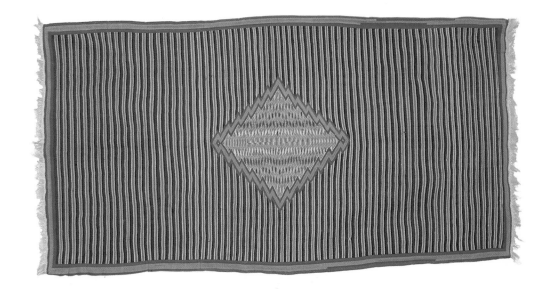

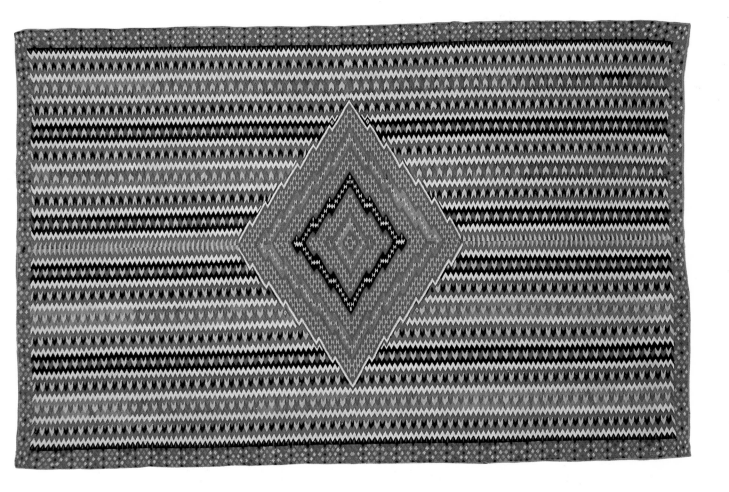

Below Partial view of a 19th-century two-web *sarape*. Tapestry-woven on a treadle loom with a cotton warp and a wool weft, it is edged with red silk braid; the red silk fringe is sewn along both ends. w. 49 in (124.5 cm); L. 89 in (225.5 cm). Maudslay Bequest. Victoria and Albert Museum (T.19–1931).

Opposite top (*left and right*) Brocaded Tzotzil draw-string bags. San Andrés Larrainzar, Chiapas; (*centre*) cross-stitched Huichol shoulder-bag. Jalisco. *Middle* (*left*) embroidered Tepehua shoulder-bag; (*right*) double-woven Otomí draw-string bag. Mezquital Valley, Hidalgo. *Bottom* (*left*) painted Nahua shoulder-bag of *ixtle*. Guerrero; (*right*) double-woven Huichol shoulder-bag. Jalisco.

Below Huichol Indian braiding palm-leaf strips to make a hat. His calico garments are cross-stitched; his sash is woven. San Andrés Cohamiata, Jalisco.

Opposite Huichol couple in *fiesta* attire. The man wears a flannel-edged cape, several bags and sashes, and bead jewellery. The woman's *quechquémitl*, made from bandanna handkerchiefs, is worn on the head. San Andrés Cohamiata, Jalisco.

Opposite Tzotzil women wearing one-web brocaded *huipiles.* Indigo-blue cotton skirts are embroidered in wool with outline and satin stitches, and secured without a sash to form a bag. Venustiano Carranza, Chiapas.

Left Male Tarahumara dancer with rattle during *La Danza de los Matachines.* His head is swathed in *paliacates* (bandanna handkerchiefs) and crowned with an image of the Virgin of Guadalupe. Chihuahua.

Below Nahua girls in *fiesta* attire which includes costly blouses sewn with beads, wrap-around skirts and *ikat*-dyed *rebozos.* Plaits are entwined with ribbons. Atlixco, Puebla.

Opposite Zapotec girl crocheting. Satin-stitched blouses and heavy wrap-around skirts dyed with cochineal are now worn almost solely for *fiestas*. San Antonino Ocotlán, Oaxaca.

Right Section of a blouse embroidered by Faustina Sumano de Sánchez. Flowers are satin-stitched with silk thread, and crocheted lace is used to join blouse sections. San Juan Chilateca, Oaxaca.

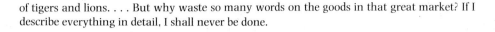

Opposite Adornments of netted beadwork: (*left*) Huichol bag, earrings, pectoral, bracelet and hatband, Jalisco; (*right*) Otomí woman's hair-cord, or *techomite*. Worn during festivals, it is wrapped around a single plait. San Pablito, Puebla.

of tigers and lions. . . . But why waste so many words on the goods in that great market? If I describe everything in detail, I shall never be done.

Yet Díaz does continue with his enumeration to mention, among other things, 'much cochineal, which is for sale too under the arcades of that market'.

Because theirs was the last of the great pre-Conquest civilisations to evolve in Mexico, the Aztec were able to draw freely on the cultural legacy of earlier peoples. Traditions and skills were assimilated, together with a concern for beauty and fine craftsmanship. Most of the exotic raw materials imported into the Aztec capital were converted into highly coveted luxury goods by professional artisans. Subdivided into groups like 'guilds', they honoured their own patron gods and lived in specially designated areas within the inner city. Goldsmiths, lapidaries, feather-workers and other groups with similarly prestigious skills were known collectively as *tolteca*, because they were thought to have inherited their skills from the Toltec who, under the guidance of the legendary god-king Quetzalcóatl, excelled in fine craftsmanship. There were, in addition, a number of less specialised skills which were practised as a part of everyday life by the rank and file.

The textile arts cut across all boundaries, however, for spinning and weaving were seen as indispensable at every level of society. The sole domain of women, they were passed down from generation to generation, and we are told by Motolinía that it was customary, soon after the birth of a baby girl, to place in her hand 'a spindle and weaving stick, as a sign that she should be diligent and housewifely, a good spinner and a better weaver'. Instruction as to the use of these implements could only be symbolic at such an early age, but later on teaching began in earnest as illustrated in the Codex Mendoza. Even girls of noble birth received training in the textile arts and attended special seminaries annexed to the temples. The invention of spinning and weaving was attributed to the goddess Xochiquetzal, and during her feast Aztec women were burnt in her honour. Sahagún, who describes these rituals, recounts how victims burned their spinning and weaving equipment beforehand, in the belief that it would await them in the next world. The goddess Tlazoltéotl-Toci was also closely linked with spinning and weaving, while Mayahuel was associated with the agave.

Textiles had many uses within Aztec society. Vast quantities were offered each year to the gods, and Durán's writings abound with detailed descriptions of the hangings that adorned the inner chambers of the temples, or the draperies used during religious processions. In the emperor's palace and in the houses of the nobility textiles also served as canopies, wall-hangings and bed-coverings. In addition, weavings were needed as dowry payments, for marriage ceremonies, and as wrappings for the dead. Textiles too were important as media of exchange. Lengths of cloth known as *quachtli* were an intrinsic feature of the Aztec economy, which operated according to a barter system.

It was the production of clothing, however, which took up the most considerable part of a weaver's time and energy, regardless of rank. Ordinary women were expected to dress themselves and their families, while noblewomen often took great pride in knowing how to weave and embroider rich textiles. According to Díaz del Castillo, 'women of the family of the great Moctezuma also, of all ranks, were extremely ingenious in these works, and were constantly employed; as was a certain description of females who lived together in the manner of nuns'. The role played by costume was more than just functional, however: Aztec society had become highly stratified by the time of the Conquest, and it was dress which best served to reinforce this hierarchical structure through a rigid series of rulings. The uncomplicated construction of Indian garments made it necessary to emphasise status by restricting the materials and types of fibre used, and by barring all but the noble and privileged from wearing certain adornments and design motifs. This fitted in well with the Aztec outlook, for believing as they did in predestination they were accustomed to searching for signs and symbols, and to vesting all things, even a feather, a jewel or a colour, with an inner meaning.

Aztec society was divided into several categories. At the top were the aristocratic lineages which included the emperor, his relatives and other noble families. It was at this level that the full complexity and sophistication of costume were reflected. As Patricia Anawalt has pointed out in a study of Aztec sumptuary laws entitled 'Costume and Control', it was the constant supply of exotic raw materials and luxury fabrics obtained from trade and tribute that made possible the dazzling variety of decorations and styles required to set this élite apart from the rank and file. Cotton, both the white variety known as *ichcatl* and the coyote-coloured strain named *coyoichcatl*, was reserved for the nobility; according to Durán, the common people were prohibited from wearing it 'under pain of death'. For greater splendour and warmth cotton cloth was interwoven with feathers, or else woven from cotton which had been interspun with feathers or rabbit fur. Although such clothing was often imported, it was also produced locally by skilled Aztec weavers.

In the codices high-ranking personages are often shown wearing richly coloured and elaborately patterned garments, but as is the case with the Mixtec or the Maya, it is difficult to be sure how specific designs were achieved. Several illustrations point to the probable use of *plangi*, or tie-dyeing, and it is possible that the Aztec also employed *batik*- and *ikat*-patterned cloth, or imprinted garments with clay stamps. Freehand painting may have been widely practised, for the Codex Florentino contains references to such garments as cloaks 'painted with bloodied faces'. It is certain that many designs were the result of weaving, however. While investigating the weavers' craft, Sahagún noted that 'They made excellent textiles from cotton, some thick and others as thin and delicate as holland. . . . These cloths they fashioned with different weaves and colours so as to represent in them various animals and flowers'. Excavations carried out during the late 1960s at Tlatelolco have produced burnt fragments of cloth exhibiting plain, basket, semi-basket, twill and brocade techniques, but the range practised by Aztec weavers probably included most other Middle American skills. Tapestry-work, mentioned and praised by the chroniclers, may have been responsible for popular geometric motifs such as the step-fret, while a reference to coloured cloaks that were 'fleecy like plush' on the top side, but smooth and colourless on the other, suggests the use of weft-loop, or pile weaving.

Embroidery was clearly a source of rich and intricate patterning in late pre-Conquest Mexico. Again it is Sahagún, so informative on the subject of the textile arts, who gives us the description of a 'loincloth with an ivy design embroidered along the ends', and a 'cloak embroidered with sun-rays', although we are not told which stitches were used. Onlay work with feathers afforded yet another method for decorating luxury clothing; this was done by sewing or gluing them to the cloth. When Durán mentioned 'an elaborate feather mantle done in black, red and white, designed like the jewel – a butterfly wing', he was surely evoking one of these two types of work. For added magnificence garments were edged with fringes and tassels, or embellished with precious stones, shells, copper bells and ornaments of gold or silver.

Aztec feather-worker from the Codex
Florentino.

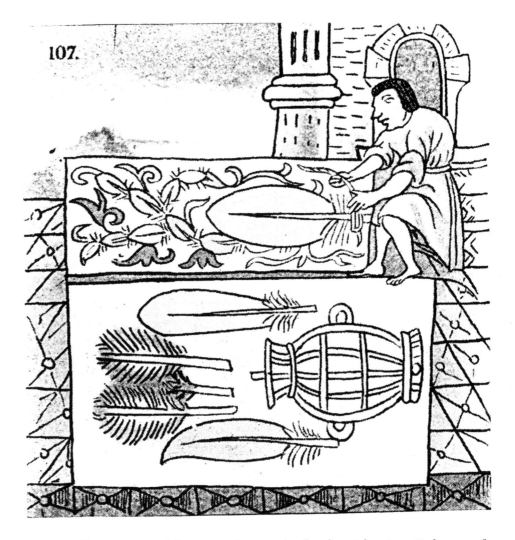

Codex illustrations and frequent references by the chroniclers to netted capes of
henequén, some of which were dyed, confirm the importance of this ancient technique.
Although the wearers were often of low status, such garments were also worn by the
élite. Decorative examples incorporated beads, shells and ribbon, and it seems certain
that feathered mantles sometimes depended on a netted ground. The Codex Florentino
contains an interesting reference to 'capes of plaited paper bordered with butterflies'.
By 'paper' Sahagún presumably meant *amatl* (bark paper), which was extensively
used by the Aztec for their ceremonial garments and offerings.

In assimilating the textile skills of other cultures the Aztec also adopted a wide
range of garments – ceremonial and military as well as secular – and today it is
Náhuatl terminology which is most often used when describing indigenous dress.
Chief among male garments was the *maxtlatl*, or loincloth. Generally both ends were
tied in a knot at the front, but it is clear from codices and other representations that
gods and those ritually impersonating them were distinguished by having the ends
hanging to the back and front. Some of the rich designs adorning the *maxtlatl* of the
nobility were listed by Sahagún, and they included 'a butterfly design at the ends' and
'a market-place design', while one example was described as a 'coyote fur breechclout
with an eagle head'. In addition men of high rank occasionally wore a hip-cloth.

The most important guide to masculine status was the *tilmatli*, or mantle, which was basically a rectangular web of cloth varying in size. The Codex Florentino lists as many as fifty-four different styles. Some dignitaries apparently wore two and even three together, or used a netted cloak over a woven one so that the colour could be glimpsed through the mesh. These were almost certainly marks of privilege, for cloaks were subject to strict controls even among the highest echelons of Aztec society. According to Durán, one of Moctezuma's regulations on dress stated that 'Only the King may wear the fine mantles of cotton embroidered with designs and threads of different colours and feather-work. He is to decide which cloak is to be worn by the royal person to distinguish him from the rest. . . . The great lords, who are twelve, may wear certain mantles, and the minor lords wear others'. It was not only the decorative elements that were prescribed, however; the length of cloaks was fixed and also the manner of wearing, for although it was usual to knot the extremities over the right shoulder, as a mark of special status the emperor and a few high-ranking nobles were entitled to tie their cloaks in front.

The use of *cactli*, or sandals, was also strictly regulated. We know from the codices and other sources that footwear could assume a great many varieties of shape and decoration. Gold, gems, the skins of wild animals such as ocelots and jaguars, the feathers of tropical birds and rich embroidery all entered into the making of sandals for the privileged. Head-dresses, jewellery and other adornments were similarly determined by the wearer's rank. These included plumes of *quetzal* feathers, fans, earspools, necklaces, bracelets, anklets and ornaments worn through the septum of the nose. Some dignitaries also pierced the skin beneath the lower lip to take rich jewels fashioned from crystal, shell, amber, turquoise, jade or gold.

Status within Aztec society was not restricted solely to those of noble birth, however; service to the State was respected, and achievement rewarded. Civil officials who administered justice and saw to the running of the empire enjoyed various privileges, and so did the *pochteca*, or professional merchants, whose long-distance trading missions enabled them on occasion to serve the State as spies. On feast days successful *pochteca* were therefore permitted to display their often considerable wealth and to abandon the simple cloaks which they were otherwise obliged to wear.

The priests, who by selfless and dedicated service to the temples won divine favour for the entire Aztec people, had their own hierarchy with appropriate costumes. Basic dress included the loincloth and the mantle, often tied in front and patterned according to status, but Durán's writings refer also to 'wide tunics', 'surplices', 'dalmatics' and to a 'sleeveless jacket of red leather'. It was stated by some chroniclers that the priests never cleansed their bodies of the blood of sacrificial victims, while according to Francisco J. Clavijero they also anointed themselves with red and yellow ochre and soot. Their hair, uncut and unwashed, was apparently braided with thick cotton cords, and sometimes a black cloth was worn over the head like a veil. Yet it is clearly a misapprehension to suppose that Aztec priests were always the sombre figures described in popular history books. Durán's descriptions prove that priestly costume was frequently colourful and magnificent. Of the priest appointed to kill a victim during an important ceremony he wrote: 'These were his garments: a red mantle similar to a dalmatic, fringed in green; a head-dress of splendid green and yellow feathers; in his ears, golden ear-plugs inlaid with green jade; in his lower lip a labret of blue stone'.

Inseparably linked with religion was war, for there could be no greater service to the State than to capture victims for sacrifice or to extend the frontiers of the empire. The battlefield offered nobles and free-born commoners alike the chance to earn the costume rewards which only the emperor could bestow. This link between dress and military achievement was underlined by Durán, who quoted the utterances of Tlacaelel, adviser to the Aztec ruler:

Know now that the King . . . has willed that lip-plugs, golden garlands, many-coloured feathers, ear-plugs, armbands, shields, weapons, insignia, mantles and loincloths are not to be bought in the market any longer by brave men. From now on the sovereign will deliver them as payment for memorable deeds. . . . He who does not dare go to war, even though he be the king's son, from now on will be deprived of all these things.

The Codex Mendoza is an invaluable guide to military attire and to the mantles awarded to different warrior grades. Many of these sought-after garments appear in the tribute section, together with limb-encasing costumes known as *tlahuitztli*. The Anonymous Conqueror defined these as 'suits all of one piece and of a heavy cloth, which they tie at the back; these are covered with feathers of different colours and look very splendid'. Protective tunics and jackets were termed *ichcahuipilli*. Made, according to Sahagún, from 'fluffed up cotton covered with cloth', they were painted or, in the words of Díaz del Castillo, 'richly ornamented on the outside with many coloured feathers'. Further description by the Anonymous Conqueror stated that 'the strength of their feather-covered garments is proportionate to their weapons, so that they resist spears, arrows, and even the sword.' In her book *Indian Clothing before Cortés: Mesoamerican Costume from the Codices* Patricia Anawalt identifies another military garment called an *ehuatl*. Made without padding and covered with feathers, it was occasionally worn over tight-fitting *ichcahuipilli* and seems to have incorporated a feathered skirt. Sculptures of warriors confirm that the triangular Toltec-style apron was also regarded as a military garment.

Military head-dresses were often highly elaborate, as recorded by the Anonymous Conqueror: 'To defend the head they wear things like heads of serpents, or tigers, or lions, or wolves, and the man's head lies inside the animal's jaws as though it were devouring him. These heads are of wood covered on the outside with feathers or incrustations of gold or precious stones, and are something wonderful to behold'. Although wood is mentioned here, when describing these same head-dresses Durán speaks of 'quilted cotton'. Zoomorphic helmets appear in the tribute lists of the Codex Mendoza, together with pointed headpieces, magnificent feather head-dresses and hair ornaments such as the *quetzaltalpiloni*.

Resplendent though the costumes of the bravest warriors and chief priests must have been, however, their luxury was never comparable with that of the emperor. His ornaments and rich weavings symbolised his power and his ability to govern, and the writings of the chroniclers abound with references to his exquisite and varied apparel. Describing Moctezuma's many capes, the historian Hernando Alvarado Tezozomoc mentioned one 'in the manner of blue net, with in the knots of it . . . rich gems delicately attached', while Díaz del Castillo spoke of his sandals 'the soles of which are gold and the upper parts ornamented with precious stones'. Such splendour was enhanced by the drab appearance of all those who entered the palace, for according to Díaz del Castillo courtiers and foreign chiefs alike 'were compelled to take off their rich cloaks and put on others of little value'. Even in death the emperor was richly robed. In Sahagún's words 'his corpse was clothed in fifteen to twenty of the finest cotton

Replica of the head-dress given by Moctezuma to Hernán Cortés, made from iridescent green *quetzal* plumes and trimmed with gold ornaments and blue, brown, red and white feathers. H. 48¾ in (124 cm). Museo Nacional de Antropología, Mexico.

garments woven in various styles. He was decked out in jewellery of gold, silver and precious stones'. Little remains today of so much magnificence, but one head-dress, preserved in the Museum für Völkerkunde in Vienna, serves as a tangible reminder of a vanished world where fine clothing and elaborate adornment could, in the words of Jacques Soustelle, 'make of a man something greater than a man, almost a divine being, hieratic and filled with splendour'.

The consorts of high-born and powerful men were also richly dressed, and although little mention was made by chroniclers of sumptuary laws governing female costume, it is to be supposed that it reflected the status of fathers and husbands. As with other pre-Conquest cultures, the chief garment was the wrap-around skirt, or *cueitl*. Tied at the waist with a sash, or *nelpiloni*, it reached almost to the ankles. Especially ornate clothing was reserved for ceremonial occasions; according to Sahagún, skirts worn during ritual dances were patterned with hearts, spirals, leaves and other motifs. The torso-garment in general use among Aztec women was the *huipil*. Tributary examples described by Durán included many 'with designs and feather-work on the front; . . . and on the back of others embroidered flowers . . . imperial eagles . . . flowers

Late Post-Classic Aztec stone statue of Chalchiuhtlicue, goddess of sweet water, with a tasselled *quechquémitl*. H. 11 in (28 cm). Museum of Mankind, London.

embroidered and so enriched with feather-work that they were a joy to behold'. In the Codex Mendoza even the simplest adult *huipil* was shown with a decorative lower border and a rectangular motif below the neck. The *quechquémitl* was found only in ceremonial contexts, when it was worn alone or over a *huipil*. Goddesses in Aztec sculpture were often shown with *quechquémitl* edged with tassels or pom-poms.

Various sections in the Codex Florentino were devoted to neighbouring peoples. The nomadic 'barbarians' of the north, for example, had only 'limited' clothing. According to Sahagún's informants, 'all the clothing of the Chichimeca was of skins, and the skirts of their women were of skins. They tanned the skins; they cut them into thongs'. The Tamime, on the other hand, were regarded as only semi-Chichimeca, for they wore 'tattered capes' and had 'learnt a more civilised way of life' which probably included weaving. The Michoaque (known today as Tarascans or Purépecha) inhabited western Mexico and were never conquered by the Aztec. They 'were real artisans, real feather-workers . . . lapidaries. The Michoaca women understood well the working of cotton thread'. Women wore 'only a skirt; they lacked a shift', while men covered themselves 'only with their *cicuilli*, the so-called sleeveless jacket'.

Late Post-Classic Huastec statue. Although Sahagún noted that Huastec men went without loincloths, this male youth wears a finely decorated example. Museo Nacional de Antropología, Mexico.

Aztec women from the Codex Florentino with *huipiles* and wrap-around skirts. The figure on the right wears her hair in a horn-like style.

Within the Aztec empire the Totonac women of the Gulf Coast drew high praise for their elegance. Skilled weavers, their dress consisted of 'vari-coloured skirts' and 'vari-coloured shoulder shawls . . . of netting' which were probably *quechquémitl*. The Aztec also admired the Huastec women, who 'dressed themselves well in skirts, in shifts'. Their weaving skills were clearly considerable, and Sahagún described some of the many fine capes which came from their looms. Huastec women were apparently fond of personal adornment, for they 'coloured their hair diverse colours – some yellow, some red'. Men also filed their teeth 'like gourd seeds'. Otomí women were even more given to ornamentation, however. Described as skilled 'weavers of designs', they were also 'very gaudy dressers'. In addition they 'darkened their teeth', 'painted their faces', 'pasted themselves with red feathers', and tattooed their arms and breasts with 'painting' that 'was well scratched, well scarified, very green, bluish, very beautiful'.

In Tenochtitlan, by contrast, over-conspicuous dressing was frowned upon, and well-bred women were supposed to rely upon cleanliness to enhance their charms. 'Never paint your face', began a father's advice to his daughter, as recorded by Sahagún. 'If you want your husband to love you, dress well, wash yourself and wash your clothes'. This fits in well with Aztec views on the family, for according to Sahagún a good daughter was one who was 'modest', while a bad daughter was described as 'showy, pompous, gaudy of dress'. The courtesans who kept company with young warriors apparently cared little for the disapproval of society, however, but used all the known aids to beauty. Sahagún, in a long and evocative passage, wrote of the 'harlot':

She appears like a flower . . . arrays herself gaudily . . . anoints herself with *axin* [a waxy yellow ointment] . . . her face is covered with rouge, her cheeks are coloured, her teeth are darkened – rubbed with cochineal. [Half] her hair falls loose, half is wound round about her head. She arranges her hair in horns. . . . She perfumes herself, casts incense about her, uses rose water. . . . She chews *chicle* [gum]. . . . She promenades . . . goes about laughing.

Accompanying illustrations show that the skirts and *huipiles* of these 'shameless' and 'lascivious' women were handsomely decorated. Such ostentation was in theory denied to women of the lower classes, however, while male costume had likewise to reflect the humble status of the wearer. Barred from wearing cotton, the common people were accustomed to using both yucca and *ixtle*, or agave fibre. Fine thread and remarkably supple cloth were produced from this last plant by weavers such as the Otomí, who specialised in working with it. Interestingly, the method in use today differs little from the one ascribed to the Otomí by Sahagún. According to him, the green leaves 'were toasted, dressed, scraped. They pressed the water [out of the fibre], treated it with maize dough, spun it, placed it over the shoulder, wove it'.

Basic garments worn by members of the lower orders were the same as those commonly worn among the nobility but without the wealth of ornamentation. Women wore the wrap-around skirt and waist-sash together with the *huipil*. The loincloth was essential for all Aztec men; the Huastec, like the Michoaque, attracted strong criticism because, according to Sahagún, they 'did not provide themselves with breech-clouts'. Some men of low rank, like the porters shown in the Codex Mendoza, apparently used netted hip-cloths of *ixtle*. The common man's cloak, or *tilmatli*, stopped above the knee; if it reached the ankles, according to Durán, the penalty was death. The codices show tightly woven white cloaks, as well as coarser examples of loosely netted mesh or knotted cords. Tied over one shoulder, such cloaks were often worn below the opposite arm to allow freedom of movement.

Despite the ban on cotton, the seller of coarse *maguey*-fibre cloaks described by Sahagún had a surprisingly wide range of merchandise to offer his clients. The best capes, 'burnished with a stone' and ringing when tapped 'like a pottery rattle', were decorated with 'whirlpool designs, as if with eyes painted', and many others such as 'the ocelot design' and 'the small face'. Even the looser and coarser capes could be 'flowered'. Patricia Anawalt, in her article entitled 'Costume and Control', takes descriptions such as these to indicate that lower-class clothing was possibly not as drab as the sumptuary laws imply. Did they, she asks, apply principally to the ritualistic and official side of Aztec life, and represent a somewhat idealised image of the military and political order in pre-Conquest Tenochtitlan? In her view the masses may well have been 'bedazzled' by the richly dressed nobles who 'served as forms of symbolic control for the State', yet they surely had ways of imitating the costume of their superiors, as in other parts of the world where an élite has sought to regulate the clothing of the rank and file. She concludes that 'authoritarian efforts to govern artistic expression as reflected in dress have seldom been successful and personal adornment irrepressibly appears to be people's favourite art'.

Scene from the Codex Florentino showing the *telpochcalli*, or military school for commoners' sons. Unadorned loincloths and *tilmatli* can be seen. One pupil, termed a 'shorn one', wears a lock of hair, or *piochtli*, on the nape of his neck; his netted cape is 'hung with very large fibre balls'.

Mexican embroidered sampler, 1850,
with sections of beading. $14\frac{1}{2} \times 29\frac{1}{2}$ in
(36.8×74.9 cm). Victoria and Albert
Museum, London (T.92–1954).

PART II

THE POST-CONQUEST HERITAGE

Scene from the Lienzo de Tlaxcala:
Hernán Cortés and Doña Marina (his
Indian interpreter and mistress) wear
Old- and New-World clothing. When
Aztec emissaries first saw the round hats
of the *conquistadores*, they likened them
to small *comales*, or clay griddles.

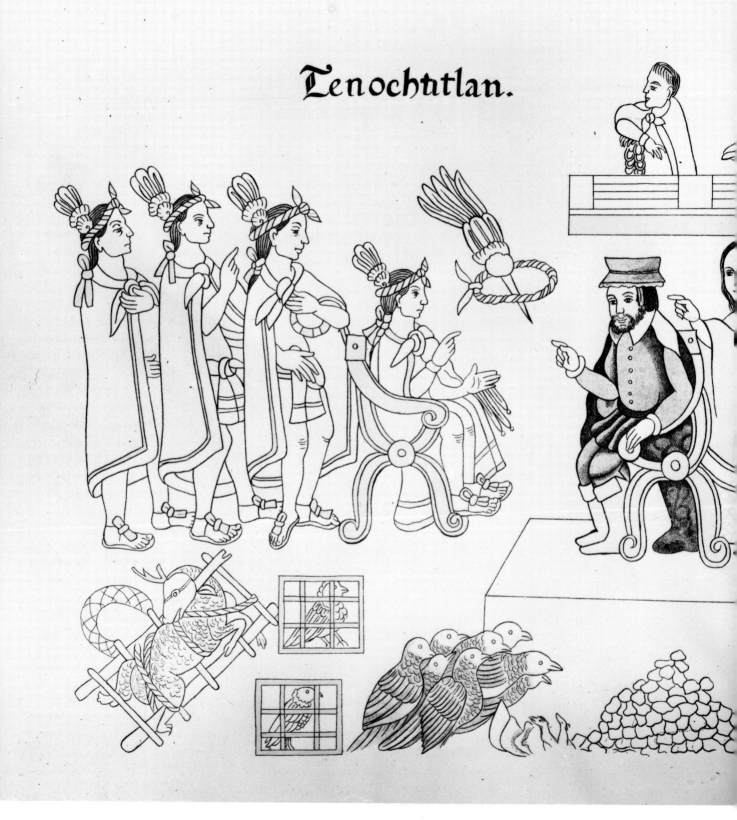

Tenochtitlan.

3 Costume in New Spain (1521–1821)

'I saw the things which have been brought to the King from the new golden land', wrote Albrecht Dürer, the German painter and engraver, in 1520. This now famous entry in his journal referred to the exhibition in Brussels of treasures and curiosities sent from Mexico by Hernán Cortés to Charles V, king of Spain and the Netherlands. Among the wonders which impressed Dürer were exquisite examples of gold and silverworking, but there were also 'strange garments, bedspreads, and all manner of marvellous things for many uses . . .'. So moved was Dürer by this collection that he concluded: 'In all the days of my life I have seen nothing that so rejoiced my heart as these things, for I saw among them strange and artful things, and I marvelled at the subtle genius of men in distant lands.'

It is ironic that this precious shipment, destined to be melted down for bullion or dispersed without trace, should have represented some of the highest technological achievements of ancient Mexican civilisation, while at the same time heralding its overthrow. For these objects, so admired by Dürer, were the first gifts which Cortés received from Moctezuma after landing at what is today Veracruz in 1519. According to Aztec informants, the emperor was greatly disturbed at hearing from his messengers of the arrival of fair-skinned and bearded strangers who travelled in 'small mountains that floated on the waves of the sea'. Already unnerved by a series of seemingly threatening portents thought to foretell the imminent return of the god Quetzalcóatl, Moctezuma sent these rich presents in the hope of placating the invaders and deterring them from advancing on the Aztec capital. They had the reverse effect, however. The sight of such wealth only hardened the resolve of Cortés and his followers to take possession of this land, soon to be thought of throughout Europe as 'golden'.

For more than a quarter of a century previously Spanish ships had been exploring the seas in search of new territories and trade openings. Almost 800 years of Moorish occupation and Christian resistance had accustomed the Spaniards to an economy largely based on booty wrested from their 'pagan' enemies. As Christopher Columbus was to point out in the dedication of his logbook, the long struggle to drive the Moors out of Spain had been successfully concluded on the very eve of his discovery of America. Spain, united and mighty, was free to deploy her military powers in the New World and to secure for herself an alternative source of wealth.

The writings of Bernal Díaz del Castillo and others chronicled the seemingly impossible victories won in Mexico by Cortés and a relatively small fighting force in the face of the massive and hitherto invincible Aztec army. Although well served by their metal weapons, gunpowder and horses, the Spaniards were greatly assisted in their conquest by the Tlaxcalans, who had long been rivals of the Aztec, as well as by subjugated peoples anxious to free themselves. Within only two years of Cortés' arrival in Mexico the Aztec empire had been destroyed and Tenochtitlan reduced to ruins.

There had been many earlier wars in Mexico: during such confrontations the vanquished had found themselves to be on much the same intellectual, spiritual and technological level as their conquerors. However, as those Indians who had contributed to the overthrow of the old order were soon to realise, they had exchanged one form of oppression for another so far-reaching that within only a short period of time it was to transform their lives totally.

The contradictions underlying the early years of Spanish rule were many. Based on private enterprise, the Conquest was carried out by brave and ambitious men eager to reap their reward, while the Crown also required its percentage of all revenue, officially termed the Royal Fifth. Charles V was not only king of Spain, however; as emperor of the Holy Roman Empire it was his moral duty to justify military conquest in terms of religious conquest, however incompatible these aims might seem today. Inevitably, greed often clashed with Christian obligations. On the one hand were those whom Díaz del Castillo described as 'poor and greedy with a dog's hunger for wealth and slaves'; on the other, often in direct opposition, were the crusading friars, genuinely anxious to spread and promote the teachings of the Catholic Church. In their desire to save the souls of their new charges they dedicated themselves to eradicating pagan beliefs and native forms of worship. Many were also tireless campaigners for the Indians' material welfare, arguing vociferously against the widely held view that Indians, as unreasoning and inferior beings, were fit only to be the slaves of Spaniards. One of their most influential defenders was Bartolomé de las Casas, Bishop for the then Guatemalan province of Chiapas, who carried his protest to Spain, complaining that Indians were being treated as 'of less worth than bedbugs'.

The lot of Indians in easily accessible areas was indeed a miserable one. According to some estimates, between one-third and a half of the native population was wiped out by European diseases such as smallpox. Within the *encomienda* system groups of Indians were entrusted to Spanish settlers, who commanded their labour and exacted tribute in exchange for religious instruction. Virtual slaves, Indians were often worked to exhaustion. In the mines large numbers also died digging for silver and gold. Harsh

Indian woman (*right*) and nobleman (*left*) drawn by Cristoph Weiditz. In 1528 Cortés took a group of princes, jugglers and ball-players to Spain, where their accoutrements and facial jewellery aroused great curiosity.

conditions and an unfamiliar climate on the newly created plantations accounted for further deaths among Indians brought in from other regions.

The arrival in 1535 of the first viceroy marked the start of the Colonial period in New Spain, as Mexico became officially known, and nearly three centuries of political stability followed. With the implementation of stricter controls many of the *conquistadores* were displaced from their positions of privilege, and some of the more extreme forms of exploitation were prohibited, but the *haciendas* which eventually replaced the *encomiendas* posed yet another threat to the Indians' liberty. As greater and greater areas of land passed out of their grasp into Spanish ownership, Indians had little alternative but to seek work as labourers on these vast and profitable estates where low wages forced them to contract debts which bound them to the *haciendas* for the rest of their lives.

By contrast, the undertakings of the Spanish colonists were richly rewarded. Vast fortunes accrued, founded on the shipments of silver which regularly left the port of Veracruz for Spain, together with less precious but important cargoes that included vanilla, balsam, cocoa beans and dyestuffs such as indigo, logwood and cochineal. In the same way that Spain welcomed many of the natural products of the New World, Mexico benefited by the introduction of European cereals and cattle, both of which represented yet another source of wealth for Spanish landholders. Predictably, this new-found affluence was accompanied by a keen appetite for luxury. Prosperous settlers were eager to proclaim their riches, and costume was the ideal vehicle for such a display.

Ready-made clothing, in extremely short supply during the early years of conquest, figured prominently in the list of imports. Spain, anxious to capitalise on her captive market, barred other European nations from trading independently with the colonies: foreign goods were only exempted from this ban if they passed through Sevilla and later Cádiz where steep tariffs were applied. The long sea-voyage, and the necessity of providing an armed escort to protect ships from attack by pirates, pushed up the price of merchandise still further. In addition, it was customary for traders in Mexico to buy up large consignments which were later resold at an even more inflated cost to the purchaser. This last practice was also applied to the shipments of more exotic merchandise which began to reach Acapulco after 1565 when The Philippines came under Spanish rule. With Mexico as the transit point for trade between Spain and the Orient consumers could now enjoy a wide range of luxury produce that included porcelain, ivory and bronze as well as satins, velvets, brocades and rich silks from China which rivalled Spanish textiles and were sold for lower prices. The middle decades of the sixteenth century saw a large number of Spanish tailors established in Mexico. Their skills enabled them to work with these imported fabrics and to provide their clients with well-made clothing based on Spanish models and reflecting fashion trends in the Old World.

Mexico's new colonists had no intention of remaining dependent on sporadic and often expensive imports of cloth, however. Given the intricacy and richness of so many Indian textiles, it is hardly surprising that they should have called on local weavers to meet a large number of their requirements. The *encomienda* system enabled landholders to exact sizeable payments of cloth and finished garments from their taxpaying vassals, just as Aztec rulers had done previously. Indeed, the old Aztec tribute records proved invaluable during this time, providing information about gold deposits and also listing the textile and other contributions of each region. In their greed for cloth, which they not only sold nationally at great profit but also exported to Spain, landholders often overworked those in their charge. This is indicated by the following edict issued in 1549: 'No *encomendero* or other person shall in any case force Indian women to be shut up in corrals or elsewhere to spin and weave the clothing that they are to be given as tribute, and they shall have freedom to do this in their houses so that they will not be exploited.' Early records itemise the taxes paid by large numbers of villages. One entry for the year 1528 assessed the tribute payable by the villagers of Cuzumala (now Cutzamala in Guerrero) at 'twelve loads of heavy clothing and twelve loads of medium cotton clothing every eighty days' and 'Six hundred slave blankets sent to the mines every eighty days'.

Throughout the Colonial period the cultivation of cotton continued unabated. Impressed by the quality and abundance of native cotton, the new settlers promoted its growth in all the traditional cotton-growing areas. They were understandably keen, however, to introduce some of the other raw materials to which they had been accustomed in Spain. By the 1530s hemp and flax for making linen were being regularly cultivated in Mexico. As for silk, the efforts of the Dominican order met with great success in the Mixteca region of Oaxaca, which soon became one of the most important centres for silk production in the New World. Plantations established in Puebla's Atlixco Valley and other parts also prospered, and the general standard of Mexican silk rose so high that Motolinía, the Franciscan friar, registered these words of praise: 'The silk that is made here . . . is so excellent that it does not deteriorate even if cast into strong bleach'. Mulberry trees, first introduced into Mexico on the orders of Cortés, 'thrive to such an extent that they become larger in one year than in five years in Spain'. The silkworms proved unusually resilient and silk could be harvested twice yearly. These considerations led Motolinía in 1540 to predict '. . . so much silk will be cultivated here [in the Atlixco Valley] that in this respect this region will be one of the richest in the world . . . in a few years more silk will be produced in New Spain than in all Christendom . . .' Thomas Gage, an English friar who visited Mexico during the first half of the seventeenth century, provided further information: the state of Michoacán was 'abounding in mulberry trees, silk . . .', while the silk towns of the Mixteca did 'trade with the best silk that there is in all that country'.

Success was ultimately destined to bring about the downfall of such ventures, however. In 1679 a Spanish decree ordered the uprooting of all mulberry trees and the destruction of Mexico's silk looms. Flax cultivation too was banned, and similar embargoes were placed on wine and olive production by the king, who feared that strong competition would weaken Spain's industries and lose her her captive Colonial market. The ban on flax achieved the desired effect, and an attempt at the end of the eighteenth century to revive its cultivation met with little success: linen was to remain a costly luxury, imported from Spain, Holland and Rouen in France. Silk culture fared marginally better, however. Many mulberry trees survived the decree in Mexico's remoter areas, enabling the local population to continue small-scale silk production into the twentieth century.

The introduction of wool into Mexico apparently gave the king less cause for concern. The first wool-flocks arrived in 1526 at the instigation of Cortés. Within a few years they were followed by merino sheep, this time at the request of the first viceroy, and this new strain greatly improved existing stock. Flocks adapted well to conditions in central Mexico and Oaxaca, and sheep farmers were allowed to concentrate on wool production unimpeded by royal restrictions.

To accompany these new materials Spanish settlers also introduced various features of European technology: these included a number of dyestuffs, the spinning-wheel, the distaff for use when preparing flax fibres, wool cards for untangling newly shorn wool, winding frames for spun yarn, European-style warping frames, scissors and needles of steel. By far the most important innovation in the textile field, however, was the treadle, or shaft, loom with its ingenious interplay of pulleys, shuttles and multiple heddle bars. It not only had the advantage of speed, but was also capable of weaving cloth in far broader widths than was possible with the traditional backstrap loom, and within only a few decades of the Conquest it had become the mainstay of the new clothing industry.

Far from being dismayed by the introduction of so many alien materials and appliances, Mexico's Indian population was quick to recognise their uses and, in some regions, to master the new skills. A remarkable story told by Motolinía illustrates this: two male Indians were sent to Mexico City to learn wool processing and treadle-loom weaving; they watched each stage of production, measured all the implements, and were ready after little more than twenty days to return to their village, where they constructed looms and set about weaving woollen cloth. The creation of textiles had traditionally been a female task in Mexico, but work patterns underwent a change as increasingly large numbers of men were initiated into the new technology. Operating European-style looms, first within the *encomienda* system and later on the great *haciendas*, they provided their overlords with fine blankets and bales of cloth using cotton and wool from local flocks.

Not all colonists chose to remain in the country, however. The seventeenth century saw the continued expansion of towns and cities where the rich and privileged shared an appetite for fine clothing and the other trappings of wealth. Controlling the various trades which catered for their needs were the guilds. Set up soon after the Conquest, they adhered to strict rulings which in many cases prohibited entry to Indians. According to a sixteenth-century decree, Indians were barred from working, using, or even possessing gold and silver – metals which they had once dominated with such skill. Initially textile-working was similarly closed to Indians, but their labour was needed and the ban was soon lifted. When the great migration to the towns began in the seventeenth century, the clothing industry offered employment to many who had been driven off their dwindling plots of land by the spread of the *haciendas* and by increasing poverty.

Although guild-operated workshops lasted until the early nineteenth century, they faced increasing competition from *obrajes*. Also dating from the sixteenth century, these textile factories came to play a leading role throughout the seventeenth and eighteenth centuries. Quality was high, maintained as in the workshops by a series of regulations for each stage of production. Mexico City became an important textile centre. So too did Puebla de los Angeles, and after a visit in 1625 Gage wrote:

That which maketh it most famous is the cloth which is made in it, and is sent far and near, and judged now to be as good as the cloth of Segovia, which is the best that is made in Spain, but now is not so much esteemed of nor sent so much from Spain to America by reason of the abundance of fine cloth which is made in this City of Angels. The felts likewise that are made are the best of all that country.

Spain placed no embargo on Mexico's weaving industry, which had the potential seriously to threaten her own, but she did prevent it from becoming too powerful by

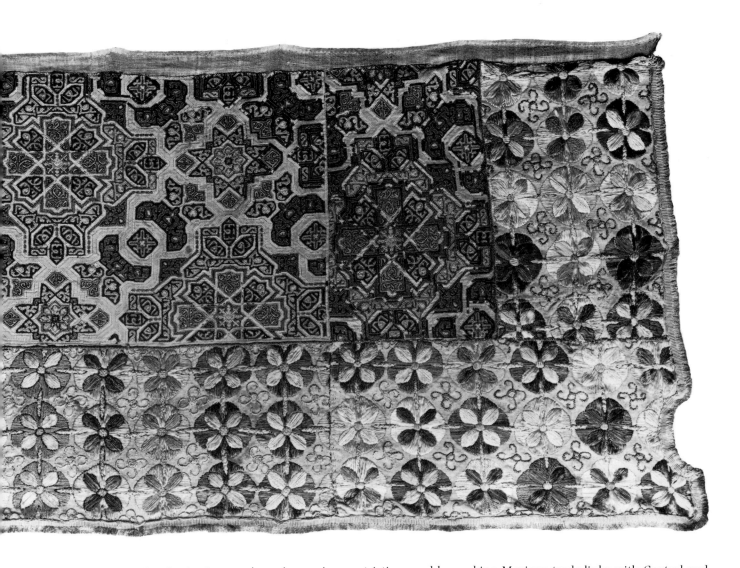

18th-century Spanish silk-embroidered linen panel from Mexico. Stitches are laid satin, stem, darning and herringbone; zig-zag chain is used as a couching stitch for the flowers. European materials, textile techniques and design motifs had a profound effect throughout the New World. w. 20 in (50.8 cm); l. 52 in (132 cm). Victoria and Albert Museum, London (T.46–1931).

imposing various restrictions and by curbing Mexican trade links with Central and South America. Imports from The Philippines, although highly taxed, and contraband textiles from Europe, Jamaica and Louisiana further threatened expansion. A new and fast-growing urban public kept the *obrajes* in business, however. Ideally suited to this poorer market were coarsely woven fabrics combining cotton with wool and unbleached cotton cloth known as *manta*. Produced as cheaply as possible in vast quantities, these textiles were the result of much human suffering. Hours were cruelly long, payment was minimal and the workers, who often included children, were frequently locked in the factories overnight. It also became accepted practice for owners to recruit Indian convicts who worked out their sentences at the mercy of terrible exploitation.

A far gentler initiation into European textile techniques was provided for Indians in the mission centres which existed in many parts of the viceroyalty. Founded not long after the Conquest by the various religious orders, they offered training in a wide range of crafts. The famous school set up by Bishop Vasco de Quiroga in Michoacán taught a great many skills including shoe-making, hide-tanning and treadle-loom weaving. In his writings Motolinía mentioned the convent-training which large numbers of Indian girls received: 'These girls, at least the daughters of lords, were assembled in many provinces of New Spain and placed in the charge of devout Spanish women. . . . They learned how to sew and embroider (they all knew how to weave), how to make fabrics of a thousand designs and how to produce these fabrics in colours.'

The Conquest led inevitably to the disappearance of some native textile traditions, but newly introduced European techniques were destined to give fine results in Mexico. Spain had an impressive and varied heritage which was shared in part with her European neighbours but which also owed much to nearly eight centuries of occupation by the Moors who brought with them skills acquired in Asia Minor and Egypt. With such a diversity of traditions to follow it is hardly surprising that weavers in sixteenth-century Spain should have been so proficient, specialising, according to region, in delicate figured gauzes, elaborate looped-pile fabrics and other styles of work. As Motolinía noted, however, convent tuition focused chiefly on embroidery and sewing.

Spanish needlework at the time of the Conquest included a wide variety of stitches, many of which are thought to have originated in ancient Egypt, Persia and other parts of the Near East, but further impetus was given to this popular craft when imported textiles began to arrive from China and The Philippines. The majority of these techniques were adopted in Mexico, which already had its own history of native embroidery. Teaching was done with the help of examplers, or samplers. These not only allowed pupils to practise their newly acquired skills but also provided them with useful memoranda of stitches and designs which could be passed on to future generations. Few if any samplers have survived from the early period of Colonial rule, but London's Victoria and Albert Museum owns several fine examples which range from the end of the eighteenth century to the start of the twentieth, and these exhibit many of the stitches and sewing skills which became current in Mexico.

Embroidery threads were most often of silk, cotton or linen. In sixteenth-century Spanish court circles colours were generally used with restraint, and there was a vogue for blackwork. This style, introduced by the Arabs and deriving originally from the Persians, consisted of coal-black embroidery worked with a variety of stitches on a white ground. Mexican needlework duly incorporated this fashion, although bright colours were destined to exert a strong fascination. Mexico's élite also acquired a taste for gilt thread and purl (very fine gold or silver wire). This fashion reached its height in Europe in the sixteenth century but lasted much longer in Mexico.

A wide range of satin, or flat, stitches found popularity (see Appendix 3). Animals, birds, flowers and foliage were often worked in satin stitch, while shading devices such as long and short were employed for subtle colour changes. Also included within this category are stem, outline and running stitches. This last technique, which adorned ancient textile fragments from Chichén Itzá, led after the Conquest to *pepenado* – the term applied to pattern running stitches on an often gathered ground.

Blanket stitching had served before the arrival of the Spaniards to reinforce frayed selvages of cloth, and the technique was subsequently used to provide ornamental borders. Related stitches such as chain and feather, which were probably not native, were employed after the Conquest, while nationality alone suggests that the lyrically named Spanish coral, or teardrop stitch, might have found favour in Spain's colonies. Couching was an important skill during the Colonial era, when church textiles displayed a wealth of metallic thread.

Late 18th-century Mexican linen sampler embroidered with silver-gilt thread, purl, spangles and coloured silks. French knots, long and short, satin and stem stitching have been used. Designs suggest European and Oriental influence. W. 15¼ in (38.7 cm); L. 12 in (30.5 cm). Victoria and Albert Museum, London (T.91–1954).

Crossed stitches have had enormous impact in Mexico. By counting the warp and weft threads of the ground, embroideresses could build up symmetrical landscapes replete with highly stylised animal, bird and plant motifs. Extremely fashionable in Europe during the eighteenth century, cross stitch became so popular that it over-shadowed most other stitches, and many samplers were subsequently worked almost entirely in this style. French knots also appear on Mexican samplers.

Because of the scarcity of pre-Conquest textiles it is impossible to say which stitches other than running were used in embroidery, and the same doubts attach to more

Within the sampler image:

DE MANO DE
VIRGINIA SAN
TIBAÑES A-
ÑO DE 1870

19th-century Mexican linen sampler with satin and cross stitching in silk, and drawn threadwork. Printed pattern books – current through most of Europe after the 16th century – remained rare in Spain and Mexico where samplers continued to serve as design inventories. 17¼ in (43.8 cm) square. Given by A.P. Maudslay, Victoria and Albert Museum, London (T.288–1928).

functional aspects of needlework. We have archaeological evidence for the use of blanket, darning and whipping stitches, but pre-Conquest weavers were not in the habit of cutting cloth, so the Spaniards were presumably responsible for the introduction of hemming methods. The *randa* seems to have been a particularly welcome innovation. This is the Spanish term for decorative cloth joins which employ a range of overlying or insertion stitches.

These were by no means the only ornamental skills acquired by Mexican textile workers, however. High on the list of European accomplishments was *deshilado*, or

Middle section of a 19th-century
Mexican linen altar cloth featuring
deshilado, or drawn threadwork.
Maudslay Bequest. Victoria and Albert
Museum, London (T.67–1931).

drawn threadwork, popularly used in Spain for embellishing articles of white linen
such as wedding shirts or altar cloths. As its name implies, this technique relies on
individual threads being drawn out from the material. The rest are then regrouped,
bound to produce a square-meshed ground, and reinforced with decorative stitching.
Although the intersection of warp and weft imposes a certain angularity on designs
and favours geometric patterning, skilled workers can portray plants and flowers, or
even animals and people. Closely allied to this technique and often combined with it
was cutwork, whereby portions of the cloth were actually cut away and filled in with
ornamental stitching.

Both skills led to the development in the Old World of needlepoint lace, and by the
seventeenth century *punto de España*, or Spanish needlepoint, was in demand throughout Europe. Made from gossamer-fine flax and occasionally enriched with gold and
silver thread, it displayed many designs including the double-headed imperial eagle

adopted by the Hapsburg kings. Bobbin lace, thought to derive not from embroidery but from weaving, was achieved by twisting threads together in pairs or groups, according to a pattern marked out by pins set in a cushion. In this sphere too Spain achieved eminence by producing a distinctive style known as Spanish bobbin which was used chiefly for *mantillas* and stoles. Worked in glistening black silk, these generally featured floral motifs. During the long period of Colonial rule both types of lace were imported into Mexico for use by the élite, but in addition these skills were widely taught, and Mexico eventually evolved variations of her own such as Tucuman. This style, which worked on the same principle as 'Sun Lace' from Spain, relied on diagonal threads secured by pins; circular patterns were then built up using a needle and thread.

Another important textile art was *appliqué*. By this technique silk ribbons and other ornamental layers of fabric were sewn on to the basic ground. When extremely fine cloths were involved, Mexican *appliqué* could achieve a remarkable delicacy, as may be seen from a mid-nineteenth-century example in the Victoria and Albert Museum.

Detail of a mid-19th-century Mexican chalice veil. Cotton cloth has been cut and appliquéd with minute stitches on to a fine linen ground. The border of bobbin lace has a repeating pattern of floral sprigs, blossoms and tendrils on a plaited ground of circular mesh. Given by A.P. Maudslay, Victoria and Albert Museum, London (T.286–1928).

Beaded sections from the Mexican sampler shown on pp. 74–5. Colonial import restrictions kept glass beads in short supply until Independence, when increased availability made them popular for samplers, napkins and costume trimmings. (See pp. 60, 165 for contemporary uses.) Victoria and Albert Museum, London (T.92–1954).

Also represented in the same collection is pleating: the technique is exemplified by the surplice of a choirboy or church acolyte from the same period.

In Peru, where so many ancient textiles have survived, it is perhaps easier to identify skills as foreign or indigenous than it is in Mexico, where many of the techniques which are thought of as European may in fact have paralleled existing, if more rudimentary, traditions. As has already been stated, a number of early Mexican peoples were adept at netting, while the Aztec frequently wore cloaks worked in this way. Such a skill, which relied on the looping or knotting of a single element, was akin to Spanish netting and, although more distantly, to crochet. We know from archaeologists that before the Conquest various types of fringing were used to give woven fabrics a decorative finish along their edges, and this custom evidently had much in common with *macramé* – a style favoured by the Moors, who specialised in knotting elaborate fringes. As for the Spanish love of tassels and pom-poms, this also derived from the Moors and fitted in well with existing Indian traditions of trimming and ornamentation.

The continuity of another pre-Conquest style of decoration was ensured by the introduction of spangles, or sequins, which took over from the feathers, shells and tiny bells which had previously been used for onlay work. Employed in Europe from the fifteenth century onwards, spangles achieved renewed popularity in the nineteenth century. Beads, which had been used for embroidery in medieval Spain, also became extremely fashionable in the nineteenth century. Their introduction into Mexico was not a total innovation, however, for long before the Conquest the Maya had evolved – and discontinued – a method for threading large tubular beads, possibly using a textile background, to make ceremonial garments. Of course, the minuscule and brightly coloured glass beads, imported into Mexico from Bohemia and other countries, lent themselves to very different styles of work.

It is hardly surprising that the Church, which fostered the teaching of many of these skills, should have been one of the main beneficiaries. With the dissemination of these European techniques she was ensured of magnificent textiles to enhance her already spectacular display of riches. By the end of the eighteenth century the Church had acquired over half Mexico's land, as well as nearly two-thirds of all the money in circulation, and her many churches and cathedrals amply reflected this wealth. Roofs and *retablos* of gold leaf, marble pillars and candelabra of solid gold and silver vied in splendour with the silk trappings, embroidered with gold and silver thread, that adorned the altars. Even during the early half of the seventeenth century much of this splendour was in evidence, and Thomas Gage pronounced Mexico's churches 'the fairest that ever my eyes beheld'. 'Sin and wickedness abound in Mexico', he noted dourly, 'yet there are no more devout people in the world toward the Church and clergy'. However, Gage was writing these memoirs as a lapsed Catholic turned Puritan, and much of this devotion he attributed to the riches themselves, for they 'cause admiration in the common sort of people, and admiration brings on daily adoration in them to those glorious spectacles and images of saints'.

Some of the most splendid images were of the Virgin Mary. Her cult, shared by all Mexicans, centred on the dark-skinned Virgin of Guadalupe, who was reported to have miraculously appeared to an Aztec Indian just ten years after the Conquest, and imprinted her likeness on his *tilma*, or mantle. This likeness was a good deal more restrained than the richly dressed and jewel-bedecked images which followed, however. Although she remained the best-loved Virgin, particularly among the poor and oppressed, several other Virgins were also venerated, and they too became the mistresses of priceless treasures. The Virgen del Rosario in Puebla, for example, owned several costly dresses. In one painting she was shown wearing a blue dress embroidered with pearls that formed squares, in the centre of which were pearl-embroidered flowers like four-leafed clovers or the name María. Perhaps the richest image of all, however, was Nuestra Señora de los Remedios. The patroness of Spaniards in Mexico, she had such a fine collection of jewels that a special treasurer was needed to look after them. She was served in addition by a wardrobe mistress who maintained her rich apparel and dressed her for holy processions when she was carried through the streets of Mexico City.

Many of these treasures were donated by the rich, for the Mexicans strove, according to Gage, 'to exceed one another in their gifts to the cloisters of nuns and friars'. As a result the 'riches belonging to the altars are infinite in price and value, such as copes, canopies, hangings, altar cloths, candlesticks . . . all which would

Detail from an 18th-century Mexican vestment embroidered with gold tissue and silver threads. Convent of Tepotzotlán.

mount to the worth of a reasonable mine of silver. . . .' An eighteenth-century cope on display at the Convent of Tepotzotlán confirms that priestly garments were indeed lavish. Minutely embroidered with gold tissue and silk threads, it features delicately worked winged figures playing musical instruments. As for nuns of the period, descriptions exist of the black veils which they wore while taking their vows. Many were embroidered with silk, gold and pearls 'in the figures of flowers, leaves, branches and every shape that the imagination could devise', and bordered in addition with pearls or adorned with crosses of precious stones.

Although much of this ecclesiastical work was done by the nuns themselves and by the pious daughters of wealthy Spanish families, a large share was contributed by Indians, who were also responsible in the secular field for many of the decorative trimmings and costume embellishments needed to deck out the rich and powerful. Mexican society was organised according to a rigid class structure with sharply defined and inviolable divisions known as *castas*, or castes. Ruling over this hierarchy were the *peninsulares*, which was the term applied to all Spaniards born in Spain. Their clothing reflected their exalted status and closely followed the fashions of their native land, with perhaps a few regional variations recalling the styles of Andalucía and Extremadura where emigration was strongest. Loose cloaks, doublets, jerkins, shirts, puffed breeches, hose, wide-brimmed hats and caps were all included in sixteenth-century male dress, while the female wardrobe comprised chemises, doublets, detachable sleeves, dresses, underskirts, bonnets and cloaks. The range of materials was extensive, as has already been mentioned, with rich velvets, fine linens, damasks, taffetas, chamois and luxuriant Filipino silks and satins to choose from. Sleeves and breeches were often lined in contrasting colours which showed through to great decorative effect when garments were slashed. Chemises were frequently embroidered with gold and silver thread or silk, trimmed with ribbons and edged with *passementerie*. Lace was much used by men and women.

In the seventeenth century costume became still more lavish. Lace ruffs, which had been popular with both sexes, grew to enormous proportions. The vogue for rich brocades, embroidery and *passementerie* intensified. Men's puffed breeches were superseded by a close-fitting style to the knee, while hats evolved higher crowns and narrower brims which widened out again later in the century. Velvet caps set with feathers were also popular. Some idea of the elegance of male dress is provided by a description from the early part of the century relating to the ambassador, Sebastián Vizcaino, who on one occasion wore elaborately worked breeches with interlinings of different materials, a doublet worked in the same manner as the breeches, a cape of heavy material, a plumed cap with gold head-gear, white boots with buttons, a gilded sword and dagger, and a large ruff.

Such was the wealth displayed in clothing that it threatened to eclipse even that of the Spanish court, and in 1623 Philip IV issued a decree entitled 'Chapters of Reform', in which he professed his love for the inhabitants of the Indies but charged them to act wisely by spending their money on more necessary things! Although he did succeed in prohibiting ruffs, which were replaced by stiff collars and cravats, his other proposed reforms did little to curb the Mexican appetite for luxury. This is best shown by the memoirs of Thomas Gage, who visited Mexico City in 1625 and noted: 'Both men and women are excessive in their apparel, using more silks than stuffs and cloth. Precious stones and pearls further much this their vain ostentation; a hat-band and rose made of diamonds in a gentleman's hat is common . . .'

This decree, however, was only one of several attempting to control costume in New Spain, for dress was seen as a way of reinforcing the caste system, which comprised many categories beyond those of the *peninsulares* and the Indians. Second in the social hierarchy were the *criollos*, or Creoles, who came of Spanish parentage but were born in Mexico, while the rapidly growing *mestizo* class was the result of intermarriage between Spanish and Indian subjects. There was also a sizeable African slave population. Introduced into Mexico after the Conquest, Negroes were again brought in during the seventeenth century to supplement the dwindling Indian labour force. They were regarded as inferior to Indians, however, and although black slaves were often used in *obrajes*, they were barred from working in guild-operated textile workshops, as were the mulatto children of white settlers and Negroes. The descendants of Indians and Negroes were termed zambos, but there were a number of other categories for the different permutations of race. According to an edict issued in 1582, Negro, mulatto and *mestizo* women were forbidden to dress like Indians unless married to Indians: should they fail to comply they were threatened with imprisonment and one hundred lashes of the whip.

The caste system was maintained throughout the Colonial period, as is shown by a series of oil-paintings, executed by an unknown artist in the late eighteenth century and generally referred to as *Las Castas*. At the foot of every picture are words to explain the racial status of the members of each family portrayed, and it is interesting to note that costumes are in keeping with the rulings on dress, for the majority of the sitters wear European clothing.

Although apparently successful in barring non-Indians from using Indian dress styles, however, the king of Spain was once again less influential when he tried to proscribe the use of finery. According to the law of 1571, black and mulatto women were forbidden to wear gold, pearls or silk, unless they were married to Spaniards, in which case these restrictions were modified. As before, it is Thomas Gage who evokes not the theory but the reality with his recollections of Mexico City, famed according to him for its streets, its women, its horses and its apparel. His writings go further than any other source in conjuring up the wealth and luxury of the early seventeenth century – a time when 'a hat-band of pearls is ordinary in a tradesman; nay a blackamoor or tawny young maid and slave will make hard shift but she will be in fashion with her neck-chain and bracelets of pearls, and her ear-bobs of some considerable jewels'. There follows a minutely detailed and lingering description of the decadent charms of these Negresses and mulattoes:

[Their] attire . . . is so light, and their carriage so enticing, that many Spaniards even of the better sort . . . disdain their wives for them. Their clothing is a petticoat of silk or cloth, with many silver or golden laces, with a very broad ribbon of some light colour with long silver or golden tags hanging down before, the whole length of their petticoat to the ground, and the like behind; their waistcoats made like bodices, with skirts, laced likewise with gold or silver, without sleeves, and a girdle about their body of great price stuck with pearls and knots of gold (if they be any ways well esteemed of), their sleeves are broad and open at the end, of holland or of fine China linen, wrought some with coloured silks, some with silk and gold, some with silk and silver, hanging down almost unto the ground; . . . their bare, black and tawny breasts are covered with bobs hanging from their chains of pearls. And when they go abroad, they use a white mantle of lawn or cambric rounded with a broad lace . . . others instead of this mantle use some rich silk petticoat to hang upon their left shoulder. . . . Their shoes are high and of many soles, the outside whereof of the profaner sort are plaited with a list of silver, which is fastened with small nails of broad silver heads. Most of these are or have been slaves, though love have set them loose at liberty to enslave souls to sin and Satan.

Anonymous late 18th-century painting from a series known as *Las Castas*. The Indian mother wears a white *huipil* apparently trimmed with yellow ribbon. Chapultepec Castle.

According to Gage, Negroes often wore clothing of equal splendour, for it was usual for gentlemen of rank to have in their train up to a dozen black slaves in 'brave and gallant liveries, heavy with gold and silver lace, with silk stockings on their black legs, and roses on their feet, and swords by their sides'.

It is to be regretted that Gage, who wrote so evocatively of city fashions, should have devoted few lines to Indian dress. During the decades immediately following the Conquest, chroniclers had shown a deep interest in native cultures, but the seventeenth

century saw a decline in the quantity and quality of such writings. The eighteenth century produced several scholarly histories but few major studies of contemporary Indian life. It is clear from ecclesiastical and regional reports, however, that the abolition of the old social hierarchy and the imposition of the Christian religion had far-reaching effects on native dress. The noble and ceremonial status of garments such as the *quechquémitl* was eroded, while laws which before the Conquest had governed the use of cotton and *ixtle*, the insignia of warriors and the garb of rulers and priests, became redundant. This is confirmed by a *Relación* for 1580, published in 1905 in *Papeles de Nueva España*, which stated that among the Cuicatec and Chinantec of Oaxaca there was no difference in dress between those of low or high rank; each person wore what he or she could afford.

As Colonial writings show, friars and governors were inordinately concerned with modesty, and were determined to eradicate any practices which seemed to them 'uncivilised' or 'pagan'. The deformation of skulls and the incrustation of teeth died out together with tattooing, although a report by Juan María Ratkay in 1683 noted that Tarahumara men in northern Mexico still displayed facial markings which had been burned deeply into the flesh. In the south-east many Maya were equally slow to relinquish their traditions. In his *Relación* of 1639 Francisco de Cárdenas Valencia described native ear and nose ornaments as 'infernal and frightful', while Andrés de Avendaño y Loyola wrote in 1696 of 'carved, striped and painted faces made in the very likeness of the devil'. In a letter of the same year Fray Antonio Margil complained that Chol-speaking Indians were blackening themselves, and implied that whipping would be a fit punishment for body-painting.

Spanish friars were equally shocked by Indian nudity. A report for 1645 by Andrés Pérez de Ribas described the efforts of priests to obtain clothing for the nude Tepehuan of northern Mexico, but even the costumes of peoples such as the Aztec were thought to be scanty. In easily accessible areas men came under pressure to adopt shirts and to abandon the loincloth in favour of drawers; according to rare sixteenth-century illustrations, these garments were worn with the pre-Conquest *tilma*, or *tilmatli*. Colonial reports offer further information about the spread of European clothing: in the *Relación* of 1580, mentioned above, Cuicatec and Chinantec men were said to be wearing jackets of blue or green wool, boots and breeches, while according to the *Historia general* of 1601 by Antonio de Herrera y Tordesillas, the Peninsula Maya 'Now . . . wear shirts, wide breeches [*zaragüelles*], hats and cotton sandals [*alpargatas*], and they let their beards grow and have good ones except that they are harsh like horse hairs'. Female dress, by contrast, underwent few changes; the *huipil* received praise in many reports, but bare breasts were predictably discouraged.

Wigberto Jiménez Moreno has made a study of Mexican archives and has outlined the changing attitudes of Indians during the decades of transition which followed the Conquest. According to him, people who had not accepted the Christian religion in the 1540s rejected Spanish clothing styles; when they saw an Indian wearing *calzones*, or drawers, they would either cut them off or mock him as a coward. By 1570, however, the situation had reversed: large numbers of Indians had accepted many of the external elements of the new faith and had begun to dress like Spaniards. This process of acculturation was almost certainly helped by the continued existence of *caciques*, or Indian nobles. In many regions Spaniards recognised their status and entrusted them with the collection of tribute. As has already been mentioned, the children of *caciques* were given special education, but in a further effort to absorb

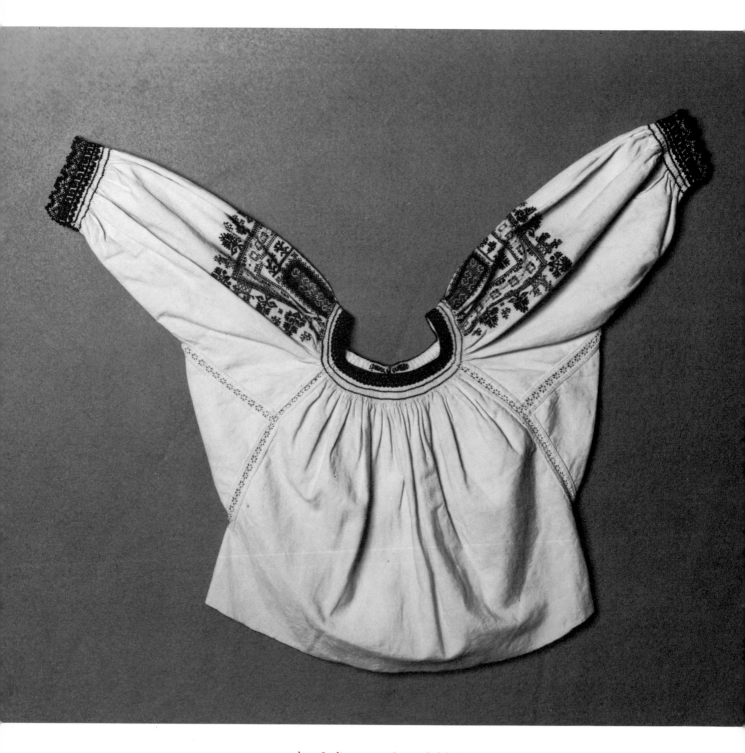

upper-class Indians into Spanish life the *conquistadores* would frequently give or sell them articles of fine clothing. In the Valley of Oaxaca, for example, Zapotec *caciques* wore Spanish dress and even rode horses. The Tlaxcalan Indians had helped Cortés to overthrow the Aztec, and in *Tlaxcala in the Sixteenth Century* Charles Gibson notes that Tlaxcalan *caciques* were permitted to apply to the viceroy for personal favours, such as licences to wear Spanish clothing or to carry a sword. The privileged status

18th-century child's cotton shirt from Spain with embroidery and *macramé*. During the Colonial period Mexican Indians adopted many Spanish textile techniques and garments; this method of sleeve construction is still seen in some communities (see pp. 170, 211). Victoria and Albert Museum, London (T.144–1924).

of Mexico's Indian *caciques* lasted in general until the early years of the seventeenth century.

In remote areas assimilation and the spread of Spanish clothing styles were very much slower. To the north the area known today as eastern Chihuahua was still populated in the eighteenth century by nomadic groups, many now extinct, who wore skins, feathers and face paint. According to William B. Griffen, many Indians took up raiding on a regular basis, often motivated by a desire to gain Spanish articles of dress, ribbons, glass earrings and other adornments. One group of attackers, thought to be Cocoyome Indians, were reported in 1715 to be wearing short jackets of baize, new hats and blankets tied around the waist. It is clear from reports that Indians sometimes made trousers from deerskin. The archives also state, by contrast, that Spaniards taken prisoner in 1726 were forced to put on cloth breechclouts by their captors, who said that trousers were 'no good'.

The eighteenth century has often been termed the grand age of portraiture. Predictably it offers few representations of Indians; instead it reflected the continuing opulence of upper-class dress, and included many fine paintings where the clothing and jewels of the sitter are depicted with care. France, which had taken over from Spain as the source of costume inspiration, led women to favour tightly waisted conical skirts with slightly raised hemlines, and these gave added emphasis to the elegant cloth shoes of the time. Hair was piled high with ribbons, while men either wore wigs or powdered their hair. The male wardrobe included breeches, occasionally buckled at the knee, cravats, three-cornered hats adorned with feathers or trimmed with gold braid, waistcoats and knee-length dress-coats embroidered with gold and silver thread and embellished with a quantity of gold buttons. There was also a great vogue for watches, which were worn with the gold chain showing. Women, on the other hand, enjoyed displaying their watches in pairs. A famous portrait of a rich Creole, Doña María Manuela Esquivel y Serruto, showed her wearing two watches pinned to her skirt, but sometimes as many as seven watches were reportedly exhibited at one time. Inventories of the period often list a truly astonishing quantity of jewellery, and many portraits illustrate the vogue. Loops and bowknots of gold set with diamonds were fashionable together with pearl necklaces, bracelets and earrings, while among men diamond coat buttons and shoe buckles were common, as were cravats set with precious stones and pearls.

Fashion trends in adornment and dress were far from being France's only contribution to Mexican life, however. Towards the end of the century many influential books were secretly imported into the country, in defiance of a ban by the Church, and the writings of Rousseau, Voltaire and others were avidly read and debated by the Creoles, whose numbers had lately been much increased by large-scale immigration from the poorer provinces of northern Spain. Together with the *mestizos* they greatly outnumbered the *peninsulares* who made up the ruling élite, and the frustration and resentment felt by both groups were further inflamed by the new political ideas from overseas. Deprived of advancement within the existing society, they advocated Mexican independence from Spain and soon won the support of the Indians, who made up over 60 per cent of the population, and the Negroes and mulattoes, who for the most part lived ignominiously outside the cities in the tropics and mining towns. War was the inevitable outcome of oppression too long endured, and after a decade of savage fighting independence was granted in 1821, whereupon New Spain was renamed Mexico in memory of her great and glorious past under the Aztec, or Mexica.

Lithograph from *México y sus alrededores*, 1855–6, showing Indians carrying their wares from Tacubaya to Chapultepec. The women wear wrap-around skirts, open-sided *huipiles* and carrying-cloths. Male garments include *calzones*, or drawers, deerskin *calzoneras*, or over-trousers, *cotones*, or long-sleeved shirts, sandals and palm hats. One man uses a folded *sarape*, or blanket; another a *gabán* over a short-sleeved shirt.

4 Independence and after (1821–1917)

Blind to the many obstacles facing the new federal republic, which soon included the state of Chiapas, Mexico's citizens welcomed their autonomy with great optimism. The Colonial system of castes was legally abolished and civil equality granted to all. From the triumph of independence, however, Mexico entered a period of chronic economic crisis, political upheavals, rebellions and foreign intervention. In the space of three decades Mexico experienced fifty governments, almost all the result of military coups. The middle class, made up largely of Creoles, consolidated its position of dominance, and the lot of the *mestizos* was much improved; but the new laws of equality did little to better conditions for factory workers or Indian peons. Meanwhile, in northern Mexico the abolition of slavery for Negroes so infuriated the cotton-growers and cattle-raisers of Texas that they rose in protest and joined the United States of America. War followed, and was only concluded by treaty in 1848 when Mexico surrendered Texas, New Mexico and California – which together made up over half her national territories – in return for a small settlement. Mexico's rulers also had internal Indian uprisings to contend with in various parts of the country, while mines and farms lay impoverished by neglect and trade came to a standstill.

Then in 1857 a period of reform began with the election of Benito Juárez. This justly celebrated president, who was a Zapotec Indian from Oaxaca, embarked on a liberal programme of education and helped to draft a new constitution which entailed the separation of Church and State. Opposition by both Church and conservatives led to three years of civil war, however, and in the economic chaos that followed Juárez was forced to suspend payment of the national debt. Anxious to protect their financial rights, the British, the Spaniards and the French sent troops into Mexico, and although the first two nations soon withdrew, the French remained and Napoleon III capitalised on this victory by appointing Archduke Maximilian of Austria emperor of Mexico. His reign lasted only four years, for in 1867 Maximilian was executed and Benito Juárez restored to power to continue his programme of reforms.

The next key figure in Mexican politics was Porfirio Díaz, whose presidency lasted from 1876 until his voluntary exile in 1911. During this long term of office, generally described as a dictatorship, peace was restored and special protection given to the upper classes, the clergy, great landowners and foreign investors. Mexican finances were put on a sound basis; railways were installed and industries built up in an effort to supplement the natural, mineral and agricultural wealth of the country. However, the mass of overworked and half-starved peasants lived in misery: their lands were taken away from them, their liberty was curtailed, and many were sent as forced labourers on to the vast tobacco and *henequén* plantations. The *haciendas* of the rich grew even larger, until by 1910 two-thirds of the country was held by just 836 proprietors. It was this open contradiction between dazzling prosperity and abject poverty that led to the Revolution. '*Tierra y Libertad*' became the cry, and revolutionaries such as Pancho Villa and Emiliano Zapata became legends in their own lifetimes. In 1917 a new constitution was drafted, bringing to an end yet another era of Mexican history.

The time-span between Independence and Revolution, with its interchange of turmoil and stability, proved to be one of the best-documented periods of Mexican life, and much information, both written and pictorial, was provided about costume by the many foreign observers who visited this newly liberated colony. Among the first was William Bullock, an Englishman, who condemned the 'jealousy of the Government of Old Spain' which had for so long sought to isolate Mexico from the rest of the world, making it 'to Europeans' an 'almost unknown country'. His impressions were published in 1824 under the title *Six Months' Residence and Travels in Mexico* and were accompanied by several colour illustrations. Bullock was followed by the Italian artist, Claudio Linati, whose highly detailed lithographs featuring a wide cross-section of Mexican dress styles were first published in 1828 in Brussels under the title *Costumes civils, militaires et religieux du Mexique*. Carlos Nebel, the German architect, was responsible for a further series of lithographs, which appeared in 1836 in Paris and were entitled *Voyage pittoresque et archéologique dans la partie la plus intéressante du Mexique* (see pp. 52–3).

No illustrations accompanied the collected letters of Frances Calderón de la Barca, the Scottish wife of the Spanish minister, but her writings displayed extraordinary powers of observation. Living in the midst of the revolts, ceasefires and government proclamations of the very early 1840s, she still found the peace of mind necessary to give her correspondents meticulous word-pictures of the customs and costumes of Mexico. *Mexico and the Mexicans*, published in 1859 and written by the German C. Sartorius, included a chapter on Indian life and a number of engravings. 1861 saw the publication of *Anahuac: or Mexico and the Mexicans, Ancient and Modern*, written by the Englishman Sir Edward B. Tylor to record the journey he made with Henry Christy during a 'lull in the civil turmoil of that lamentably disturbed Republic'. The book featured several illustrations which closely reflect the styles of dress displayed by a remarkable series of wax *genre* figurines collected by Christy and now owned by the British Museum. As Bullock had noted during his own travels, '. . . the Indians greatly excel in the modelling and working in wax. The specimens of different tribes with their costumes, with the habiliments of the gentry of the country . . . will amply testify their merits in this department'. Mexican society was evoked in the early 1880s by yet another Englishman, Thomas Unett Brocklehurst, whose book *Mexico To-day* contained further references to dress and some black and white illustrations.

These were by no means the only foreign travellers to reach Mexico's shores during

Lithograph by Claudio Linati, 1928, showing a Zapotec Indian girl with a wrap-around cotton skirt; covering her head and shoulders is a gauze garment termed a *huipil grande*.

Wax figures, purchased in Mexico by Henry Christy, 1856. The women wear *huipiles* and wrap-around skirts; the water-carrier wears a European-style shirt, long drawers and over-trousers with vertical side openings. Museum of Mankind, London.

the nineteenth century. Scientific discovery and the lure of ancient ruins attracted many other observers such as Alexander von Humboldt, Jean Frédéric Maximilien de Waldeck, John Lloyd Stephens and Frederick Catherwood, but their work had little bearing on contemporary costume, although Alfred Percival Maudslay, the celebrated British Mayanist, did collect a number of textiles which are now in the Victoria and Albert Museum. The documentation of Mexican life was not left entirely to outsiders, however. Many references to costume are to be found in national writings of the time, for example *Memorias de mis tiempos* by Guillermo Prieto. Of great importance to the study of costume is the book of lithographs *México y sus alrededores*, edited in the 1850s by Decaen. *The Republic of Mexico in 1876* by Antonio García Cubas, written 'with the view of removing the wrong impressions that may have been left on the minds of the readers of those works . . . composed and published by different foreigners in regard to the Mexican nation', was also accompanied by a number of informative colour plates (see p. 54).

Although García Cubas would probably have been pained by Tylor's judgement on Mexico as 'one of the countries in which the contrast between great riches and great poverty is most striking', he could not have taken exception to Tylor's additional comment that he had 'never noticed in any country so large a number of mixed races'. Despite their official abolition, the *castas* were still recognised and associated with certain dress styles as in the past. In the words of Linati 'Nowhere is there a greater variety of costumes than in the provinces of the Republic. Each caste has its own; not content with the diversity of their colourings, they add their differences of clothing. The Negroes, *mestizos*, Indians, Creoles and Spaniards are easily known by their attire'. For his book of lithographs, which he described as 'a panorama of the Mexican people', Linati systematically drew representatives from all these different classes, including in his vast repertoire a black man from Veracruz in his all-white Sunday best costume of European breeches, hat and shirt, and a black woman wearing only a wrap-around skirt in the African manner.

Most observers and painters, however, concentrated their attention on the white élite whose customs, according to García Cubas, 'conform in general to European civilization, and particularly to the fashions of the French with reminiscences of the Spaniards'. Bullock, who arrived in Mexico City not long after the turmoil of Independence, was struck by the reduced circumstances of some families and noted 'the woeful change which has taken place among the inhabitants of this once gay city', sadly observing that 'The profusion of jewels and the extravagant equipages are no longer to be seen in the streets. . . . The dresses of the ladies, and even of children, in the streets, is universally black'. This attire, described by Tylor as a 'church-going black silk dress and mantilla' and judged by him to be 'one of the most graceful costumes in the world', was soon offset by more lavish styles of dress as fortunes were restored and new ones accrued. With the resumption of peace women reclaimed their right to deck themselves out as they pleased, and the letters of Frances Calderón de la Barca reflect what she termed 'the extravagant notions of the ladies in point of dress'. Holy Thursday, it seems, was an occasion for 'displaying all the riches of their toilet. On this day velvets and satins are your only wear. Diamonds and pearls walk the streets. The mantillas are white or black blonde; the shoes white or coloured satin'. Balls called for an extraordinary display of wealth, and descriptions recall the ostentation of Gage's period. After one such *soirée* Frances Calderón de la Barca complained of 'a monotony of diamond earrings', 'an endless succession of China crape shawls of every colour

Plate from *The Republic of Mexico in 1876*:
'1. Mexican, or Naca [Nahua], Indians
of Tlapacoyan, Veracruz. 2. Tarascos of
the town of Chilchota, Michoacán.
3. Zoque Indians of Tuxtla Gutiérrez,
Chiapas. Ordinary and wedding
costumes.'

La Mantilla by Carlos Nebel, 1836. This 'altogether Spanish' costume was worn in the morning; after dinner upper-class city women adopted French fashions and went bare-headed.

and variety' and 'too much velvet and satin', explaining that 'the dresses were too much loaded'. This same writer was even more dismayed by the lavish style of morning attire: 'For the last two days our rooms have been filled with visitors, and my eyes are scarcely yet accustomed to the display of diamonds, pearls, silks, satins, blondes, and velvets, in which the ladies have paid their first visits of etiquette.'

Gold embroidery, according to this same tireless observer, remained an important form of decoration, and although 'beautiful gold-embroidered ball-dresses . . . are nearly out of fashion', she noted 'an amazing quantity' of this work 'used in the churches, and in military uniforms' – a fact already mentioned by Bullock, who wrote that 'The manufactory of gold and silver lace, trimmings, epaulets, & c. is carried on in the greatest perfection . . .' The military uniforms of high-ranking officers were certainly splendid, and Linati's lithograph of Mexico's president, General Guadalupe Victoria, shows him wearing white breeches with gold buttons at the knee, white hose, and a waisted black jacket with gleaming gold epaulets. This uniform, according to Linati's description, had a few Spanish trimmings but was basically French in style, and the civil dress of high-ranking Mexican male society followed this same trend, for as Tylor observed 'In the towns . . . "nous autres" wear European garments and follow the latest Paris fashion . . .' According to Bullock, long cloaks were worn in the street; light jackets of printed calico, soon to be superseded by cloth jackets, were used indoors. As in Europe, convention dictated a more austere style of dress than that of previous centuries, with a greater severity attaching to cut and colour and a decline in the use of lavish jewellery and ornamentation.

The arrival of Maximilian and his wife Charlotte in 1864 gave renewed impetus to European dress styles for both men and women. The technological advances of the age made fashion plates and magazines readily available and kept Mexican high society in touch with the latest Paris fashions, which were quickly recreated by city tailors and dressmakers. The end of the Second Empire and the triumph of the

Republican cause in no way weakened the lure of France, admired for its scientific and cultural achievements, and under the regime of Porfirio Díaz the town-dwelling élite continued to dress in the French mode.

Foreign goods, like foreign styles, were seen to confer status upon the wearer, and the withdrawal of Spanish trading restrictions left a free market. Nineteenth-century imports included French woollen cloths and silk stockings 'with ornamented clocks', German and Irish linens, and the Chinese 'crape shawls' mentioned by Frances Calderón de la Barca. This same writer also informs us wryly that during a brief vogue among society women for simpler dress styles 'half the men in Mexico were ruined . . . by the embroidered French and India muslins bought by their wives'. English goods too were in demand and included shawls and 'muslins and calicoes, printed and plain' which, according to Bullock, 'are greatly used and preferred'. In the opinion of this patriotic Englishman, however, imports could have been still higher. Ever keen to promote trade, he advised: 'It would be a good speculation for our merchants to forward a few handsome and well-dressed specimens of our countrywomen as pattern cards. . . . A few numbers of Ackermann's Fashions would probably assist in producing the same effect.'

On Mexico's country estates costume was developing in a rather different direction. Cut off from the fluctuations of city fashions, landowners had evolved their own styles of dress which relied far less on foreign influences and imported goods. Practical and often showy, their costumes were much admired by European observers, who felt them to be more intrinsically 'Mexican' than those of city-dwellers. Even the comparatively modest dress of *mestizo* smallholders came in for praise from Frances Calderón de la Barca, who noted that it was 'impossible to see anywhere a finer race of men than these rancheros – tall, strong and well-made, with their embroidered shirts, coarse sarapes, and dark blue pantaloons embroidered in gold'.

The *sarape*, described by the same writer as 'convenient and graceful, especially on horseback', was widely worn in country areas, and Tylor explained its uses to his readers as follows:

The Mexican blanket – the *serape* – is a national institution. It is wider than a Scotch plaid, and nearly as long, with a slit in the middle; and it is woven in the same gaudy Oriental patterns which are to be seen on the prayer-carpets of Turkey and Palestine to this day. It is worn as a cloak, with the end flung over the left shoulder, like the Spanish *capa*, and muffling up half the face when its owner is chilly or does not wish to be recognized. When a heavy rain comes down, and he is on horseback, he puts his head through the slit in the middle, and becomes a moving tent. At night he rolls himself up in it, and sleeps on a mat or a board, or on the stones in the open air.

It is open to debate whether this useful and decorative garment did originate in Spain, as Tylor's description implies, for although it bears similarities with Arab-inspired cloaks from the Jeréz region, its rectangular shape also suggests the Indian *tilmatli*, or – when worn – an open-sided *huipil*. Perhaps it is safest, therefore, to assume a fusion of traditions. In any case, by the middle of the seventeenth century *sarapes* were being woven and were destined eventually to displace previous styles.

The *sarape* represented the perfect match on Mexican soil of two foreign elements – namely the treadle loom and woollen yarns. Production centres grew up in many of the areas best suited to sheep farming, but the most famous was Saltillo in the northern state of Coahuila. At the end of the sixteenth century, when the region was still dominated by fierce Chichimec raiders, Spanish administrators sought to bring stability by resettling 400 Indian families from Tlaxcala. Their mastery of treadle-

Early 20th-century one-web portrait *sarape* from Zacatecas. Tapestry-woven from natural wool, aniline-dyed cotton and possibly silk, it represents George Washington. The warp fringe is not shown. W. 44 in (111.8 cm); L. 94 in (238.8 cm). Museum of Mankind, London.

loom techniques is widely thought to have fostered the *sarape de Saltillo*, which reached its apogee in the late eighteenth century and fetched increasingly high prices at the yearly Saltillo fair. Gradually the term came to be applied to similarly patterned *sarapes* from other centres such as Querétaro, Zacatecas or San Miguel Allende (then San Miguel el Grande).

Tapestry weaving was the method used to give *sarapes* their distinctive patterning. By manipulating richly coloured weft threads weavers achieved dazzling mosaic effects, which led Náhuatl-speaking Indians to talk of *acocemalotíc-tilmatli*, or 'rainbow mantles'. Characteristic designs included small triangles, rhomboids, hour-glasses and ovals grouped round a central lozenge or medallion. As with the garment itself, patterning may have evolved from a number of sources including native ones. Did the Tlaxcalans draw on their own range of designs? Did they borrow central Mexican ones of the type used in the pre-Conquest *centzontilmatli* (literally 'capes of four hundred colours'), attributed by Sahagún to the Huastec and levied in tribute by the Aztec? Or did they adopt northern designs of the type displayed by diamond-patterned archaeological remains from Chihuahua? Imported textiles may also have been influential. As Paula Maria Juelke points out, these came from The Philippines, China, the East Indies, Holland and Spain, which had in turn inherited a range of Moorish designs. A degree of mystery also attaches to the techniques used. Ramón Mena has suggested that painted pattern boards may have been used to achieve complex patterning, and it comes as no surprise to read Isabel Marín de Paalen's estimate that a master-craftsman who wished to recreate a *sarape* of the classic period would have to spend ten hours a day for eight months at his loom.

The *sarape* lost none of its splendour in nineteenth-century Mexico, as Nebel's lithographs show (see pp. 53, 55, 56). Purists consider, however, that increasing opulence during the latter half marked a decline in quality. Silk, gold and silver metallic threads, and newly invented aniline dyes were used in the creation of *sarapes* for the rich, who regarded them as prized possessions, while the lower classes made do with less costly versions.

An alternative to the *sarape* was the *manga*, which probably approximated more closely to the Spanish cape and which, according to Bullock, did 'credit to the taste of the country'. A description by Sartorius recounts how lavish this garment could be. Woven from wool, like the *sarape*, it too had an opening for the head which was 'usually trimmed with velvet, several inches broad, and bordered with gold and silver fringe'. Nebel's lithograph of an *hacienda* owner shows a splendid garment of this type being worn, with the decorative area entirely covering the shoulders, and Linati depicted a wealthy Creole landowner with a similar style of *manga* (see p. 53).

This same *hacendado*, whose opulent life-style was apparently upheld by the toil of 2,000 Indians, was also shown by Linati with a jacket and trousers of chamois leather. Trousers of this type, which had buttons down the sides, were used over a *calzoncillo*, or pair of long drawers, and may originally have been inspired by the clothing of Spanish riders in Andalucía and Extremadura. It is interesting to note that a similar costume was worn at the lower end of the social scale by the *vaqueros*, or herdsmen, of Texas. When this region was annexed to the United States, Mexican horsemen became American cowboys, and their *chaparreras*, or leather over-trousers, were abbreviated to the word 'chaps'. Tylor was able to test the practicality of such a costume for himself. During his travels he adopted not only a suit of leather but also 'a grey felt hat, as stiff as a boiler-plate, . . . a red silk sash . . . lastly, a woollen serape to sleep under, and to wear in the mornings and evenings. This is the genuine ranchero costume, and it did me good service. . . . In all the country, all Mexicans – high and low – wear this national dress'.

Originally inspired by Spanish styles, the stiff felt hat mentioned by Tylor had become an indispensable article of clothing in country areas. Indeed, its popularity was such, according to this same writer, that it was even worn in cities 'by people who adopt no other parts of the costume'. Tylor continued the description of his own hat, noting humorously that it was 'of more than quakerish lowness of crown and broadness of brim, but secularized by a silver serpent for a hat band' and concluding that 'There never were such hats as these for awkwardness. . . . The flat sharp brims of passers-by are always threatening to cut your head off in the streets. . . . But for walking and riding under a fierce sun, they are perhaps better than anything else that can be used'. Linati came to the same conclusion, adding only that in the rainy season 'the wide brimmed hat acts as a kind of umbrella'. Such hats were often extremely ornate, and one of the first articles of costume to catch the observant eye of the newly arrived Frances Calderón de la Barca was the hat of her coachman, which 'of itself was a curiosity to us; a white beaver with immense brim, lined with thick silver tissue, with two large silver rolls and tassels round it'.

It is clear from the writings of these many witnesses that the richer the wearer the more luxurious his dress became, but few descriptions are more detailed or evocative than Bullock's when he noted the following:

The dress of the country gentlemen, or paysanos, is showy and expensive; and, when mounted on their handsome and spirited little horses, they make an elegant appearance. The lower dress consists of embroidered breeches, chiefly of coloured leather, open at the knees, and ornamented with numbers of round silver buttons, and broad silver lace; a worked shirt, with high collar; and a short jacket, of printed calico, over which is generally thrown an elegant manga or cloak, of velvet, fine cloth, or fine figured cotton, the manufacture of the country; – these are often embroidered, or covered with a profusion of gold lace. On the feet are soft leather shoes or boots, over which is tied a kind of gaiter, peculiar to the country; they are commonly of cinnamon-coloured leather, wrapped round the leg, and tied with an ornamental garter: these are a very expensive article, the leather being cut in relievo in a variety of elegant patterns – which is done by the Indians, in the interior provinces, in a manner that it would be difficult to copy in Europe . . . they are an article of great consequence in the fitting-out of the Mexican beau, who often appears in this kind of boot, richly embroidered in gold and silver, which costs upwards of one hundred dollars. The stirrups and the spurs correspond, in magnificence and workmanship. . . . The hat is of various colours, large, and the crown very flat and low, bound with broad gold or silver lace, and with a large round band, and fringe of the same . . .

This costume approximated very closely to that generally associated with the *charro*, or horseman. An important national figure even today, the *charro* evolved during the Colonial era but gained maximum importance during the nineteenth century. Closely identified with the landowning class, the *charro* derived both his picturesque costume as well as his name from the Salamanca region of Spain, although a noticeable influence was also received from the horsemen of Andalucía and Navarro. The *conquistadores* had brought with them to Mexico their enthusiasm for riding contests, bullfights, processions and promenades, and under Spanish rule vast sums were lavished on horses and carriages. In the seventeenth century Thomas Gage noted the tendency among rich city-dwellers to deck out their mounts with bridles and shoes of silver, and a style of dress was elaborated to keep pace with this appetite for splendour.

After Independence riding remained the chief amusement of Creole and *mestizo* landowners. They took pride in owning good horses and in decking them out richly

Detail of a 19th-century leather gaiter embossed in relief. The riders on p. 53 wear gaiters.

with elegant saddles that had been carved, appliquéd or embroidered with heavy white, gold or silver thread. When riding, they wore clothing of the kind described by Bullock but often so loaded down with adornments that the term *charro* became synonymous with the adjectives 'loud' and 'flashy'. Tylor noted wryly:

In books of travels in Mexico up to the beginning of the present century, one of the staple articles of wondering description was the gorgeous trappings of the horses. . . . The costumes have not changed much, but the taste for such costly ornaments has abated; and it is now hardly respectable to have more than a few pounds worth of bullion on one's saddle or around one's hat, or to wear a hundred or so of buttons of solid gold down the sides of one's trousers, with a very questionable calzoncillo [pair of long drawers] underneath.

The female counterparts of Mexico's rich landowners elicited a great deal less comment among foreign visitors. One of Linati's lithographs shows a prosperous young woman on horseback, and she is dressed in a blue *manga* trimmed with gold, a small hat with a floating veil, a white skirt with flounces and white shoes. Frances Calderón de la Barca gives the impression that simplicity was preferred to the lavishness of city attire. According to her 'Some country ladies . . . were dressed in very short clear white muslin gowns, very much starched, and so disposed as to show two under-petticoats, also stiffly starched, and trimmed with lace, their shoes coloured satin. Considered as a costume of their own, I begin to think it rather pretty'. Lower down the social scale the appearance of the *mestizo* smallholders also gave her much pleasure, and she described 'the prettiest little ranchera, a farmer's wife or daughter', whom she met with on horseback, as wearing 'a short embroidered muslin petticoat [skirt], white satin shoes, a pearl necklace, and earrings, a reboso, and a large round straw hat'. Like Tylor, she found it 'the wisest plan to adopt the customs of the country one lives in', and thought this style of dressing 'about the most convenient costume that can be adopted'.

The *rebozo*, mentioned above, had become during the Colonial period one of the most important female garments in both town and country. Long and rectangular in shape, its uses were enumerated in 1794 in a report to the Crown by the current viceroy, the second count of Revillagigedo, who noted that it would be hard to find another female garment 'in such general and continuous use. They are worn without excepting nuns, the highest born and richest of ladies, and even the most unfortunate and poorest women of the lowest class. They use it like a *mantilla*, like a cape, in public buildings, during promenades, and even in the home; they wrap it diagonally about themselves, they put it on their heads, they muffle themselves up in it, and tie and knot it around their bodies . . . some are woven only of cotton and others of cotton mixed with silk, and some also have stripes of gold and silver threads, and the richest ones are additionally embroidered with other metals and coloured silks, so that there is a scale of prices which rises according to the quality of the thread, the weave, the workmanship, the materials and the embroidery'.

The origins of the *rebozo* have been described as nebulous. Like the *sarape*, it probably represents a synthesis of various cultures, although the geographic spectrum may range even further. Did the *rebozo* derive from the *mantilla* or from the small squares of cloth termed *rebozos* which were likewise used in Spain? Did it undergo Oriental influence or relate to already existing indigenous garments such as the Aztec *ayatl*, or carrying-cloth, which was used by women as well as men? Another theory proposes that the webs of cloth used as head-coverings in contemporary Indian communities may have led to the *rebozo*, although Donald and Dorothy Cordry do not support this view, believing that the practice does not date back to pre-Conquest times. They suggest that the *rebozo* may have developed from the dictates of priests who urged newly converted Indian women to cover their heads when entering churches. Lengths of cloth, such as those woven on the backstrap loom when making *huipiles*, would have suited the purpose admirably. Investigators who stress the possibility of Spanish or Oriental influences, however, feel that the *rebozo* originated not with Mexico's Indians but with her *mestizo* class. Barred by law from wearing Indian clothing, yet unable to pay the high prices Spanish styles commanded, *mestizo* women may have solved their problems in part by developing the *rebozo*.

It would be hard to prove any one of these theories, yet it is certain that the *rebozo* – however it may have evolved – was rapidly adopted by all classes. As Ruth D. Lechuga points out, the garment was named for the first time by Durán in the sixteenth century. During the first decade of the seventeenth century *rebozos* were included among gifts made by the wife of the current viceroy to her chambermaid's daughter, who was about to become a nun. By the eighteenth century the *rebozo* was being depicted with great frequency by artists, and an anonymous oil-painting of the period detailing a viceregal procession in Mexico City showed a profusion of *rebozos* worn by the onlookers, who clearly belonged to all social levels. Several very elegant eighteenth-century examples which have survived feature gold and silver threads and an abundance of embroidery, as mentioned in the viceroy's description. Motifs were

Middle section of a mid-18th-century *rebozo*. Silk-embroidered motifs include figures in contemporary costume, fountains and other Mexico City landmarks. The end section (see p. 51) shows that fringes were shorter then than now. Parham Park.

colourful and minutely worked, and included rural and city scenes, bullfights, processions and the coats of arms of wearers. It has been suggested that needlework of this type may have been inspired by the long embroidered silk scarves that were popular with female courtiers in Imperial China.

A second style of decoration frequently employed for eighteenth-century *rebozos* was derived by *ikat*-dyeing a varying number of threads. Sometimes the embroidered motifs were bordered by *ikat*-produced triangles or stepped chevrons, but often the entire *rebozo* was patterned with reptilian markings. Chapultepec Castle in Mexico City has on display a fine silk *rebozo* from this period, where the cream ground is traversed by blue, green and pale yellow *ikat*-dyed threads to create a delicately mottled effect.

The fact that Mexican *rebozos* were so often *ikat*-dyed has led the Cordrys to put forward another theory regarding the origins of the *rebozo*. Was it, they ask, introduced under Spanish rule from South-East Asia, where *ikat* was well developed and where *rebozo*-like garments were common? This suggestion seems feasible if consideration is given to the pictorial designs adorning an *ikat*-dyed *rebozo* acquired by Zelia Nuttall in 1902. This example, now with the Berkeley Museum of Anthropology in the USA, features not only zig-zag patterning but also human figures and stylised flowers reminiscent of Indonesian and even Filipino *ikat* cloths. Alternatively, patterning could denote Moorish influence, thought to have spread from the Middle East via Italy to Spain and to Mallorca, where *ikat*-dyed cloth, known as *tela de lenguas*, became popular. Jack Lenor Larson, author of *The Dyer's Art*, notes a similarity between certain *ikat* patterns from Mallorca and the geometrical markings featured in early Mexican *rebozos*. It seems most likely, however, that *ikat* was practised in Mexico before the Conquest, as it was in Peru where archaeological textiles display a variety of motifs.

Rebozos relied not only on their patterning for decorative effect but also on their fringes. These were elaborately finger-knotted and may have been inspired by the fringed ends of Manila shawls. The gamut of available finishes, colours and weaves gave rise to a range of names which allowed purchasers to distinguish between different grades and styles, and an edict issued in 1757 specified how each type should be made. *Rebozo*-producing centres grew up in a number of states, including Puebla, Oaxaca and Michoacán, but the most celebrated of all was – and still is – that of Santa María del Río in the state of San Luis Potosí. Here women weavers working with the backstrap loom specialised in creating *ikat*-dyed *rebozos* of silk. One of the tests which is still applied to these light and delicate shawls is to pass them through a finger ring. If they have been made of real silk, they will slip through easily.

By the nineteenth century the *rebozo* had become intrinsic to the Mexican way of life. Linati's panorama included a lithograph of a young Creole girl wearing a *rebozo* of deep pink cashmere, and a text explaining that 'although the French fashion has extended its empire over the dress of people of a certain rank, it has not affected their *coiffure*, because no one would dare to enter a church with the head covered by an enormous hat as in Europe'. *Rebozos* were much loved by their owners who often kept them in special inlaid wooden boxes, also made in the town of Santa María del Río. In country areas they were sometimes scented by being stored in chests with apples and quinces, or held over the smoke of burning rosemary. During a visit to a country market Frances Calderón de la Barca noted that 'rebosos had a brisk sale. A number were bought by the men for their wives, or *novias* [sweethearts], at home'. Elegant yet functional, the *rebozo* has remained a symbol of femininity. It is mentioned repeatedly in literature and popular songs, and this verse by A. León Ossorio is typical:

> 'How pretty looks my brunette
> Wrapped in her *rebozo*,
> Hanging from its fringes
> Are the hearts of a hundred *charros*.'

These flattering lines might well have been written to honour the *china poblana*, whose charms and lavish style of dressing were portrayed throughout the nineteenth century in lithographs and oil-paintings (see p. 53). Although lower down the social scale than the *charro*, she too had become a national figure and was seen to represent the *mestizo* ideal of femininity in towns and some country regions. It is not known how the name originated, although exotic tales abound which centre on the arrival in Puebla de los Angeles of an Oriental princess during the seventeenth century. Frances Toor has recorded two different versions of this story in *A Treasury of Mexican Folkways* but points out prosaically that *china* meant not only 'Chinese' but also 'maid-servant', and was extended at the end of the Colonial period to describe the colourfully dressed girls who sold refreshments in town *plazas*. As Ruth D. Lechuga notes, *china* was also one of the Colonial *castas*. Carlos Nebel, writing in the 1830s, stated that the term *poblana* 'derives from *pueblo* (village). . . . These are women from the working class, although ladies of the upper class often adopt this apparel indoors'.

The distinctive costume associated with the *china poblana* is thought by Electra and Tonatiúh Gutiérrez to have evolved during the late eighteenth or early nineteenth century, inspired by Spanish peasant styles from Andalucía and Lagartera in the province of Toledo. The resulting ensemble was often far costlier than these rather lowly antecedents might warrant, however, for Frances Calderón de la Barca saw several which 'could not have cost less than five hundred dollars'. So impressed was she indeed that she referred to this 'rich and magnificent' costume on various occasions, noting that it was especially decorative on fête-days. One of her best descriptions concerned a costume bought by a friend to wear at a country fair where rich girls 'disguise themselves in peasants' dresses'. It ran as follows: 'The top of the petticoat [skirt] is yellow satin; the rest, which is of scarlet cashmere, is embroidered in gold and silver. . . . Her shoes white satin, embroidered in gold; the sleeves and body of the chemise, which is of the finest cambric, trimmed with rich lace; and the petticoat, which comes below the dress, shows two flounces of Valenciennes.' Bullock's description of 'country ladies' confirms Nebel's statement. The apparel of many clearly paralleled that of the *poblana*: 'worked shifts, with a light open jacket, and a richly embroidered or spangled petticoat [skirt], of bright coloured soft cloth (often scarlet or pink), seem to be the unvarying costume'.

Frances Calderón de la Barca also provided details of the rich adornments adopted by the true *china poblana*. These included 'a diamond ring' to hold her two plaits together, 'long earrings, and all sorts of chains and medals and tinkling things worn round the neck'. In yet another passage, written to evoke an important religious festival in Mexico City, she tells how she picked out among the crowd 'here and there a flashing Poblana, with a dress of real value and much taste, and often with a face and figure of extraordinary beauty . . . the petticoat [skirt] of her dress frequently fringed and embroidered in real massive gold, and a reboso either shot with gold, or a bright-coloured China crape shawl, coquettishly thrown over the head'. It may seem surprising that women of the lower class could afford costumes of such splendour, but according to Nebel 'Their dress takes precedence, and they would rather go without a bed, a chair, a table or other household utensil, than a pair of silk stockings, a tortoiseshell comb, or other luxury object, which could set off their charms . . .'.

It was no doubt the coquettish quality remarked on by Frances Calderón de la Barca which led her to find the *poblana* costume 'more showy than respectable', but she also had the advice of high-placed friends to guide her in her judgement. There was apparently nothing misplaced in a lady of quality adopting such a dress in the country, but when she proposed to do likewise in Mexico City she was 'adjured' by a group of ministers to abandon her project. They assured her that '*Poblanas* generally were *femmes de rien*, that they wore no stockings, and that the wife of the Spanish minister should by no means assume, even for one evening, such a costume'. Ironically, now that the *china poblana* no longer exists as a national type the costume has become one of those most frequently seen at smart gala balls. Skirts are often entirely covered with sequins and recall Bullock's rather crabbed reference to nineteenth-century styles as 'more showy than elegant'.

Although a good deal less costly, the costumes of other low-class *mestizo* women were also eye-catching. According to Frances Calderón de la Barca, the dress of 'the peasants and the countrywomen' was made up of 'short petticoats [skirts] of two colours, generally scarlet and yellow (for they are most anti-quakerish in their attire), thin satin shoes and lace-trimmed chemises'. Bright colours were equally popular with many working women in the cities, and the same religious celebrations that attracted the *poblanas* also drew a 'motley crowd' which included women 'in their gaudy colours . . . like armies of living tulips' in the sunlight.

Most of the cloth needed for these costumes was woven not by individual artisans but in large factories and, to a decreasing extent, in *obrajes*. With Independence the national textile industry had entered a period of expansion, and throughout the nineteenth century it received increasing support from governments. As Tylor noted, this was a highly profitable field, and investors were able to amass sizeable fortunes. New technology meant that cloth could be produced in larger quantities and greater variety than ever before. By the 1850s modern machinery from the USA had been installed in a number of towns, losing Puebla de los Angeles its position of pre-eminence, and hydraulic energy was later adopted widely. The quality of mechanically spun yarns improved steadily. From 1842 onwards methods for whitening *manta*, or calico, were elaborated. Synthetic dyes were introduced from Europe, and several factories began using them to colour their cloth. According to Dawn Keremitsis, attempts were made in 1860 to pattern cloth by hand. Then a small business in Tenancingo imported aniline dyes and French cylinders with which to print their textiles. By 1872 advertisements were offering materials from the principal factories of Mexico 'stamped in blue and other colours', together with Mexican *indianas* [printed cotton cloths] which for their quality and designs can compete with those imported from Europe'.

Sales of factory-produced cloth escalated in town and country, overtaking those of traditionally woven textiles, but although patterned fabrics gained steadily in popularity, they never undermined the central role played by *manta*. It has been estimated that by the close of the century this staple cloth was used by approximately two-thirds of the population. Despite this pattern of growth, however, the textile industry was faced by one major problem – an often acute shortage of home-grown cotton. As a result, Mexico was compelled to import vast quantities of raw cotton, as well as bales of woven cloth which could be printed locally. In 1879, for example, Mexico produced 60 million square metres of cloth for domestic use but imported 40 million square metres. England and the USA were the chief suppliers, and their cotton was a great deal cheaper, even including transportation costs, than home-grown varieties. Tylor was extremely critical of national policy which shored up home industry, and encouraged the manufacture of Mexican cloth when imports would have cost the consumer far less, were it not for the protection duty imposed by the government.

Mexico's faith in its own industry proved justified, however, when in the 1880s the cultivation of cotton took a new direction. Importance was gradually lost by traditional cotton-growing areas such as Guerrero, where farmers had been unable to devise a system of irrigation. Even the tropical coastal regions along the Gulf and the Pacific were overshadowed by newly established and highly productive cotton plantations in the north of the country. By the end of Porfirio Díaz's presidency the national textile industry was able to meet the needs of the Mexican people without recourse to imports.

In Mexico's fast-growing cities women of the poorer classes made up a large proportion of the industrialists' market. They bought commercially produced cloth, and their clothing may be studied in nineteenth-century lithographs or in *pinturas costumbristas* which were paintings showing scenes from everyday life. Men's clothing, similarly represented in numerous pictorial sources, also relied heavily on cloth from Mexican factories.

There are many references to urban dress in the writings of nineteenth-century observers. According to Tylor, 'In the towns, it is only the lower classes who dress in the ranchero costume'; Frances Calderón de la Barca described a group of men in the capital 'dressed *à la Mexicaine*, with their large ornamented hats and serapes, or embroidered jackets'. The *sarape*, which was so highly thought of in the country, had sinister overtones in towns. 'Convenient as it is', wrote Tylor, 'the serape is as much tabooed among the "respectable" classes in the cities as the rest of the national costume.' Tylor was apparently speaking from experience, for when he wore his own *sarape* in town even his rich friends' dog took exception to it! Frances Calderón de la Barca was among those who commented on the more unsavoury uses of the *sarape* which, like the *rebozo*, provided the wearer with the opportunity 'for concealing large knives about the person, as also for enveloping both face and figure so as to be scarcely recognizable'. Tylor was not alone among Mexico's foreign visitors to feel threatened by the sight of 'three or four dirty fellows . . . wrapped in their serapes . . . the broad-brimmed Mexican sombrero . . . slouched over their eyes . . . as they stood watching us'. This has, of course, become a filmic stereotype in innumerable North American westerns.

Among men of the lowest class the *sarape* also served as a cover-up for ragged and disreputable clothing – or even for the lack of it! As Bullock noted, 'The mixed descendants of the Spaniards, in the capital, and in Tolluca, and other cities, have little more than a blanket, worn much in the fashion of the Roman toga'. Commenting on the near-naked state of many revellers at a country fair, Frances Calderón de la Barca humorously quoted a Spanish soldier who had written in a letter to his father: 'They call this place a Paradise . . . and so I think it is, it is so full of *Adams*.' The poorest of city-dwellers was the *lépero*, an often picturesque figure described by many foreign visitors including Linati, who explained that 'It is the name given in Mexico to a man from the lowest social class, of mixed Indian and Spanish lineage. The Lepero is the Lazzaroni of Naples'. Because of the warm climate he apparently had need of few clothes. 'Without shirt, without shoes, his clothing consists of a piece of leather and a woollen blanket. This same covering serves him as a bed at night . . .' In the accompanying illustration Linati's *lépero* is shown wearing his blanket and also trousers, presumably made from the leather.

Taken together, Linati's lithographs offer an invaluable insight into the lives of the lower classes. He was clearly fascinated by the bustle of Mexico City, which 'like Naples and Madrid, swarms with importunate poor'. He described the beggars, the 'hawkers of lottery tickets and sellers of scandal sheets', but he also documented many of the more respectable trades practised by the lower classes, who worked as water-carriers and street-vendors of all kinds. Some were shown with European articles of clothing such as shirts and breeches but others, like the sweet-seller or the butcher's delivery boy, went about their business swathed in a cotton sheet. Although lighter than a woollen blanket, it still weighed too heavily on the former, who 'moves and re-arranges it in a thousand ways to rid himself of the heat that annoys him'.

Important information about the lower classes is also provided by the wax *genre* figurines in the British Museum. Modelled with great precision, they take in a wide

Genre figurines from the Christy Collection showing Indians with a range of native and European-style garments. One woman wears an *ikat*-patterned *rebozo (far right)*; the charcoal-seller has an *ayate*, or carrying cloak, of *ixtle (near right)*. Museum of Mankind, London.

range of city types including a *lépero* and a *lépera* in a dress and *rebozo*. The letters of Frances Calderón de la Barca abound with references to poor women, whose tawdry clothes were often torn and dirty but who used the *rebozo* – 'the greatest cloak for all untidiness . . . that was ever invented' – as a cover-up for 'uncombed hair and raggedness'. Also represented in the collection are a number of occupations with appropriate clothing styles.

Although a few of the characters portrayed may be *mestizo*, most are clearly Indian and demonstrate the fact that large numbers of native men and women had close contact with city life. As Linati wrote, 'the squares and streets proffer the continuous motion of people, bronzed by the sun and half naked, each carrying his merchandise and announcing it with varied and high-pitched cries. Above all the Indians who . . . come down in groups, laden with firewood, charcoal, foodstuffs, gypsum, varnishes, and in a word all the different wares of their regions.' The wax figurines show male vendors of butter, violins, charcoal and spindles, as well as a hunter and a baker. Native garments include an *ayate* (*ayatl*) of *ixtle*, waist-sashes and *huaraches*, or sandals. Over-trousers, long drawers, hats and shirts fall within the European category. The collection also features female characters whose garments include a European-style blouse, *rebozos*, *huipiles* and *enredos*, or wrap-around skirts.

Apart from trade, many Indians went into service and gained their experience of city life that way. 'In all good houses they try to have *una indita*, an Indian girl for the most essential tasks of the household . . .' These words by Linati accompany a fine lithograph showing that the model had retained her native costume. Sometimes too Indians would make pilgrimages, just as they do today, to cathedrals in towns and cities. A lithograph, published in Mexico and attributed to Nebel, shows a group of *huipil*-clad women outside the shrine of the Virgin of Guadalupe – the dark-skinned Virgin and patron saint of Mexico. Yet, as Frances Calderón de la Barca realised, 'it is neither in or near the capital that we can see the Indians to perfection in their original state. It is only by travelling through the provinces that we can accomplish this' (see pp. 52, 54).

Lithograph by Carlos Nebel showing Indians outside Mexico City. The baby is carried in a *rebozo*; one man wears a *china*, or palm raincape.

Sadly, few of these nineteenth-century travellers did attempt to penetrate any very remote regions, unless motivated like Catherwood, Stephens or Maudslay to discover and excavate ancient ruins. Visual sources show only a small number of rural Indians in native dress, while written descriptions are brief, repetitive and often patronising. Most observers were struck like Bullock by the 'long raven-like tresses plaited on each side of the head' of the Indian women who, according to this same author, were 'generally clean in their appearance'. The men seen by Frances Calderón de la Barca, however, 'looked as dirty as Indians generally do', while those described by Tylor were 'dressed in the national white cotton shirts and short drawers and sandals'.

Lithograph by Carlos Nebel showing Indians from Santa María de Tlapacoya in the Puebla highlands. The women have home-woven cotton clothing; their *quechquémitl*, worn in pre-Conquest fashion without blouses, are longer than modern *quechquémitl*. Villagers perform the *Danza de los Voladores*, or Aerialists' Dance.

According to Tylor, the traditional self-sufficiency of Indian communities was being undermined by the 'law of supply and demand . . . cotton-cloth, spun and woven at home, is yielding to the cheaper materials supplied by the factories. . . . Those who leave their native place . . . bring back with them tastes and wants hitherto unknown . . .'. Other sources give a rather different picture, however, and underline the conservatism of more isolated groups. We know from Stephens, for example, that despite missionary insistence on modesty during past centuries unbaptised Indians near Palenque were still wearing no more than a cotton loincloth at the end of the 1830s, while a report on the Maya by Santiago Mendez stated in 1861 that in Yucatán unmarried girls 'wear only a petticoat of white cotton cloth' in the home; men at work in the fields 'take all their clothes off and wear only the loincloth'.

Fortunately for the study of Indian rural dress, the end of the nineteenth century brought a new type of observer with different priorities. The North American ethnographers Frederick Starr and W. J. McGee and the Norwegian anthropologist Carl

Lumholtz were among the first to travel into remote regions with the aim of studying contemporary cultures for their own sake. Between 1890 and 1910 this last writer made a series of remarkable journeys on horseback through the western Sierra Madre. Lumholtz encountered many Indians 'dressed in the ordinary garb of the working-class of Mexico'. In *New Trails in Mexico*, published in 1912, he noted that the Papago Indians had adopted 'civilised man's mode of dressing, his tools . . . sewing machines and even phonographs. . . . What the girls desire most to acquire at school is the knowledge of music and dressmaking'.

Lumholtz also visited largely unacculturated peoples such as the Tarahumara and the Huichol, however. Men in these groups were generally 'naked-legged'; in *Unknown Mexico*, published in 1902, he described a visit with some male Huichol companions to the town of Tepic, where 'the law of the Territory forbids anyone to appear in the streets of the towns without *pantalones* (trousers). This law, in operation in one or two of the States of Mexico, is intended to promote culture by improving the appearance of natives. It is argued that the loose white cotton drawers (*calzones*) worn by the working classes and the civilised Indians are not decent enough. Happily the enlightened commander of the Territory has modified the law in favour of the Indians, allowing them to wear cotton drawers. . . . To be sure, trousers may be bought very cheap, or may even be hired for the day. There are here in Tepic some enterprising speculators who rent them out to their Mexican country cousins as well as to the Huichols'.

Photography offered observers an additional method of documentation, and the works of Lumholtz and others often include fine portraits of Indians. The new art was

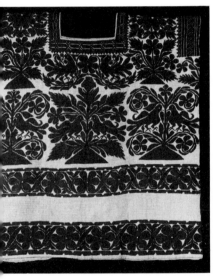

19th-century single-web white and red cotton *huipil*, possibly from the state of Oaxaca. w. 33 in (83.8 cm); L. 35½ in (90.2 cm). Victoria and Albert Museum, London (T.75–1922).

Early 20th-century hand-tinted post-card from Mexico City showing drawn threadwork.

Making linen drawnwork in the Original Hole in the Wall, Mexico Cit

Opposite Print from an acetate negative, *c.* 1900, by an unknown photographer. The woman wears an *ikat*-dyed *rebozo*; the man carries a large hat typical of the period.

practised not only by foreign visitors, however, but also by Mexican photographers, some of whom were commissioned by the government to document the Mexican nation. This undertaking encompassed all levels of society and recorded scenes from upper- and middle-class life, but it also included some evocative portraits of traditionally dressed Indians in various parts of Mexico.

After the 1910 Revolution a new attempt was made to redress the social balance in Mexico, and much was done to redistribute the land. A great wave of nationalism swept the country. The *mestizos*, who had at last emerged as the dominant class, were anxious to free themselves from the influences exerted by Europe over so many centuries, and they extolled the virtues of all things Mexican, such as traditional foods, folk arts, native and *charro* costumes, and the *rebozo*. The 1920s and 30s have often been described as Mexico's Renaissance, and under the guidance of such painters as Diego Rivera and Dr Atl a new value was set on the Indian heritage. This enthusiasm for native cultures and styles of dress has since been shared by several gifted and dedicated investigators. Faced with the national trend towards industrialisation and modernisation, distinguished Americanists such as Donald and Dorothy Cordry, Ruth D. Lechuga, Irmgard Weitlaner Johnson and Gertrude Duby have devoted their energies to documenting and photographing Indian traditions. Their work constitutes an invaluable record of the Indian Mexico which has – in spite of often tenacious resistance – begun to disappear, and which in the not too distant future may exist only as a memory.

Print from an acetate negative, *c.* 1890, by an unknown photographer, of Maya Indians on the Yucatán Peninsula.

Tzotzil president and family in Magdalenas. Chiapas, where clothing is chiefly of cotton. He wears rolled-up breeches, a bought shirt, an over-shirt and a brocaded waist-sash. Female costume comprises a wrap-around skirt and waist-sash, and an everyday two-web *huipil*. The baby wears a brocaded sun-bonnet.

PART III

TWENTIETH-CENTURY MEXICO

Tzotzil market in San Juan Chamula, Chiapas, where women specialise in weaving sheep's wool to make wrap-around skirts, shoulder- and head-cloths, and sashes; in warm weather shop-bought cotton blouses are worn. Men use woollen *chamarros* over home-woven or shop-bought cotton trousers and shirts; hats and tooled leather shoulder-bags are from San Cristóbal de las Casas.

5 Fibres, spinning and dyeing

The pressures of Spanish colonisation and twentieth-century modernisation have affected Mexico's Indian peoples to a widely varying degree. Effects have predictably been strongest in those fertile and low-lying areas which had most to offer settlers. After the Conquest groups such as the Tarascans of Michoacán, the Zapotec of the Oaxaca Valley and the Nahua – as the descendants of the Aztec are called – were swiftly drawn into the new social order, together with many other peoples whose surroundings left them vulnerable to invasion. Yet despite the inevitable adoption of certain European customs, Indian groups such as these have retained a strong sense of their own identity. Others, by contrast, gradually allowed themselves to be absorbed into the national culture, and are today virtually indistinguishable from the local *mestizo* population.

In the remoter parts of Mexico a number of Indian groups have succeeded in leading a surprisingly marginal existence, however. Relying on their inhospitable surroundings to shelter them, they escaped the more oppressive aspects of colonial domination. In the highlands of Oaxaca, for example, Spanish culture had little immediate impact on linguistic groups such as the Mixe or the Trique. Like the Tzotzil and Tzeltal, who inhabit the remoter reaches of the Chiapas highlands, they have preserved many of their traditions right up until the present time. Other peoples, over the centuries, have sought peace and seclusion in the forests of the south-east. According to Bishop Diego de Landa, many Maya Indians chose to escape the turmoil of the Conquest by scattering into the woods of Quintana Roo, while in the Chiapas rain-forests the Lacandón, who also belong to the Maya family, were so rarely seen by outsiders that many local people spoke of them as a mysterious race, and tales circulated of four-breasted women.

In the more barren regions of the north and north-west there are further outposts of indigenous culture. On the arid coast of Sonora, for instance, live the Seri Indians who maintained an independent existence as semi-nomadic hunters and gatherers right up until the 1930s. Their number now stands at around 300, but the Tarahumara of south-west Chihuahua form a much larger group, presently thought to exceed 45,000. Once they occupied a far wider area, but the curtailment of their lands has confined them to the rugged mountains of the eastern Sierra Madre where many still lead a semi-nomadic life, dividing the year between houses and cave shelters. In the north-west high mountain ranges have also served to protect the Huichol, who remain one of Mexico's most marginal groups, prizing their isolation although faced periodically with drought and famine.

The Huichol, in common with many Lacandón, have rejected Christianity, continuing instead to worship a pantheon of gods whom they identify with the forces of nature. Most other groups are nominal Catholics, however, although beliefs and ceremonies frequently hark back to the traditions of their ancestors. The Conquest was responsible for the overthrow of the old élite and the breakdown of the social hierarchy, yet many facets of collective organisation remain recognisably native even today. Groups such as the Tarahumara and the Huichol maintain their own systems of government, while comparatively acculturated villages still elect a number of dignitaries to take decisions on their behalf. It could even be argued that the power of the priestly class, which was swept away after the Conquest, has descended to the shamans who control spiritual life in pagan communities, and to the *curanderos* and *brujos* who effect cures, preside over agricultural rites and cast spells in ostensibly Catholic ones.

This continuity between past and present is reflected even more clearly by the material culture of many groups. In the remoter areas of Mexico houses are still built with roofs of palm thatch, earth floors, and walls of wood, adobe or wattle and daub. Natural surroundings also provide the raw materials for a number of crafts, many of which have changed very little in hundreds of years. In some regions communities still specialise in a particular skill such as potting or wood-carving, and Indians from different villages are able to complement one another's needs by trading their wares at markets and festivals as in pre-Conquest times.

Such traditionalism has been frequently criticised by Mexican and foreign observers alike, and the comments of Sir Edward B. Tylor are typical of many when he wrote during the last century of 'obstinate conservatism' in the face of 'progress' by people who 'hardly understand any reason for what they do, except that their ancestors did things so'. Yet this judgement is far from accurate, for Indians will often welcome new things if they feel it is in their interest to do so. Nowhere is Indian selectivity better demonstrated than in the field of costume, where native traditions have merged with European innovations to give a wide range of styles, methods and materials.

Before the Conquest the clothing of settled and nomadic peoples differed widely, and it is clear from Colonial reports that while culturally advanced groups in central and southern Mexico continued to produce magnificent weavings many northern tribes were slow to abandon their more rudimentary styles of dress which depended very largely on the pelts of animals. According to Andrés Pérez de Ribas, for example, women in the Laguna area were still wearing skins adorned with other small pieces of the same skin in 1645. Deerskin was frequently mentioned in reports, while others referred to buffalo hides and rabbit skins. In most cases the lure of Spanish clothing styles and the teachings of missionaries were eventually sufficient to bring about a change in northern dress, but the Seri remained an exception to this rule. In the late 1800s men and women from this marginal group were still wearing skirts made from the skins of pelicans, and even today the Seri continue to use pelican skins as bedding.

Leather also had its uses, both before and after the Conquest, and most Indian groups evolved ways of scraping and curing skins. With the introduction of livestock and the growth of the Colonial leather industry, however, many Indians were taught European tanning methods, and they became adept at manufacturing the saddlery and leather garments required by rich landowners at prices which, according to Bullock the nineteenth-century traveller, 'yielded a poor remuneration to the makers'. Native communities did continue to produce leather articles for their own use, however. Leather sandals have remained the standard form of footwear for countless Indians, while the Lacandón of the Chiapas forest still cure the skins of wild animals with the bark of the mahogany tree to make shoulder-bags. In 1902 in *Unknown Mexico* Lumholtz gave especial praise to the Tarahumara for their 'excellent buckskin', and today the hides of deer, cows, oxen and goats are tanned in the same way that he described. Staked out to dry, they are later scraped with sharp stones or knives, smeared with brains or squash seeds, and left to dry yet again before being soaked in water for several days and worked by hand until soft. This method is probably indigenous, although an alternative technique involving prolonged soaking first with lime and secondly with oak bark may well have been introduced into the area by missionaries. Eighteenth-century accounts of the Tarahumara carry several references to buckskin clothing, and today they still manufacture their own sandals, mats for sitting and sleeping on, and bags in different shapes and sizes.

Another ancient, though rare, survival in the costume field is bark cloth. Like fur and leather, it can provide articles of clothing without recourse to spinning or weaving. The writings of Durán and Sahagún provide detailed information about the vestments of *amatl*, or bark paper, that were worn during Aztec ceremonies, and the art of paper-making survives today in the borderline area where the states of Puebla, Hidalgo and Veracruz meet. There bark strips from wild fig-trees are pounded to make paper which serves as a magic ingredient in various pagan rites. True bark cloth, which has a more net-like texture, persists among the Mazatec Indians of Tenango Teotitlán in northern Oaxaca, where it is used for *brujería*, or witchcraft. The chief exponents of the craft, however, are the Najá-based Lacandón, whose native forests are rich in wild fig-trees. By splitting the bark to the wood they are able to strip off long portions which are later immersed in water and spread over freshly cut trunks from the same species of tree – known by the Lacandón as *bits'kal*. The bark fibres are then beaten with a wooden mallet until they unite and stretch, often to double their original size. When finished, the cloth is washed and hung out to dry on cords.

Bark cloth probably pre-dated the art of weaving among the Lacandón and may have evolved from the use of skins. It seems significant that bark should symbolise the skin of an animal, as Robert D. Bruce has noted in *Lacandon Dream Symbolism*, and a dream which involves the stripping of tree bark is thought to foretell the skinning of an animal. Fray Diego de Ribas, writing in 1695, reported the use of bark-cloth loincloths, and until recently Lacandón men continued to use bark cloth in the form of tunics which they donned during important rituals. Made from two long sections, they were sewn together with bast fibres. Bark-cloth headbands, according to Bishop Diego de Landa, were worn by sixteenth-century priests on the Yucatán Peninsula. During present-day ceremonies in Chiapas the Lacandón gods, represented by clay censers with heads, are offered red bark-cloth headbands which have been boiled with logwood. Known as 'god hats', the bands are wrapped first round the censers, then round the heads of the worshippers. Bark beating, undertaken by both men and women, is a laborious and often painful process because the sap can sting the hands, yet the recent interest taken by collectors and museum curators has prompted a few families in Najá to produce bark cloth for sale to outsiders (see p. 163).

Tree bark is just one of many traditional materials afforded to Indian communities by their natural habitat, however. Archaeological findings show that basketry was one of the earliest skills to have evolved in Mexico, which is hardly surprising since all peoples, particularly nomadic ones, need to devise ways of storing and transporting their food and belongings. Bags and baskets have remained a major necessity and a significant costume accessory, with styles of workmanship that vary from region to region. Reeds, bamboo, flexible twigs and branches, agave fibres, strong grasses and palm leaves are all important materials, and techniques include coiling, twining, wickerwork, checker- and twill-weaving (see p. 17). This last skill is not restricted to basketry, however. The *soyate* is a highly functional sash, worn by many women in the states of Puebla and Oaxaca; it derives its name from *zoyate*, which is the Aztec word for palm, and is twill-woven to resemble a flattened tube (see p. 172).

Palm is also the material most commonly used for hats, and the technique employed is so close to mat-making, or *petate*-plaiting, that the term *sombrero de petate* is generally applied to this type of hat. Texture, like size and form, is extremely variable, and the finest hats are reputed to come from Becal in Campeche. Made from *jipijapa*, a palm-like species known to botanists as *Carludovica palmata*, they are called *jipi* hats, and are worked in caves where the cool, damp atmosphere protects the moisture of the leaves and prevents them from becoming brittle. The palms and allied species that grow in other parts of Mexico are less rarified, however, and in certain regions of Guerrero or Oaxaca one may see men, women and children all engaged in braiding narrow leaf strips; even as they walk or sit talking in the shade, their fingers move ceaselessly to produce a constant supply of flexible cream-coloured strips. Sometimes hat-making is used to measure time, and if a stranger were to ask the way to the next village he might be told that it lay 'half a hat' or even 'a whole hat' away, according to the amount of work that could be accomplished on the way. Large quantities of braided palm are bought in by semi-industrialised hat-making centres in towns, but numerous Indian groups continue to assemble their own hats, sewing the flattened strips to shape by hand or even by sewing-machine (see p. 58).

A different type of skill is required to make the palm-leaf raincapes that are worn in several parts of Mexico. Among the many local names which apply to this ingenious garment is the word *china*, which may be an indication of the Oriental ancestry that some investigators ascribe to it. Despite its Far Eastern appearance, however, there seems little reason why the raincape should not have evolved independently before contact with The Philippines. In communities where tradition has withstood the lure of plastic sheeting there are still a number of men who specialise in cape-making, cutting the palm leaves into 1 in (2.54 cm) wide strips and tying them in horizontal rows with spacings of approximately 2 in (5 cm) between each row. When finished, the outside of the cape displays evenly placed layers of palm ends which are super-imposed in the manner of tiles to keep the wearer dry during the heaviest downpour (see p. 113).

Another pre-weaving technique which could be counted as a modern-day survival is netting. Practised in several areas, it is responsible for a variety of carrying-bags. In Chiapas a number of communities make use of hard-wearing shoulder-bags that expand the more they have to carry. Highland men make *pita* twine by rolling agave fibres on their legs with the palms of their hands, just as the forest Lacandón of both sexes do with the *majagua* fibres that they use for hammocks, nets and carrying-bags. Informants recall that as novices they suffered from the pull of the fibres on their leg-hairs, but those who work regularly have bald patches and feel no discomfort. On the contrary, bag-making is looked on as a pleasantly social activity in many villages, and visitors are often surprised to see groups of splendidly dressed Indian officials sitting on the steps of their presidential building rolling *pita* twine and discussing community matters. A wooden frame small enough to rest on the knee is generally used to support the netting which is held in place with nails.

Vegetable fibres are also used, albeit rarely today, for footwear. In Morelos Nahua women from several villages still wear coarsely fashioned but durable sandals of *ixtle* with heel supports. Made locally in San Felipe Ixcatlán or in Puebla in the village of Tepemaxalco, they are reminiscent of backless archaeological examples from the Tehuacán Valley and other regions. Sandals from Cavedweller sites in Chihuahua show that sections of yucca trunk were sometimes used, and although the modern Tarahumara employ a different technique, they do provide a continuity with the past by occasionally twisting and interweaving yucca leaves to form a hard-wearing sole which is anchored to the foot with an agave-fibre cord. The mountains of Guerrero have sheltered another survival in this field, for near Xonacatlán men still wear sandals of palm, which they make by plaiting strands to form a pointed sole and two narrow straps.

With these exceptions, however, most articles of dress depend today on loom weav-

Nahua woman's *ixcatles*, or sandals of *ixtle*, from Morelos.

ing. Among the bast and leaf yarns which were formerly employed in northern Mexico *apocynum* and yucca have fallen into disuse, but in a small area of Oaxaca the fibres of the *chichicastle* shrub are still spun and woven. Francisco Hernández saw the plant growing near Tepoztlán in Morelos during the 1570s and described it as follows: 'It is a sort of nettle . . . as high as a tree. It has serrated . . . leaves . . . is covered with thorns that prick when touched. . . . The bark of the stalks is soaked, spun like linen, and made into garments which are neither different from nor inferior to those of linen.' Despite its thorns, which have won for it the conflicting nicknames of *mala mujer* ('evil woman') and *mal hombre* ('evil man'), its fibres were clearly much appreciated both before the Conquest and during the decades that followed it. Now, however, its uses are confined to just a few Zapotec and Chontal communities where, according to Ruth D. Lechuga, the upper branches are boiled in water with oak ashes to act as a bleaching and softening agent.

Plants belonging to the agave family have fared very differently, with many species retaining a high level of importance. In Veracruz, for example, *Agave zapupe* continues to serve as a source of fine and durable fibres for the Huastec, who strip them of pulp with the aid of two sticks. Long and white, *zapupe* fibres are left to dry and occasionally dyed. When ready for weaving they are twisted together, wound into a figure of eight, and knotted to form the warp. *Agave lecheguilla* also provides plant fibres which are used, like those of *Agave zapupe*, to make shoulder-bags and household articles. During preparation the *lechuguilla* spikes are beaten with a wooden implement, then scraped with a metal blade to clean and separate the fibres. These are dried, carded and later spun.

Numerous other agave species provide fibres, indiscriminately termed *ixtle*. During the Colonial period the *maguey*, or Mexican agave, received extravagant praise from several writers including Thomas Gage, who spoke of it as 'that excellent tree . . . which they plant and dress as they do their vines in Europe'. As for Francisco Hernández, it was his opinion that 'if men were to live with reasonable moderation and temperance, this plant alone would provide them with all the things necessary for human life, for the advantages and uses which it affords are without number'.

The environment in the Mezquital Valley of Hidalgo is arid and inhospitable, yet the Otomí who live there are still able to rely on the *maguey* for house-building materials, natural fencing for their small plots of land, food, *aguamiel* (sweet sap), soap pulp, nails, needles, pins and textile yarns. According to Sahagún, Otomí women before the Conquest 'concerned themselves only with *maguey* fibres', and despite the introduction of other materials they continue to spin and weave them today to make shoulder-bags and *ayates*, or carrying-cloaks. Men are generally responsible for stripping the fibres, however – a task requiring considerable strength. Methods in the Mezquital Valley differ little from those described on page 73 by Sahagún. The spikes are severed, usually from plants which no longer yield *aguamiel*, baked until soft and left in water until they rot. They are then beaten with a mallet, spread across an inclined board and scraped. When the fibres are free of pulp, they are soaked in water with local seeds, soap or maize dough, dried in the sun and combed.

The use of agave fibre clothing persisted well into the Colonial period. The Tarahumara, whose early *pita* garments have been excavated from archaeological cave sites, were reported in 1645 by Pérez de Ribas to be still wearing clothing of *pita* 'which the women knew very well how to make', and historical references confirm that this custom continued into the 1700s. The introduction of sheep's wool and the spread of cotton cloth changed dress habits throughout Mexico, however: clothing restrictions, which had barred many people within the Aztec empire from wearing cotton, disappeared with the old hierarchy, and the peasant classes found themselves free to adopt the garb once associated only with the rich and powerful. Today cotton is spun and woven in many of the central states, while numerous groups in Oaxaca, Guerrero and Chiapas carry on the textile traditions of their ancestors.

Among Indians the cultivation of cotton has remained a marginal pursuit, quite divorced from the high production levels of industry. Weavers who live along the coastlines of the Atlantic and the Pacific, or in hot and humid valleys, like whenever possible to grow their own plants, but in highland areas trade is still a vital link enabling women to buy cotton from lowland communities during visits to markets and religious festivals. The long, white fibres of *Gossypium hirsutum* are valued everywhere, but the tawny species known as *coyuche* and defined by botanists as *Gossypium mexicanum* is becoming rare. Industry has shown no interest in developing or cultivating the genus, and in some areas Indians have allowed their stock of plants to dwindle or die out. *Coyuche* was once widely used in the Puebla highlands, for example, but a decline in cultivation has led many weavers to substitute white cotton which they dye mat brown. Oaxacan groups such as the Mixtec, the Trique and the Amuzgo continue, like the Tzotzil of Chiapas, to make regular use of *coyuche*, however, and to appreciate its warm and subtle colouring.

Preparation methods for both kinds of cotton are long and laborious. When the bolls are ripe and ready for gathering, the fibres are carefully separated from the seed and picked over by hand to remove all impurities. They are then fluffed out and spread on a palm mat, hide or thick woollen blanket which usually rests on a cushion of corn husks and other plant material. Next the cotton is pounded, slowly but firmly, with

Tzotzil president and family in Magdalenas, Chiapas, where clothing is chiefly of cotton (see also illustration on pp. 118–19).

wooden beaters. These are held in both hands and range from carefully polished rods in some communities to rough y-shaped branches in others. As the fibres begin to adhere to one another, the blows become stronger, and after the cotton has been turned to ensure regular beating, it is shaped into a smooth and even strip ready for the spindle. Patience and skill are essential at this early stage, for without clean yarn it is impossible to produce delicately textured cloth.

After cotton, the fibre most frequently woven among contemporary Indian groups is wool. Acceptance of this advantageous new material was rapid, and when Motolinía recorded his observations between 1523 and 1540 he noted that 'fine articles' of merino were being made in convents by native weavers and that 'the Indians esteem them highly'. Over the centuries esteem turned to practical skill, as missionaries introduced wool-flocks into many of Mexico's remotest areas. In the Mezquital Valley of Hidalgo, for instance, the enthusiasm of the Otomí was such that they abandoned their garments of *ixtle* in favour of wool – until the availability of cotton cloth caused them to transfer their allegiance yet again. In high regions wool has remained an invaluable fibre, however. The Tarahumara of Chihuahua specialise in weaving thick blankets as protection against the cold of winter, and other mountain peoples have put wool to even more extensive use. Wrap-around skirts, *rebozos*, *sarapes*, *quechquémitl* and *huipiles* are among the many garments used in the upland areas of Puebla, Morelos, Mexico State, Oaxaca and Chiapas.

In conservative Tzotzil communities such as San Juan Chamula or Zinacantán sheep are tended entirely by women and girls, whose responsibility it is to graze and sheer them. The wool is washed with a special soap made from a local plant, and carded with a pair of crude boards inset with short wire bristles in accordance with Conquest technology. Wool cards are occasionally omitted by the Tarahumara, however. Robert M. Zingg, who made a close study of their material culture in the 1930s, noted that the shorn wool was washed in running water where it was beaten with a smooth stick. When dry, the wool was carded by hand to become a light, fluffy mass, then hand-twisted into loose strands. These strands were later twisted on the thigh, before being wound on to the spindle. In Morelos the Nahua weavers of Hueyapan have evolved a very different procedure. After cleaning the wool they use two large teasels to card it, and even on occasion to mix fibres of different shades. This is done by softening the right-hand teasel in hot water, then rubbing it against the left-hand teasel where the fibres are lodged. In this way white is merged with black or brown to give grey or beige. This method of treating wool is unique in Mexico, although it has been reported that the Navajo used long ago to clamp several burrs together to make cards.

The adoption of sheep's wool contributed ultimately to the decline and disappearance of spun rabbit hair and feathered yarns, both extravagantly praised by the Spanish *conquistadores* for their smooth texture and warmth. Surprisingly one village has retained the use of feathered textiles, however. This is Zinacantán in Chiapas, where the wedding *huipil* incorporates white chicken feathers spun into the weft thread and serves as a last reminder of the luxuriant feathered textiles of ancient times.

After the Conquest fine weavings were frequently compared with silk by chroniclers who commented on the absence of this fibre in the New World. Recent investigators have questioned this assumption, however. It is Irmgard W. Johnson's opinion that wild silk may have been spun and woven on a small scale before the arrival of the Spaniards. According to her, contemporary weavers from a few highland communities

Tapestry-patterned *sarape* of undyed wool, spun with a spinning wheel and woven on a treadle loom, from Coatepec Harinas, Mexico. The warp yarns form a fringe at both ends (not shown). w. 38½ in (97.8 cm); L. 67½ in (171.5 cm).

in Oaxaca and Puebla make use of the fibres provided by *Eutachyptera psiddi* Sallé, which feeds on oak trees, and those of a second species which lives on the leaves of the *madroño*, or *Arbutus menziesii* tree. This practice could be extremely ancient, for methods and implements fit clearly within a native tradition. When the cocoons have been boiled in water, the fibres are picked over by hand and then spun. Wild silk was also collected until recently by the Otomí of the Puebla highlands where, according to Bodil Christensen, a species of night moth now known as *Malacosoma incurvum Azteca* Neumoegan provided weavers with cocoons in the late spring.

It is the domesticated Asiatic genus, *Bombyx mori*, that is responsible for most of the silk woven in modern Mexico, however. The importation of Chinese and Italian silk came to an end during the Second World War, but Mexican sericulture persists in Oaxaca's Mixteca Alta, which achieved fame for its silk production in the sixteenth century. Widespread spraying against malaria during the 1930s killed off large numbers of silkworms, yet enough survived to meet local demand. While on a visit to San Sebastián Peñoles in the 1960s, Donald and Dorothy Cordry watched silk being prepared. First the cocoons were boiled with ashes in a large pot on the weaver's hearth to turn them from yellow to white; then they were allowed to dry and pulled apart ready for spinning. The Cordrys also traced some of the trade links involving silk. They noted, for example, that silk continued to travel long distances within the Mixteca region, and that it had even been used until recently by Nahua weavers in San Sebastián Zinacatepec, Puebla, for the narrow weft stripes and embroidered yokes of their fine *huipiles*. Today, after a lapse of twenty years, silk commands ever higher prices but a number of predominantly Oaxacan villages continue to employ it, reserving it for small items such as sashes or using it to decorate areas of cotton garments.

All these different materials, native and foreign, accord well with Mexico's many variations in climate and habitat, and contribute substantially to the richness of Indian costume. Often a short distance between two villages can involve fundamental changes in dress styles, as in Chiapas where the contrasts are striking and numerous. Huistán, for example, lies in a temperate basin, and villagers wear mostly cotton, while the inhabitants of San Juan Chamula – who are also Tzotzil – live high up and rely on wool to protect them against the cold (see p. 120).

Methods and implements for spinning these different fibres also range from the indigenous to the European. In many areas agave fibres are twisted with the aid of a *carreta*, or wooden wheel, but the resulting cord is generally too thick to be used for anything except carrying-bags and articles such as hammocks for home use. The spinning-wheel, or *redina*, is widely used with wool, however, to produce fine textiles that are nearly always treadle-loomed. An early photograph published by Frederick Starr in 1899 shows a young Tarascan man on the island of Janitzio, Michoacán. Standing beside his wheel, he turns it with one hand and feeds carded wool into the thread on the spindle with the other. The procedure remains unchanged today in innumerable wool-weaving centres, where wheels are home-made from local wood and have little in common with the highly polished specimens displayed in tea shops or antique fairs in England.

According to Ruth D. Lechuga, Mixtec women in San Mateo Peñasco twist the silk they produce with their fingers, but this is very unusual, for in areas where the backstrap loom predominates yarn is almost always spun with a spindle. The whorls and their wooden shafts vary in size and shape to suit the fibre and the width of thread current among different groups. The Tarahumara, who now weave only wool, employ a stick some 14 in (35.6 cm) long with a 6 in (15.3 cm) whorl of wood, although Lumholtz noted the use of pine bark at the end of the last century. The modelling of clay whorls is also widespread. Unlike pre-Conquest examples these are rarely decorated, but the pastel-painted whorls of Jamiltepec, Oaxaca, are one exception: carried by traders throughout the Mixteca region and beyond, spindles are sold at religious festivals and used in countless villages to spin cotton, silk and even wool. Archaeological whorls are occasionally used in Hueyapan, Morelos, by Nahua weavers who find them in their fields and fit them with new shafts. As for the Otomí of the Mezquital Valley, they too make use of archaeological whorls, but their shafts – which are uniquely carved to spin *ixtle* – are arrow-shaped instead of pointed. Great resourcefulness is also to be met with among the Huichol, who have been known to fashion whorls from bone, gourd and even – according to Donald and Dorothy Cordry – from a piece of white china belonging to a broken factory-made plate.

The quality of finished cloth depends on the smoothness and resistance of the spun thread, which should be 'of even thickness' and not – as Sahagún recorded – 'lumpy' or 'poorly twisted'. Pre-Conquest techniques illustrated in the codices remain unchanged today, and spinners generally own a number of spindles which they keep in a gourd or special basket like the ones shown in the Codex Florentino (see p. 18). Yarn is spun by whirling the stick-and-whorl in a pottery bowl, half-gourd or even on the ground. The first few inches are the most difficult, and the spinner frequently moistens the top of the spindle so that strands will adhere when applied. After this the spindle revolves rapidly. Sahagún and Hernández both mentioned lime as an aid to spinning, and women often use either lime or ash on their fingers and in the bottom of the gourd or dish to make the spindle turn smoothly. Spun yarns range from the very coarse to the very fine, and the time taken varies accordingly. It could take a weaver about three days to turn two pounds of wool into thick thread, for example, but up to two weeks to spin the same amount finely.

Although most spinners kneel on a palm mat as they work, there are those who prefer to sit on a low stool, a log or even a stone. Indian houses are traditionally windowless, and interiors are often too dark to permit close work, so women perform most of their tasks in the open air. After his travels through nineteenth-century Mexico, Tylor gave readers a cheerful pen-picture of Indian women 'sitting at their doors in groups, spinning cotton thread with the *malacates* [spindles], and apparently finding as much material for gossip here as elsewhere'. These lines would still apply in countless weaving communities, although Otomí spinners in the Mezquital region have the advantage of mobility: their uniquely shaped shafts are designed to spin not on the ground but in the air, and throughout the valley women are to be seen with hanks of *ixtle* over their right shoulders, their spindles turning rhythmically as they walk along the roads to market or accompany their goats and sheep to graze.

Although some Otomí men from the Mezquital Valley are skilled spinners, the task is nearly always undertaken by women, as in pre-Conquest times. Experience may make the work seem effortless and mechanical, yet most women remember their training when young and the scoldings they received. The following confidences, published in *Indian Education in the Chiapas Highlands*, were recorded by Nancy Modiano just a few years ago in the Tzotzil community of San Pedro Chenalhó:

When I was about fifteen I began to use the spindle. . . . 'Do it this way', my mother would say, 'Don't make it too soft or too hard'. When my spindle didn't turn right she would hit me with it. . . . My mother would say 'Where did you come from, woman, that you don't know how to

Zapotec wool-spinner from Oaxaca. The raw fibre, washed and dried, has been carded in the European manner with wool cards. With her left hand she pulls each roll of wool and feeds it on to the tip of the spindle-shaft. Spun yarn is rolled in a ball.

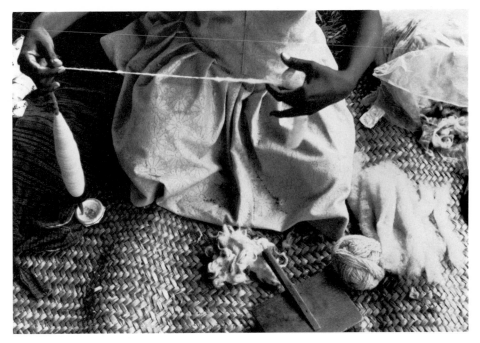

Otomí *ixtle*-spinner from the Mezquital Valley, Hidalgo. The spindle has a clay whorl; the wooden shaft is arrow-shaped at the upper end. She spins the *ixtle* in the air as she walks and wears a two-web *ixtle ayate* on her head as protection against the sun.

handle your spindle? Women have to learn. You'll probably have a strict mother-in-law who knows how to weave very well, and she'll scold you. She'll hit you on your head with the spindle and whorl if you don't know how to use them. . . .' It was hard to make thread; in those days we had to spin it ourselves, but now we can buy it all ready for the loom.

There is, as this last statement indicates, a growing tendency among Indian weavers to bypass the preparation and spinning of yarns and to rely on factory-made threads. These were first marketed in the second half of the nineteenth century, and in 1902 Lumholtz reported the existence of Nahua and Otomí pedlars who made five-yearly ex- peditions into the Sierra Madre to visit the Northern Tepehuan of southern Chihuahua with needles and thread. Today traders are generally *mestizo*, and their visits to Mexico's more isolated communities, like those in the Chiapas highlands, are undertaken with far greater frequency. Sales of commercial weaving and embroidery threads are high, and these are transported up mountain inclines by animal train or by van along dirt tracks. In less remote areas these materials may even be stocked by village shops run by the local *mestizo* population. Frequently, however, weavers prefer to journey to the nearest town where the choice is greater, and if they sell their work to stall-holders or shop-keepers, they may accept commercial yarns in part-payment.

Hilaza is the term used for the coarsest type of factory-spun cotton, and many weavers in acculturated areas now rely almost exclusively on this, or on mercerised thread for fine work. Commercial wools too are in high demand, even among the Huichol and other groups who also continue to spin their own home-produced wool. Occasionally Indian weavers will combine these bought materials with local ones or even modify them to suit their requirements. The Huichol, for example, are given to opening up and re-spinning some yarns by hand to produce fine embroidery and sew- ing threads. The Tarascan Indians, on the other hand, will often double commercial wool on a spinning-wheel to get a thicker yarn.

Sad to say in Mexico, as throughout the rest of the world, the last decade has seen a general trend towards synthetic fibres. Acrylics are fast replacing wool in a number of Indian communities, and artificial fibres are taking over from silk and even cotton. Older, more conservative weavers are quick to point out that factory-produced fibres, whether synthetic or traditional, rarely wear as well as home-spun yarns and that resulting textiles are frequently inferior in quality and texture. The other disadvantage is expense: as soon as a weaver starts to buy her materials, she becomes part of the national economy and vulnerable to inflation. Price rises over the past few years have affected several communities, leading weavers to cut corners by economising on ma- terials, and any outsider who questions these falling standards will surely be told '*Pero el hilo es muy caro . . .*' ('But yarn is very costly . . .').

Despite these drawbacks, however, the majority of weavers welcome the chance to buy their fibres, many of which come ready coloured and entail an even greater saving of time and effort. Modern technology has, it seems, brought an element of truth to Aztec legend. For among the many marvels attributed in the Annals of Cuauhtitlán to Quetzalcóatl, ruler of Tula, was a miraculous cotton which 'grew in many colours: red, yellow, pink, purple, green, pale green, reddish yellow, and spotted like a jaguar. All these colours it had by nature. . . . No one had to dye it'. Yet for all their advantages, factory-coloured yarns do have serious shortcomings: many syn- thetic dyes fail to match the subtle shades obtainable with natural methods. In the Chiapas highlands, for example, where red predominates in many textiles, weavers have difficulty finding commercial threads with the tonalities they desire.

Factory yarns are also responsible in many cases for changing native tastes. In a number of areas Indians have become accustomed to, and even acquired a liking for, a range of strident colours such as lime green, acid yellow and shocking pink, known colloquially as *rosa mexicano*. This last colour was already popular among townspeople in 1911 when Mary Barton, English traveller and author of *Impressions of Mexico with Brush and Pen*, confided to her readers: 'I regret to say that there is a horrible bluish-pink of a most unpleasant brilliancy which is distinctly a favourite for skirts.' Moved in the same book to pronounce the Mexicans 'fond of colour' but without 'the fine sense of it', this fastidious observer would have been still more offended by the luminescence that so often characterises acrylic fibres today. Yarns of this type are much used in treadle-loom workshops for the manufacture of modern-style *sarapes* but they are gaining increasing acceptance among backstrap weavers. In Oaxaca Trique women from San Martín Itunyoso and San Juan Copala often brocade their magnificent *huipiles* with acrylic weft threads, while in the western Sierra Madre many Huichol employ them to weave brightly patterned bags and sashes, as well as for ceremonial offerings such as yarn pictures and gods' eyes (see p. 152).

The spread of factory-dyed thread has affected Indian textiles in another way, however, for poor quality is often indicated by a lack of colour-fastness. After the first wash, many a finely woven garment might be described as spoilt by outsiders, because the dyes have run, causing the designs to become confused. In the case of predominantly white textiles results are particularly sad, with delicately brocaded or embroidered motifs streaking the background. In the Zapotec village of Yalalag, Oaxaca, most weavers now take special steps to protect their white cotton *huipiles*. These feature long threads, braided below the neck slit to form a horizontal bar with a long tassel at either end (see p. 219). Formerly this was twined into the cloth during weaving, but since the adoption of brightly coloured artificial silk it is generally made separately and sewn on after each washing to prevent staining.

Artificial dyes are also used by large numbers of weavers who still prefer to home-dye their hand-spun fibres. Sold even in remote regions by itinerant traders or village shop-keepers, they have largely overtaken natural colouring methods. Most commercial dyes are still aniline, and they work on all the traditional fibres including those of the agave family. In Veracruz, for example, the Huastec weavers of Tantoyuca incorporate brightly coloured strands into their *zapupe* shoulder-bags to make decorative stripes. Brown colourants are also used to imitate *coyuche* cotton, as in Yalalag where the traditional wrap-around skirt continues to feature tan and white warp stripes. In areas where indigenous dyes such as cochineal have become expensive and scarce synthetic dyes have taken on their role, and several communities in Chiapas now rely on a red aniline known as *cochina*, while many weavers in Oaxaca have adopted a purple aniline named *fuchina*. According to Francisco Santamaría, *fuchina* was once extracted from varieties of the fuchsia plant, but today it is chemically manufactured and bought by numerous weavers to replace shellfish colouring. In the Mixtec village of San Sebastián Peñoles women used, until recently, to weave belts and bags with stripes of *fuchina*-dyed silk which softened to lavender after repeated washings and became indistinguishable from shellfish-coloured cloth. The Tacuate of Ixtayutla and the Chinantec of San Felipe Usila are among those who continue to make regular use of *fuchina* (see p. 173).

Each year large quantities of synthetic dyestuffs are required by Mexico's many treadle-loom workshops, and while natural colourants are often recognised as superior their use is becoming increasingly rare. If a customer should desire a traditionally dyed *sarape*, he is generally obliged to place a special order. In family workshops dyeing is usually carried out by the women of the house, although helpers may also be taken on. Commercial products are often combined to get intermediate shades: to colour white wool a deep blue, for example, a dyer might mix three parts blue with two parts purple, increasing the amounts to get a deeper hue; if dark wool is used, the dyer must also take this into consideration.

Methods are similar in many *sarape* centres to those described by María García Vargas for San Bernardino Contla, Tlaxcala. There yarns are dyed in large galvanised cauldrons which are heated by petrol burners. In order to achieve colour-fastness dyers add sulphuric acid to the boiling water, and this acts as a fixative for the colourants, which are measured in accordance with the amount of yarn required. When this mixture is ready, dyers immerse the yarns, moving them constantly to ensure even absorption and only removing them when the water is clear of colour. The yarns are then wrung out and left to dry in the open air. When preparing for cheaper, low-quality textiles, however, dyers frequently leave out the fixative and soak the yarns for only five or ten minutes. Completed weavings are not always colour-fast, therefore, but in the case of *saltillos* this is seen to contribute to the design. Named after the famous northern town of Saltillo, these *sarapes* present a rainbow appearance with a succession of differently coloured weft threads. At the first wash the narrow bands of colour merge together, heightening the rainbow effect and causing people to say evocatively '*los saltillos se lloran*', which means that they have 'dissolved in tears' and run.

This haphazard method of patterning is a modern substitute for *ombré* dyeing – a procedure described in 1937 by Elsie McDougall. While visiting a *sarape* workshop in Jalisco, she watched dyers achieve delicately shaded yarn:

The yarn was wound in skeins; one end of each skein was looped and used as a handle and so remained white. The skein was then dipped in the blue, dyed, taken out, and dried. The dye was strengthened, and re-boiled and the dry skein partly dipped again, the handle and some of the light blue being reserved. Successive dippings produced the shaded yarn.

Since the 1930s, when Elsie McDougall did much of her research, dyeing techniques have declined not only in treadle-loom centres but also among backstrap weavers. Yet despite the popularity of bought thread and synthetic dyes, weavers in a few communities do still rely on natural colourants. Although some dyestuffs are traded across long distances, many are confined to small areas and may be used by just one or two villages. Recent years have seen a considerable awakening of interest among collectors and investigators in these native dyeing methods, and some attempts have been made to prevent their disappearance. One of the most successful has been that undertaken in the Chiapas highlands during the late 1970s by Walter F. Morris, whose exceptional rapport with local Maya communities has enabled him to persuade several to establish weaving co-operatives. Members are encouraged to pursue traditional methods and to ask prices that will adequately reward them for their labours. Weavers who belong to these co-operatives are therefore freed from haggling with intermediaries, whose prime concern is not quality but profit. The meticulous investigations carried out by Amber Spark into local dyes have also proved important to the success of this project. Today rich and subtle hues are still produced in communities such as Magdalenas, where they testify to the wealth of natural colourants which must once have existed in the region (see p. 161).

Weavers in Oaxaca have also retained a number of native dyestuffs, especially in the mountain areas, while in the lowland community of Santa Ana del Valle it is still possible to buy fine treadle-loomed *sarapes* with naturally dyed weft threads that form elegant landscapes replete with birds and flowers. In northern Mexico a broad spectrum of vegetable colourants is used by the Tarahumara, and in his book on their material culture Campbell W. Pennington describes dyeing methods in considerable detail: the study of archaeological finds suggests, according to him, that such an extensive range of colourants may have developed only in late pre-Columbian times, or even after the introduction of wool. Today this is the only type of fibre dyed, and preparations vary according to the plants which grow at different altitudes. It is heartening that so many natural dyes should continue to hold their own, even though most Indian groups now buy commercial products from traders as well.

Traditional methods require considerable skill, patience and hard work, with operations often taking several hours, or even days. Ingredients need to be accurately judged, but weavers rarely measure them in a scientific way, preferring instead to work *al tanteo*, or by guesswork. The structure of wool makes it particularly receptive to colour, and in San Juan Chamula, Chiapas, this staple fibre is often dyed while still unspun. Such a procedure is extremely rare, however, as most weavers prepare their yarn for weaving first. Treadle-loom centres generally dye skeins which have been reeled on winding frames. As in the past, natural colourants derive from vegetable, animal and mineral sources. While some dyes are substantive and stain fibres directly, others require mordants to fix the colour in the yarn. With this second category materials are dipped first in the mordant and secondly in the dye bath, or alternatively soaked in a solution that combines both. Although used with the same dyestuff, different mordants can produce a wide range of shades and substantially enlarge the dyer's spectrum. There is also a third dye category requiring oxidisation.

Flowers, fruits, barks, roots, leaves and various types of wood all provide important regional dyes, but the plant species most widely employed today is *Indigofera anil*. During the early years of Conquest its rich blue-black tones achieved great popularity in Europe, and brought sizeable fortunes to those who exploited it. Some, according to reports analysed by Murdo J. MacLeod, were so greedy for profit that they collected not only leaves but also stalks, twigs and hacked-off branches, severely maiming acres of shrubs. Neglect followed this initial craze, however, causing Bullock to comment in the nineteenth century on the decline in cultivation and to note that Guatemala had become the best source for indigo, or *añil*. Despite the recent ban on foreign imports, many contemporary weavers in Chiapas use Guatemalan indigo, smuggled across the border by pedlars. Before they are traded across such long distances indigo leaves are generally soaked in hot water, strained, dried and compressed into small cakes of the type described long ago by Sahagún and Clavijero. These cakes, or *piedritas* ('little stones'), can then be dissolved by the purchaser.

In Chiapas indigo is chiefly used for the wrap-around skirts, or *enredos*, worn in most communities (see pp. 61, 166), but while some women continue to dye their own cotton, others prefer to weave skirts from natural cotton – home-grown or bought – and to take them for dyeing to one of the *mestizo* workshops which operate in the town of San Cristóbal de las Casas. For Doña Esperanza Morales de Ruiz, who runs one such centre, work abounds in October when Tzotzil women from Zinacantán bring her their skirts to be indigo-dyed in readiness for the Feast of All Souls. These small businesses also concentrate on treadle-loom weaving, however, and a large part of their revenue derives from providing Indian women with skirt-lengths in the style they require. Trade with the Tzeltal of Amatenango del Valle is confined to the town of Comitán, where skirts are distinctively striped and priced ever higher because of the indigo shortage. Other communities rely instead on the textile workshops of San Cristóbal, and Doña Esperanza has no shortage of clients.

A specialist in indigo-dyeing, she leaves the weaving to a male employee and devotes her time to colouring. To break down the indigo Doña Esperanza soaks it in an alkaline solution of lye which she makes with lime, wood and charcoal ashes of pine and oak. After three or four days a doughlike consistency is achieved, and the indigo is beaten to paste. A third vital ingredient is *sacatinta*, or *muicle*, known to botanists as *Jacobinia spicigera*. This Doña Esperanza buys from the Tzotzil villages of San Pedro Chenalhó and San Miguel Mitontic. *Sacatinta* plants are left to rot for three days in a vat of sugared water, then combined with the indigo and the lye in the dyeing vat. Into this peacock-green solution the yarns are dipped twice and even three times daily for up to five days. After each soaking they are wrung out and hung up to dry, so that the dye can oxidise and the colour deepen. To reactivate this liquid, which can last for several months, Doña Esperanza adds periodic measures of newly processed *sacatinta*.

Another source of indigo for Chiapas weavers is Oaxaca, where a plentiful supply still exists. Fine skirts incorporating horizontal indigo-dyed stripes are worn in several Mixtec communities, while neighbouring groups such as the Trique still favour this same dye. In central Mexico indigo is also used by the Nahua of Morelos, the Otomí of Hidalgo and the Totonac of the Puebla highlands. Even the Huichol, who have given up virtually all other dyes, continue to cultivate indigo. The same is true of the Tarascan Indians, referred to as indigo dyers by Lumholtz in 1902, when men of the trade were still known in some parts as *'Tecos'*, or 'finger nails', because theirs were so indelibly stained with blue. In northern Mexico the Tarahumara too make use of indigo, steeping the leaves for several days in a clay jar and transferring the liquid to a second jar. Human urine is added as a mordant, or alternatively alum – the metallic substance referred to by Sahagún as 'the alum stone' and praised by Hernández for its great value to dyers.

Further enhancing this continuity between past and present is a broad spectrum of more localised dyes such as *sacatinta*. Mentioned earlier as an adjunct to indigo, it is often used in the Chiapas highlands where it is mordanted with lime, alum and chrome to produce a dark grey with purplish-blue overtones. Blackberries are also used in this same region to give a purple colour which verges on green when mordanted with lime. In hot areas the seeds of *Bixa orellana* continue to furnish inhabitants with an orange-red food colourant and textile dye known as *achiote*, or annatto. Mordanted with urine or alum by weavers or even used alone, it is – as Hernández noted – extremely fast and difficult to remove. Berries of a different variety are still gathered by a few Trique women, who rely on the fruit of the *madroño* and lime water to provide them with a range of red and yellow shades. Red is also obtained by some Tarahumara from the scrapings of the *Haematoxylum brasiletto* tree. These are collected from the trunk and branches, then boiled and combined with alum or lime. This same tree, known as *palo de Brasil*, or brazilwood, is also exploited in the south of Mexico. On the coast of Oaxaca, for example, it is occasionally used by the Huave of San Mateo del Mar to give a deep tan ground to their brocade-patterned *servilletas*, and by the Chontal of Huamelula whose waist-sashes are sometimes dyed with a combination of brazilwood and *fuchina*. Logwood, known to botanists as *Haematoxylum campechianum*,

Mixtec *posahuanco*, or three-web wrap-around skirt, from Pinotepa de Don Luis, Oaxaca. The horizontally worn warp stripes incorporate *hiladillo*, or cochineal-dyed silk, dark blue cotton dyed with indigo, and lilac cotton dyed with the secretion of shellfish. w. 60½ in (153.7 cm); L. 45½ in (115.6 cm). Museum of Mankind, London.

is to be found in the south-east, where its dark red pulp affords another important colourant.

Rust shades are obtained in several ways. In the canyons of Chihuahua grow three types of tree with dye-rich barks which the Tarahumara combine with lime, urine or alum. Of these the best known is *Erythrina flabelliformis*, or *colorín*. Lichens offer another rewarding range of colourants, and upland species are mixed with alum by Tarahumara weavers requiring rusty yellow hues. In the Chiapas highlands lichens are gathered from the bark and branches of oak and alder trees or fence posts, then ground and soaked to give a firm reddish-brown. As for the tawny tones of *coyuche*, these are imitated with various dyes, one source being the *huixtololo* root which is favoured among Nahua weavers in the Puebla highlands.

Yellow is achieved with a range of colourants. A parasitic plant, known to the Aztec in pre-Conquest times as *zacatlaxcalli* but to modern botanists as *Cuscuta americana* or *Cuscuta tinctoria*, is still occasionally used in Oaxaca to give a mustard tone to yarn. Methods mentioned by Campbell W. Pennington for the Tarahumara include the boiling of flowers from *Acacia farnesiana* with lime, and the boiling of an entire plant of the *Manihot* family with scrapings from *alcaparra* branches. Research by Amber Spark shows that dogwood leaves are a source of yellow in the Chiapas highlands, where strong and opaque shades are obtained with alum and chrome respectively. Gold is provided in this same region by leaves from the peach tree, or by leaves and twigs taken from the red alder and combined with lime, alum or chrome. Alder bark also affords a reddish-brown, while the roof soot from alder fires is occasionally used to dye yarns dark brown.

Black results from a variety of methods: in San Juan Chamula, for example, weavers often boil their unspun wool for several days with black earth and a species of plant known as *huele de noche*, translatable as 'smells at night'. This process is also used to over-dye wool that is naturally black so as to intensify its appearance. In some regions oak galls are used, while according to Isabel Kelly and Angel Palerm a few Totonac continue to rely on three shrubs which outsiders group under the Spanish term *capulín*, but which botanists know as *Ardisia escallonioides* and *Eugenia capuli*. Green is also derived in several ways: high up in the Oaxaca mountains greenish-blue, herb-dyed clothing is still worn by a few Mixe women in the villages of Yacochi and Mixistlán; while in Chihuahua the Tarahumara occasionally make use of a local plant which they call *siyóname*. *Manzanilla* (camomile) leaves are a source in Chiapas for greenish-gold.

This list could be continued to include green walnuts, *pitahaya* juice and a number of other colourants – some as yet unidentified by botanists – which meet local needs. Combinations are varied and may even entail over-dyeing, as in Zinacantán where woollen sashes incorporate green threads which have been stained yellow and then re-immersed in an indigo bath. Several minerals and earth colourants have already been mentioned, for their role is vital in many dyeing processes, and to this category should also be added iron oxide, gypsum, ochres and similar substances which are found in natural deposits and mixed with other elements to furnish stable pigments. In *Las técnicas textiles en el México indígena* Ruth D. Lechuga describes an interesting procedure used by *rebozo* producers in Santa María del Río and Tejupilco in the states of San Luis Potosí and Mexico. There old iron, left to rot and to decompose in water, provides the basis for a black and strong-smelling dye. The resulting *rebozos*, with their permanent odour, are termed *de olor*.

Mexico's two animal dyes, greatly valued before and after the Conquest, have both persisted to the present time, despite growing rarity and high prices. *Purpura patula pansa* is exploited today only along isolated coastal stretches of southern Oaxaca, but the yarn which it dyes is prized in several communities for its 'beautiful and intense violet'. This colour definition by Zelia Nuttall, the American scholar, accompanied an important investigation into shellfish dyeing in 1909, published after a visit to Tehuantepec. Her findings document not only the procedures but also the decline of an industry which she saw as 'invested with all the romance and charm of historical and classical associations'. During this period *purpura*-dyed skirts were still worn by Zapotec women, 'who appeared to be in better circumstances than the rest', and women in 'primitive weaving establishments'. When interviewed, the owner of one such establishment described how she sent fine cotton thread to Huamelula on the coast. This was dyed by the local fishermen, then returned to her on mule-back. The scarcity of shellfish was forcing up prices, however, and the market value of finished skirts was fixed at 'not less than ten dollars gold'.

In 1946, when Miguel Covarrubias published his book *Mexico South*, *caracol*-dyed wrap-around skirts were worn in Tehuantepec only on ceremonial occasions by old women. Thread was still dyed by the Chontal of Huamelula and Astata, then later reinforced in Tehuantepec by being boiled with alum and cochineal. A skirt cost the equivalent of a husband or son's monthly wage, and women 'would not sell it for its value in gold. They become so attached to these skirts that they often include among their last wishes one to be buried in a purple skirt, because, they claim, snail-dyed thread never rots away'.

Today the Chontal of Huamelula and Astata rarely dye yarn with shellfish, while the neighbouring Huave dye only on a small scale. Indeed, disturbing reports from this stretch of coast suggest that increasing oil pollution is threatening the future of shellfish in the vicinity. The tradition has been upheld further along the coast, however, by Mixtec dyers from the inland village of Pinotepa de Don Luis. Each winter a band of men make their way to the Pacific shore, carrying a quantity of spun cotton thread. When the tide is low, colonies of molluscs are exposed to the searching gaze of the dyers, who pick them off the wet rocks in order to squeeze and blow on them. Distress causes *Purpura patula* to give off a foamy secretion from the mouth, and this is rubbed directly on to the yarn. Although it is colourless at first, the liquid soon turns when exposed to the air to a dirty yellow, then to a brilliant green, and finally to a strong and irregular purple. This sequence occurs in less than three minutes in bright sunlight but takes longer in the shade. Once each mollusc has yielded up its dye, it is returned unharmed to the rock and left for a month while dyers work their way along the coast. After this period it is 'milked' again to procure a second, though diminished, supply of dye. With repeated washings shellfish-dyed yarn, or *caracolillo*, may soften to a delicate lavender, but it will never lose its characteristic aroma, described by some as 'strongly fishy' or more flatteringly by others as 'imbued with the tang of the sea'. In Pinotepa de Don Luis this valuable thread provides weavers with the lilac stripes which decorate not only their own skirts but also those which they sell to surrounding Mixtec villages (see p. 137). A few male costumes in the region incorporate brocaded shellfish designs, but as with female clothing there is a growing tendency to rely on other, less expensive, sources to recreate this traditionally important colour.

Cochineal has suffered a similar decline since Colonial times, when shipments to Europe ranked second only to precious metals and accumulated vast fortunes for Spanish landlords. During this time native cultivation continued unabated in many regions including Chiapas where, according to Gage, there were 'few Indians who have not their orchards planted with the trees whereon breed the worms which yield unto us that rich commodity'. Tylor's nineteenth-century writings confirm the continued appeal of cochineal in Oaxaca where 'Indians cultivate great plantations of *Nopals*, and spread the insects over them with immense care, even removing them, and carrying them up into the mountains in baskets when the rainy season begins in the plains, and bringing them back when it is over'. With the subsequent rise of synthetic dyes the cochineal industry was abandoned by landholders and neglected by many Indians. In a few remote communities, however, cultivation and dyeing methods have continued unchanged, while in recent years government-backed schemes have been introduced in Oaxaca to revive production.

Domesticated cochineal is a delicate insect, and host cacti, which belong to the *Opuntia* or *Nopalea* genus, are planted in rows and carefully tended. 'Seeding', as the process is termed, occurs when nests of pregnant females are attached to the joints of the plant. As the new parasites hatch, they spread across the *nopal* and settle, embedding their proboscises in the tissue. After approximately 100 days they are harvested with a pointed stick, and enough females retained to initiate a new cycle. Tylor reported the custom of transferring parasites from one habitat to another, but it is more usual to store them under the roofs of houses during the rainy season. Although the best yield of dye is thought to come from this domesticated variety, known to botanists as *Dactylopius coccus* and popularly referred to as *grana fina*, Indians also collect wild cochineal, or *grana silvestre*, throughout the year from untended *nopales*. The eventual colour of the dyestuff is partly determined by the methods used to treat the insects. When sun-dried for up to two weeks they give carmine red, but if toasted on griddles or boiled they become black and brownish-red respectively.

Alum, lime juice and salt are popular fixatives, contributing greatly to the colour achieved. According to Amber Spark, weavers in Chiapas begin their dyeing operations by mordanting their wool with alum. It is then added to a mixture of ground cochineal, water and lime juice, and boiled. Dyed in this way, yarns do not fade but turn darker with age. In Oaxaca various communities have also retained the use of cochineal, especially in the Mixteca where dyed silk called *hiladillo* is still included, together with indigo- and *purpura*-coloured cotton, in many of the striped skirts intended for gala wear. Pinotepa de Don Luis, where skirt production is centred, hosts three important yearly markets. Here *hiladillo* is sold by Mixtec dyers from the distant highland region of San Mateo Peñasco and bought by local women, as well as by weavers from other villages such as Ixtayutla, which lies two days away on foot. There this much valued thread is used, albeit more rarely than formerly, to brocade designs and to decorate men's ceremonial belts.

In the valley of Oaxaca, however, heavy cochineal-dyed skirts are little more than a memory shared by old women. Abandoned around the 1940s, they are remembered with nostalgia by Doña Sabina Sánchez de Mateos of San Antonino Ocotlán. Now in her seventies, this famous Zapotec embroideress recalls as a girl taking spun wool to be dyed; later it was loomed with lozenge patterning by a skilled male weaver. According to Doña Sabina, skirts in the region ranged from coral-red, deep pink and even purple to near-black. Dyers were very secretive about their methods for obtaining this last colour, which was much admired. On the coast of Oaxaca the custom of reinforcing shellfish-dyed yarn by boiling it with cochineal and alum has virtually disappeared, while the Otomí of Santiago Temoaya in the state of Mexico now rarely combine cochineal with fruit from the red *capulín* tree to create dark reds and browns. Cochineal continues, however, to serve in many areas as a colourant for traditional foods such as *tortillas* and *tamales*, or even post-Conquest ones such as rice.

Until recently many of these natural dyes were used in conjunction with *ikat*. This method of resist-dyeing requires the future warp yarns to be stretched between two sticks and tightly bound with *ixtle* fibre at predetermined intervals. When the skein is immersed in the dye bath, the covered portions are reserved. If further dyeing is

Ikat-patterned Otomí *quechquémitl*, photographed in the 1930s by Elsie McDougall. This style, according to her, was traditional among the Otomí of Querétaro, Hidalgo and the Toluca Valley.

Indian woman with an *ikat*-patterned *rebozo* photographed in the market of Acaxochitlán, Hidalgo. She wears a wrap-around skirt and sash, a man's hat, a *quechquémitl*, and a blouse of cotton cloth embroidered in green and red with hand and machine stitching.

desired, the weaver allows the yarns to dry out thoroughly and binds new sections, allowing the skeins to absorb the colours in successive stages.

This technique, which demands great skill and accuracy, was formerly the speciality of Otomí weavers from Tolimán in Querétaro, and from Ixmiquilpan and Zimapán in Hidalgo. In this last state dark blue, *ikat*-dyed *quechquémitl* of cotton were worn until comparatively recently, while *ikat*-patterned sashes and *gabanes* (locally termed *jergas*) were also popular. A fine woollen example of this last garment is included in the collection donated by Elsie McDougall to the Pitt Rivers Museum, Oxford. Dating from the 1930s, it features trees, crosses and lozenges which have been reserved in white against a twice dyed background. In Tolimán *ikat* was performed with silk and later *artisela* (artificial silk) or cotton to make multi-coloured *quechquémitl* and sashes (see p. 172).

Sadly, *ikat* has now all but died out among the Otomí, but nationally it remains the most admired form of decoration for *rebozos*. Bought by Indian women and *mestizas* alike, *ikat*-patterned shawls are widely sold throughout Mexico. At the cheaper end of the scale are the treadle- or power-loomed variety, commercially produced from *artisela* and offered for sale in most markets, but in Santa María del Río delicately dappled *rebozos* are woven from Chinese silk on the backstrap loom and sold for high prices. Many may even end up in the smart shops of Mexico City, together with others from Tenancingo in the Toluca Valley. Here *ikat*-dyed *rebozos* of fine cotton are also created on the backstrap and treadle loom, and elegantly patterned in a style which closely recalls the markings of snakes.

In Western culture, where most yarns are machine-spun or chemically prepared, synthetically dyed and patterned by printing, it is easy to take textiles for granted and to consider their manufacture as removed from daily life. In many parts of Mexico, however, the textures afforded by hand-spun yarns, the varying shades produced by home-dyeing, and even the inbuilt patterns of *ikat* are still an integral part of life, making the resulting garments a matter for pride among creators and purchasers alike.

6 Weaving, embroidery and other decorative techniques

Tzotzil weaver in San Juan Chamula, Chiapas, reeling warp yarn off a winding frame on to a warping frame in a figure of eight. The length and width of future garments are established at the warping stage.

Mixtec weaver in Pinotepa de Don Luis, Oaxaca, winding warp yarn on to stakes set in the ground and organising the stripes of a future *posahuanco* (see p. 137). Until recently women in the area went bare-breasted, but bibbed aprons are now widely worn.

Paramount in the preparation of Indian costume is weaving. Assembled without tailoring as in pre-Conquest times, traditional garments depend for their beauty on their surface decoration rather than on their simple though graceful lines. In conservative villages where inhabitants share a common form of dress weavers compete not by originality of design but by expertness of execution, and the work of each is readily recognised as hers by other weavers. Photographs or descriptions of costumes from different regions generally elicit small response, but if a textile is shown weavers are invariably roused by curiosity to determine the techniques involved.

Setting up a backstrap loom is a lengthy process, and spun thread is ordinarily rolled into balls for ease of handling. A few peoples such as the Zoque or the Tzotzil of San Juan Chamula use a winding frame, but in most communities the yarns are wound directly on to a warping frame. This device may take the form of a wooden I or consist more commonly of stakes. The number used varies from village to village, in accordance with the length of textile desired. Some communities employ only two stakes which stand in the earth, but others require as many as fifteen, slotting them into holes in a movable wooden frame. The warp yarns are wound in a figure of eight to create the cross, or lease, which will ultimately form the shed. Before they are attached to the loom, however, these yarns are often dipped in maize water to stiffen them. As for the weft threads, these are wound on to long and slender cane bobbins, or shuttle sticks (see p. 208).

The parts that go to make up the loom demand very little elaboration (see Appendix 1). The strap, or *mecapal*, consists of woven *ixtle*, plaited palm or leather, while the wooden end bars, heddles and shed sticks are cut to the right length and polished. Particular care is taken when smoothing the battens, for it is their even pressure that produces even cloth. In the Mixtec village of San Sebastián Peñoles loom sticks are occasionally carved at one end to suggest deer heads. If a tenter is required it is generally a hollow reed held in place with thorns or, less traditionally, with small nails. Combs, which are frequently used like battens to tighten weft threads, are still carved from wood in many communities.

During plain weaving the loom requires a minimum of parts, but specialist weavers often rely on additional tools. Among the Otomí, for example, open-meshed *ayates* of *ixtle* are woven with the aid of a uniquely fashioned bar featuring teeth several centimetres long. The rigid heddle is another interesting device. Probably inspired by European treadle looms, it is used instead of a stick heddle by many sash-weavers including the Nahua of Altepexi in Puebla and the Zapotec of Santo Tomás Jalieza in Oaxaca. Many patterning techniques require weavers to subdivide their warps and create further sheds. This may be achieved with additional heddles and shed sticks. Pattern sticks or brocading sticks also serve to separate selected warps. Picks have several functions: narrow and pointed, these may be used to lift warps and to pull up or push down wefts. Most picks are carved from wood or deerbone; few are decorated, but in the Cuicatec village of San Andrés Teotilalpan in Oaxaca bone picks are embellished with bird-shaped handles. Bird motifs are equally favoured by the Mixtec of Pinotepa de Don Luis, where local blacksmith forge elegantly handled picks from iron. Long and tough thorns, afforded by *maguey* plants or lime-trees, are also used in some regions, but darning needles and strips of pointed plastic provide more modern alternatives.

When setting up the loom, weavers ensure the number of selvages they require by the use or non-use of heading cords. Procedures, together with those relating to the double start, have been described in Chapter 1 (see also Appendix 1). In addition, the various rods have to be positioned and the heddle tied. While manipulating the wefts, the weaver controls the tension of the warps with her body, and this often demands considerable strength. During the production of lighter fabrics women generally prefer to sit on a mat or low chair, but heavy cloths may demand a kneeling or even standing position. Dark interiors and lack of space lead most weavers to work out of doors, and the far end of the loom is attached to a tree or post. Because backstrap looms are so easy to roll up and transport, however, some weavers carry them long distances. In the countryside surrounding San Andrés Chicahuaxtla, for example, brightly dressed Trique girls can often be seen herding goats while they weave. Yet the most novel location must surely be that described during the nineteenth century by Bullock. While on a visit to the floating market at Lake Chalco – now dried out to make way for housing developments and the excavation of mineral salts – he watched flat-bottomed boats transporting vegetables, fruit and flowers, and observed entire families, sitting under cover in the centre of each, busily occupied in 'either spinning cotton or weaving it, in their simple portable looms'.

Flexibly constructed, native looms often vary considerably in both length and breadth. In Chiapas, for example, broad red sashes measuring nearly 15 ft (5 m) are worn by the Tzotzil men of Huistán. Most garments require a warp which is very much shorter, however, but in a few villages long looms are a matter of choice and not necessity. Unlike most weavers, who set up their looms separately for each web, Nahua women in Cuetzalán prefer to weave several *quechquémitl* sections using the

Tzotzil backstrap weaver wearing an embroidered everyday *huipil* in San Andrés Larrainzar, Chiapas. The cloth, plain-woven with brocaded geometric motifs, will be part of a three-web gala *huipil*; a woven central section keeps the warp in position.

same long warp, while in Oaxaca it is customary for Amuzgo weavers to produce a single length of cloth which is cut to provide *huipil* strips and hemmed. Different garments determine the width of the loom. Although 20 in (51 cm) constitute a comfortable armspan, broader textiles may stretch to around 30 in (76 cm) with thin sashes demanding no more than 4 – 5 in (10 – 13 cm). This last width allows for great sociability among weavers, who frequently take advantage of the narrowness of their looms to sit side by side round a single post or tree. As for Huichol sash-weavers, they sometimes prefer to dispense altogether with traditional supports and to tie the loom's end bar to the big toe of their outstretched foot.

Sash warps are often wound directly round the end bars of the loom. When weaving is completed the warp ends are cut and twisted or knotted to prevent unravelling. Occasionally, however, as in the Nahua village of Tetelcingo in Morelos, belts are ring-woven to form a continuous web and severed. Tubular weaving is a speciality with Otomí women in Santiago Temoaya in the state of Mexico. Here single skirt webs, approximately 24 in (60 cm) by 140 in (355 cm) are ring-woven and released intact, then bordered at the top with a narrow strip of calico. According to Donald and Dorothy Cordry, the Tzotzil of San Juan Chamula, Chiapas, are also able to produce tubular cloth.

Ring weaving is more generally associated with the rigid loom, however, which is used in northern Mexico by the Mayo of Sonora, as well as by the Tarahumara and Northern Tepehuan of Chihuahua. Among these last two groups the horizontal frame is built close to the ground from four crudely finished logs, two of which are notched

Tarahumara women positioning the wool warp of a future blanket on a rigid loom of logs in Norogachic, Chihuahua.

to support the other two which serve as raised end bars. Square or rectangular in shape, this frame lends itself to the weaving of blankets and sashes, but a triangular version just for sashes was observed by Lumholtz at the turn of this century. While working, women sit with their legs stretched out in front beneath the loom. When the tubular web is nearly completed, the warp is severed leaving a fringe at each end. This principle is the same for Mayo looms, although they are constructed rather differently with the end bars supported by four posts set in the ground. Mayo weaving is done from a kneeling or squatting position.

As in pre-Conquest and Colonial times, a wide range of patterning is achieved on ring looms and backstrap looms alike. Simple in their parts and primitive in their appearance, both are capable of producing textiles which it would be hard to imitate on commercial looms (see Appendix 2). Plain weaving allows the construction of warp and weft stripes, which remain popular with skirt and *rebozo* weavers. The texture of cloth is open to variation. Crêpé weft stripes frequently decorate *quechquémitl* in villages such as Atla and Huilacapixtla, Puebla, where Nahua weavers compress thick and unnecessarily long rows of weft into puckered bands. In many regions horizontal patterning is also created by introducing thick or additional weft threads to make raised lines in the cloth. The corded weft stripes which adorn the yokes of Zapotec *huipiles* in Yalalag, Oaxaca, demand the manipulation of both warp and weft threads, however.

Twill techniques offer further scope, enabling many skirt and blanket weavers of wool to pattern cloth diagonally with lozenges and zig-zag lines. According to Irmgard W. Johnson, Chocho women in Teotongo, Oaxaca, produce their two-and-two twilled blankets using three heddles, a single shed stick, and two complementary pattern sticks. Mayo and Tarahumara ring weavers also make use of twill techniques, but their speciality is tapestry which allows them to pattern blankets with elaborate geometric motifs.

Double weaving requires great skill and is found today only among the Otomí of Hidalgo, the Cora of Nayarit and their closely related neighbours, the Huichol. The complexity of the technique requires additional heddles, and all three groups succeed in adorning their cotton or wool shoulder-bags with wonderfully varied geometric and figurative designs (see p. 57). Huichol weavers also produce uniquely patterned double-cloth sashes for men. Another highly advanced loom construction practised by the Otomí is that of curved weaving: in several communities including Santa Ana Hueytlalpan and Tenango de Doria in Hidalgo and San Pablito in Puebla *quechquémitl* incorporate two webs shaped at one corner of one end (see p. 165). This effect is created on the loom by using part of the warp as weft, and when the two webs are joined they give the effect of a gently rounded shoulder-cape. This technique, which is apparently unknown outside the Americas, is shared in Puebla by the Nahua of the Cuetzalán region and the Totonac of Pantepec and Mecapalapa. Although confined today to one small area, curved weaving may once have been employed by the Maya and the Zapotec to create their curved garments. In *El traje indígena de México* Ruth D. Lechuga offers an alternative explanation, however, based on a quite different method of shaping cloth on the loom which she observed recently in the Huave village of San Mateo del Mar, Oaxaca.

Gauze weaving has a wide distribution in modern Mexico. Fine *huipiles* which combine gauze with other techniques are worn in Oaxaca by the Mixe of San Juan Cotzocón, the Trique of San Andrés Chicahuaxtla, the Cuicatec of San Andrés

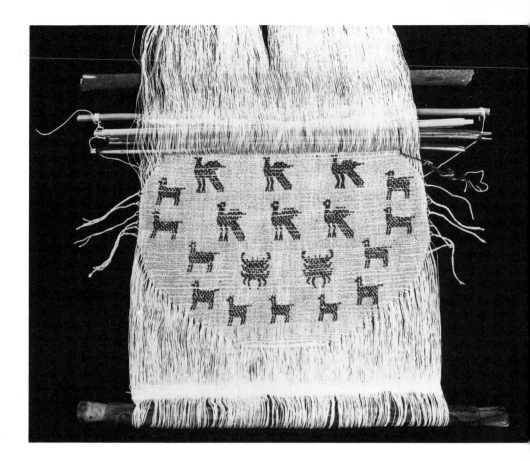

Huave backstrap loom from San Mateo del Mar, Oaxaca. Weaver Justina Oviedo has evolved a way of making circular cloth: weft yarns are inserted to form a curve; warps will be severed and knotted. Each side of the cloth features different motifs brocaded in red and lilac respectively.

Close-up of a white gauze-woven Tarascan *servilleta* from Aranza, Michoacán, seen against a black background.

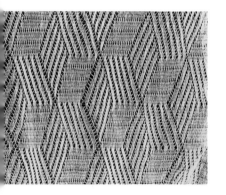

Teotilalpan, the Chinantec of the western Chinantla, and the Amuzgo who also inhabit a stretch of Guerrero. It is interesting to note that the weaving sequences used for many of these garments recall those of the Chilapa *huipil*, described in Chapter 2. Puebla is another important centre for gauze weaving. Here the skill is largely practised by Nahua women to create *quechquémitl*. Cuetzalán is famed for its all-white geometric patterning, worked in cotton thread and, more recently, strands of gleaming *artisela*. Weavers need to memorise complex manipulations in correct sequence, and may use up to twenty heddles to separate and lift the warps. In Atla and near Huauchinango elaborately figured gauze is produced with a range of motifs that includes double-headed birds, people on horseback, animals and flowers. The *quechquémitl* of the Totonac are, by contrast, often made today from machine-embroidered shop-bought organdy, although we know from Sahagún that at the time of the Conquest 'their shoulder shawls were of netting', which was in all likelihood a reference to gauze. The Tepehua of Huehuetla, in the neighbouring state of Hidalgo, continue to weave their *quechquémitl*, however, and to incorporate gauze sections. In Chiapas the skills of the Zoque have suffered a decline, but in Michoacán the gauze-weavers of Aranza continue to create white *servilletas* with geometric patterning suggesting the delicacy of fine lace.

Weft-wrap openwork is another technique demanding great skill and laborious finger manipulations. It seems likely that the art reached its peak with the exquisite gala *huipiles* of Santiago Choapan. Now sadly extinct, these unique Zapotec garments combined weft-wrap and plain weaving to feature birds, animals, flowers and human motifs intricately worked in white on a white ground.

The versatility of native looms is further demonstrated by warp-patterned textiles, which require weavers to position floating warps by hand. The technique was formerly used in Oaxaca by skirt-weavers in the Zapotec village of Mitla to create elegantly patterned, cochineal-coloured cloth, and in the Mixtec village of San Pedro Tututepec to pattern selected warp stripes with a range of animal and plant motifs. Warp-patterning persists today, however, in many sash-weaving centres. In Santo

Thomás Jalieza, for example, Zapotec sashes display plant, animal and human motifs, while those of the Tarahumara feature geometric designs (see p. 172). The technique is also used by the Huichol and several other groups for the straps of shoulder-bags. As for the Otomí of San Juan Tuxtepec in the state of Mexico, they warp-pattern bands for the hair. A rare and interesting custom has been noted by Ruth D. Lechuga for the Huastec of Tancanhuitz, San Luis Potosí. There *zapupe*-weavers pattern shoulder-bags with colourful motifs created with floating warps which are dyed as they are woven.

Perhaps the most widespread style of decoration employed among backstrap weavers today is brocading. It is commonly used in conjunction with plain or gauze weaves for almost all categories of Indian clothing. These include Tepehua *quechquémitl* from Huehuetla, with bands of geometric patterning, Mixtec wrap-around skirts from Jamiltepec in Oaxaca, with stripes featuring zig-zags and chevrons, and Chinantec head-cloths from San Felipe Usila, distinguished by their bird and animal designs. Often brocading is done in a different fibre from the background, as in the Otomí village of Zacamulpa in the state of Mexico, where *ayates*, or carrying-cloths, of *ixtle* are adorned with wool motifs.

Huipiles, bags and *servilletas* offer the broadest spectrum of brocade-woven designs. In the highlands of Guerrero richly patterned *huipiles* from San Miguel Metlatonoc and neighbouring Mixtec villages display colourful geometric motifs, together with a host of squirrels, rearing horses, flowers and birds with outstretched wings. Stylised plant designs are the speciality of Amuzgo weavers, whose *huipiles* feature eight-petalled flowers, vines and ferns, while the Mixe of San Juan Cotzocón often favour red birds, dogs and geometric forms on a white ground. The Huave excel at brocading *servilletas* with a range of creatures that includes seagulls, crabs, deer and scorpions. Skilled Huave are even able to produce different designs in different colours on either side of the cloth. In Trique villages brilliant bands of geometric patterning decorate increasingly large areas of both *huipiles* and *servilletas* (see pp. 164, 176). According to Irmgard W. Johnson, this is achieved in San Martín Itunyoso through wrapped brocading.

In Chiapas, where men have retained their indigenous clothing to a greater extent than is usual elsewhere, male as well as female garments are often distinguished by magnificent brocading. Tzeltal and Tzotzil weavers from a number of highland villages, such as Tenejapa, Magdalenas and San Andrés Larrainzar, demonstrate extraordinary mathematical powers by building up large areas of patterning which incorporate perfectly interlocking geometric and stylised plant and animal motifs (see pp. 161, 229). No less gifted are the Tzotzil weavers of Venustiano Carranza. Formerly known as San Bartolomé de los Llanos, this low-lying town was visited at the turn of this century by Starr. He described the cloth, replete with 'rosettes, flowers, geometrical figures, birds, animals or men . . . wrought with red, green or yellow wools', and noted his surprise 'to find that the designs . . . are not embroidered upon the finished fabric, but are worked in . . . during weaving'. Today these basic motifs remain the same, and so do the reactions of most uninitiated observers, who invariably mistake brocading for embroidery (see p. 61).

Weavers in hot regions frequently specialise in brocading in white on a white ground, and many women in Venustiano Carranza carry on this tradition. Fine white *huipiles* are also woven in several Amuzgo communities, but exquisitely patterned examples from the Mixteca area of Oaxaca have become increasingly rare. With their

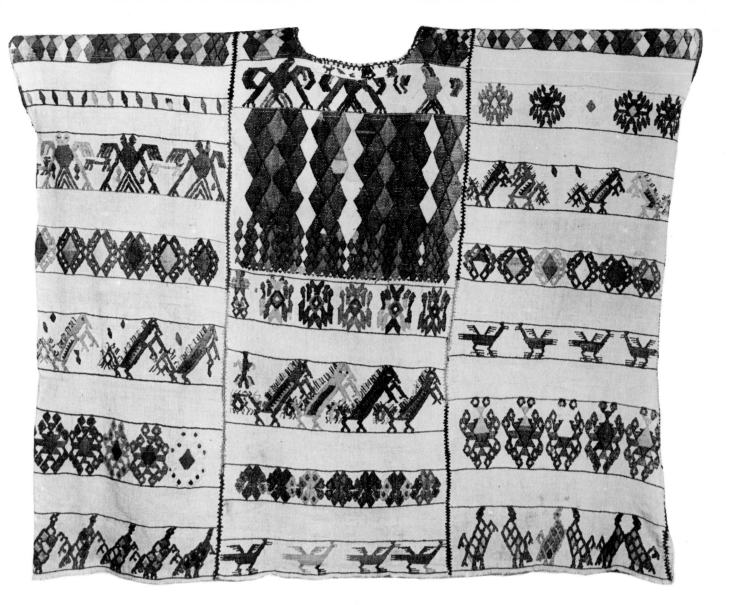

Mixtec gala *huipil* of cotton from San Miguel Metlatonoc, Guerrero. Brightly coloured brocaded motifs include plume-tailed horses and double-headed birds; webs are joined with decorative insertion stitching. W. $37\frac{1}{2}$ in (95.3 cm); L. 30 in (76.2 cm). Museum of Mankind, London.

Close-up of the Tzotzil weaver shown on p. 144. When brocading she subdivides the warp with a pointed stick; completed cloth is wound on to a rolling stick.

Tarascan woman's warp-patterned waist-sash from Cuanajo, Michoacán. The pattern board of twigs and wool shows the complex warp manipulations weavers must achieve (see also p. 172). Museum of Mankind, London.

wealth of anthropomorphic, zoomorphic and geometric designs *huipiles* from this region survive in a few private collections where they testify to the truly remarkable skills of their creators. Like figured gauze, cloth of this type is best examined against the light, and it is a sad fact that women who devote themselves to weaving such complicated white-on-white motifs often go blind in middle age.

Although the examples mentioned so far feature weft brocading, warp brocading also occurs in several sash-weaving communities. Geometrical vine motifs are worked by this method in the Nahua village of San Francisco Atotonilco, Hidalgo, while Otomí weavers in San Juan Tuxtepec, in the state of Mexico, specialise in birds, plants and stylised doll motifs. Sashes from the rigid looms of the Tarahumara may also feature warp-brocaded patterning.

Closely related to brocading is the looped weft technique of pile weaving, or *confite*, which is chiefly used today for *servilletas*. Among the lowland Totonac of Veracruz, and the highland Otomí of San Pablito, Puebla, this style of cloth is traditionally worked in white on white. It seems possible that this native technique may have been reinforced after the Conquest by examples of Spanish *confite*, also worked entirely in white.

Twining, which pre-dated weaving in Mexico, is still used in a few communities to reinforce webs while they are on the loom. The technique has been observed by Irmgard W. Johnson in the Tarahumara region, where woollen blankets sometimes display twined edges along all four sides, and by Donald and Dorothy Cordry in the village of San Sebastián Peñoles in Oaxaca's Mixteca Alta. Here two-web woollen blankets are twill-woven, and reinforced at both ends with a narrow twined weft stripe. Worked by hand, these modern-day examples of twining recall archaeological specimens from the Tehuacán Valley, Chihuahua and the Mixteca Alta.

The time taken by different weavers to complete their weavings varies enormously: in the rainy season many do not weave at all, and during the rest of the year household tasks leave most women with only a few hours each day to give to their looms. An average *huipil* advances only a few inches daily and could take between two and three months to complete depending on the type of weave used. There is considerable diversity even with plain or tabby techniques. These produce thick and coarsely woven woollen cloth as well as fine cotton fabrics like those of the Zoque that can incorporate as many as seventy-five warp and sixty-four weft threads to one square inch. Patterned weaves are extremely time- and energy-consuming. The intricate weft-wrapped *huipil* from Santiago Choapan, for example, comprised two webs, each of which demanded an estimated four months. It is also recorded by Donald and Dorothy Cordry that in the past, when Zoque weavers were working on figured gauze, they would remain at the loom from dawn to dusk, receiving their food from relatives. 'These designs are so complicated and difficult', they write, 'that one can think of nothing else while weaving, and for this reason most women do not make them after they are married.'

Most weavers carry their designs in their head, although a small bag or a fragment from an old garment may serve as a *muestra*, or sampler, for occasional consultation. In Michoacán, however, Tarascan sash-weavers from Cuanajo refer while they work to 'pattern cards', fashioned from twigs and reeds. Interwoven with wool, these display design motifs on both sides. In communities which specialise in patterned weaving the prestige value of garments is determined by their ornateness, and many weavers astound the outsider by the precision of their work. Often illiterate and without formal education, they reveal an intuitive grasp of mathematics as they divide and subdivide their warps to form different groups of motifs. Ana Cecilia Cruz Alberto, an Otomí weaver from San Miguel Ameyalco in the state of Mexico, carries on the weaving traditions of her village by brocading cloth with a multitude of animals, people, houses and flowers. When asked to explain her rapid calculations, she replied simply, 'But it is my fingers – not my head – that do the counting. They think for me.' (See p. 224.)

As in pre-Conquest times, native weaving methods remain an almost exclusively female pursuit. According to Lumholtz, when Tarahumara mothers taught their daughters to spin and weave, they assured them that if they did not learn they would 'become men', while in the highlands of Chiapas many ceremonies persist to link girl children with their future duties. Among the Tzotzil of Zinacantán, for example, newly-born infants are given the tools of adult life to hold. A digging-stick and a hoe are among the implements presented to a male baby, but a girl receives a *mano*, or pestle, for grinding and parts from a backstrap loom. A similar dedication is also performed by the Lacandón of Najá, where small children are taken to the god-house and held astride the mother's hip. Girls are shown a spindle and formally counselled not to spin coarse thread.

In Chiapas, as elsewhere, Indian children learn adult skills by imitation, and Nancy Modiano has described the games played by highland girls, who commonly make *tortillas* of mud and construct toy looms with sticks, beginning their first weavings with wisps of yarn left over from their mothers' work. By the age of twelve they are expected to adopt a serious attitude to the skill, however, and to master it fully by sixteen – often after marriage. A young woman from San Juan Chamula, when interviewed by Nancy Modiano, had the following recollections of her training:

My mother had told me that it was time for me to begin to learn my work. . . . She prepared the loom. . . . I wove with a lot of fear. . . . My shawl ended up with lots of threads and almost without any form. It was hard for me to learn. . . . Sometimes I would get so angry I wanted to rip my weaving apart with a knife or something sharp. . . . I suffered a great deal. . . . I felt that I wasn't capable of learning. . . . My mother told me not to lose patience, that I would learn little by little. . . . When she began to show me how to prepare the looms a new era of suffering began. . . . it seemed impossible to do. . . . After all of this my mother said that the least I could do was make a blouse [*huipil*] for myself. I don't know how old I was, but I do know that I trembled with fear because my mother scolded me; she said she wasn't going to be around to make my clothing for me for the rest of my life. She told me . . . that this was woman's work. . . . When I first began to weave, my mother and I went to the Virgin who lives in our town. . . . We offered some little candles and asked the Virgin to put the art of weaving into my heart. . . .'

Throughout the Chiapas region the Virgin and the female saints are often appealed to in this way, and in communities where their images are dressed in Indian-style garments mothers may pass a daughter's hands along the saints' brocaded clothing and across her eyes. Even in later life accomplished weavers may continue to rely on divine assistance. When beginning a complicated weaving, Huichol women in the western Sierra Madre frequently enlist the help and goodwill of the gods, while in Atla, Puebla, Nahua women are still in the habit of creating diminutive garments which they leave on the hillside as offerings. In highly traditional societies Indians do not confine themselves to the laws of cause and effect; they believe instead that magic forces accompany man from birth to death and that the supernatural permeates every aspect of life. As a result, numerous ancient weaving beliefs and practices have persisted. It has been reported by Calixta Guiteras-Holmes, for example, that Tzotzil

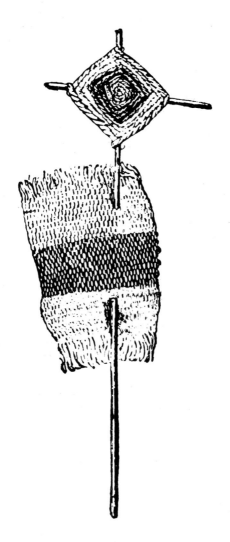

Huichol votive offering, drawn by Carl Lumholtz, termed a *tsikuri*, or gods' eye. The lozenge of coloured wool allows gods to view their followers; the weaving is a woman's prayer for luck in textile work. H. 6¼ in (16 cm).

women in San Pedro Chenalhó, Chiapas, measure the warp yarns for the loom, then symbolically 'feed' them with beans or maize to ensure that they will not run out. Another interesting Huichol custom was recorded by Lumholtz, who noted that when a woman was weaving a sash her husband would catch a live serpent and bring it to her. While he held it on the ground beside her, she would pass her hand over its back, then over her eyes, thereby transferring the design to the sash.

Given the close links which have always existed between women and weaving, it is hardly surprising, as Donald and Dorothy Cordry have pointed out, that the loom and its attributes should frequently serve as symbols of fertility. Weaving implements, spindles, combs and thread are connected with hair, which in turn is connected with rain, agriculture and life force. It is only fitting, therefore, that the tools which have accompanied weavers throughout their lives should accompany them to the grave. In many Indian societies death is still visualised as a long journey, for which the traveller must be prepared. The Tarahumara accordingly bury women with their spindles, while in San Pedro Chenalhó each woman is given a bag with her textile accessories including spindle, needle and thread so that she can mend her clothes on the voyage to the next world.

Men's tasks, like those of women, are prescribed at birth and include agriculture and hunting, yet in a few communities they too may learn to weave on a backstrap loom. A late nineteenth-century illustration by Thomas Unett Brocklehurst showed prisoners in Cholula gaol engaged in weaving 'bright scarlet-coloured cotton sashes', and today in the Nahua village of Altepexi, Puebla, men commonly weave women's belts as well as their own. There are also male weavers of *rebozos* in Tenancingo in the Valley of Toluca, and in Mitla in Oaxaca. As for the tough *ayates* of *ixtle* which are current in Hidalgo, these are occasionally woven by Otomí men.

With only a few such exceptions, however, male weavers confine themselves to the treadle loom, described by many even today as the 'Spanish' loom. Weaving is usually carried out in small family-run workshops which are very often *mestizo*. Located in countless towns throughout Mexico, these small businesses provide the local Indian population with cloth, which has the advantage of being wider than any single web from a backstrap loom. Production includes not only *manta*, or calico, but also skirt-lengths, *rebozos* and *sarapes*, patterned to meet local demand. Twill is a speciality with many weavers and so is tapestry. Many of these centres have also found favour with tourists and export companies by producing attractive cloths of rustic appearance such as *cambaya*, which serves to make tablecloths and other items for home furnishing.

Competition from power looms is strong, however, and an ever-growing number of Indian women now rely on commercial factory-made cloth and on finished articles of dress. Sold in most market-places and carried into remote regions by travelling vans, cheap acrylic *sarapes*, rayon *rebozos*, aprons and inexpensive lengths of material are gaining increasing acceptance. Even in relatively conservative communities these garments may be teamed with traditional costumes, or the cloth tailored to suit Indian requirements. In the Tancanhuitz region of San Luis Potosí, for example, Huastec women who formerly wove their wrap-around skirts from black wool now buy black poplin, while the Zapotec of Tehuantepec and Juchitán in Oaxaca have come to depend almost entirely on commercially produced cloth. This last trend was apparent as early as 1909, when Zelia Nuttall noted the decline of shellfish-dyed clothing in favour of 'imported and cheaper European stuffs'. Manchester in England

Male weaver and home-made treadle loom from Santa Ana del Valle, Oaxaca, where wool *sarapes* feature tapestry-woven geometric motifs. Pattern wefts are wound on to small cane bobbins.

was a source for dark purple or red cotton cloth, with a white polka dot or repeat motif, but today, when all materials are of Mexican manufacture, Zapotec taste has broadened to encompass vivid flower-patterned prints and a range of dark velvets and sateens. Here, as in many other places, factory cloths are welcomed for their modernity, as well as for the saving which they offer in time and effort.

A fondness for brilliantly coloured rayons and synthetic silks is shared by several groups, including the Mazatec of Oaxaca. In Jalapa de Díaz women have retained the form of the *huipil*, yet have largely abandoned weaving, preferring instead to seam together sections of cheap satin and artificial lace. Among the Mazahua who inhabit the state of Mexico European-style blouses, skirts and aprons are worn by a number of women, and the same is true of Tarascan women from villages such as Ocumicho, where their rainbow appearance is rendered still more colourful by the use of bright acrylic shawls. Trique men from San Juan Copala have also acquired a taste for

colourful and shiny sateens, and many now display flamboyant shirts on festive occasions.

Patterned cottons have found even wider popularity. Zapotec women from Mitla, Tlacolula and Teotitlán del Valle habitually wear wrap-around skirts featuring blue and white, or green and white checks, while young women from a number of Chinantec communities are abandoning their woven skirt lengths in favour of garish commercial prints, which detract from the detail of their richly patterned *huipiles*. In the north the Seri and the Tarahumara also enjoy dressing in brightly coloured factory cloth, which they tailor in semi-Victorian fashion (see p. 168), while at Najá the gathered skirts of the Lacandón exhibit floral patterns in which blue and red predominate (see p. 163).

The Huichol too have acquired a taste for printed materials and for *paliacates*, or bandanna handkerchiefs, which they seam together, but commercially woven *manta* was for many decades their chief source for clothing. Red flannel played a similarly important role, and when Robert M. Zingg visited the Huichol during the 1930s he found that they had developed a legend to explain the existence of these by now necessary fabrics. According to this legend, which he cited as proof of Huichol ability to incorporate alien features into their own culture, it was on the orders of their god, the Sun Father, that the Mexicans had begun to cultivate cotton and the North Americans to found factories for making cloth! Today there is a scarcity of *manta* in the region, which explains in part the shift to printed cottons, and much of the *manta* which the Huichol adorn with embroidered motifs is distractingly stamped with blue brand markings, betraying its previous industrial life as a *costal*, or sack (see pp. 58–9).

Having captured a large share of the Indian market during the nineteenth century, *manta* has retained its prominent position in the field of Indian costume, and the Huichol are far from being the only group to use it regularly. In some regions male clothing consists almost entirely of unbleached calico, while many women employ it to make European-style blouses. This is the case in Hidalgo's semi-desertic Mezquital Valley where, according to Carlota Mapelli Mozzi, *manta* is peddled to remote Otomí communities by travelling salesmen known as *varilleros*, because they still rely on *varas*, or measuring-rods, in the tradition of the Aztec *pochteca*. Wrap-around skirts of *manta* may also be worn in areas where they were formerly hand-woven, and the same is true of *huipiles*. Bleached cotton cloth, which has achieved equal popularity, is put to similar uses in a number of states.

The transition from home-woven to factory cloth was marked, in a few communities, by attempts to recreate visually the traditional appearance of garments. Until the 1960s, for example, Zapotec women from Santo Tomás Mazaltepec in Oaxaca were careful to gather the commercial cloth of their *huipiles* into two wide tucks, one running over each shoulder, to suggest the use of three separate webs. This effect was further heightened by the use of coloured running stitches to secure the pleats. A similar preoccupation also characterised the fine gala *huipiles* of the Nahua of Amatlán de los Reyes in Veracruz. Here imported linen, and later *manta*, was decorated with two fake seams colourfully worked in satin-stitching, A third instance of visual trickery still occurs in Tetelcingo, Morelos, where Nahua women manufacture their clothing from bought woollen cloth. Known as *paño de lana*, this dark blue fabric came initially from England but is produced today in Mexico. Used by villagers to make tubular skirts and *huipiles*, it is given a gratuitous line of dark blue handstitching, implying that two separate webs have been used instead of a single length.

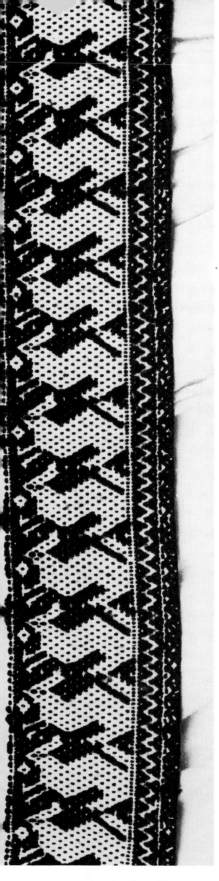

Embroidery is one of the methods most often used to personalise bought cloth. Deprived of the decorative control which weavers exert when manufacturing garments on a loom, consumers often resort to magnificent displays of needlework, and the availability of brightly coloured factory thread acts as a further incentive to creativity. Few women have access to, or can afford, embroidery silks, but shiny substitutes such as *artisela* are popular, together with mercerised cotton and woollen yarns. This last type of thread is much used among the Huichol, who re-spin it before decorating their costumes with a wide range of conventionalised flower, animal, bird and geometric motifs. Worked in cross stitch, long-armed cross stitch, running stitch and very occasionally Holbein stitch, these designs adorn male and female garments alike. Sometimes negative techniques may also be used, whereby the off-white background of the *manta* contributes directly to the patterning. Although black, red and blue were once popular, Huichol embroidery now takes in a wide range of colours, and the areas which are decorated have grown in size. The borders on women's skirts, for example, have become noticeably wider in recent years.

A special talent for embroidery is also displayed by the Huastec of San Luis Potosí. Praised for their weaving skills by Sahagún, women from this group have largely abandoned that art of late, preferring instead to devote their energies to needlework. In Huastec villages the traditional *quechquémitl* is made today from *manta*, and decorated with a profusion of fanciful or locally observed animals, birds and flowers, which are elegantly and colourfully stylised in cross stitch with either cotton or woollen thread. Women very often carry matching shoulder-bags, and *servilletas* or baby's bonnets may be adorned in a similar way.

Although the Huastec rarely decorate their skirts with embroidery today, there are several groups in addition to the Huichol who do. In Hidalgo, for example, gathered *manta* skirts with handsome deep-pile borders are worn in a number of Nahua villages such as Huautla, where embellishments are worked in looped herringbone stitch with re-spun wool, or Atlapexco where looped long-armed cross stitch is used to create arrangements of diamonds, chevrons and s-shaped motifs, with occasional instances of negative patterning. In Guerrero the Cuitlatec of San Miguel Totolapan also embroider their white skirts with borders of stylised flower and vine motifs, worked in cross, long-armed cross and Holbein stitching with commercial cotton. In the neighbouring state of Oaxaca a distinctive style of wrap-around skirt is still worn on gala occasions by the Mazatec of Huautla de Jiménez. Here *manta* or, more rarely, home-woven cloth is bordered along the bottom with a solid band of dark red wool, broken only by black triangles. Cross and long-armed cross stitching are used for this, as well as for scattered motifs, such as conventionalised flowers and human figures which adorn the white ground above the border.

In conservative communities where women continue to fashion *huipiles* from factory cloth a broad spectrum of techniques is also employed. In San José Miahuatlán, Puebla, these garments have not been hand-woven for many years, yet contemporary examples of *manta* are richly embroidered with horizontal bands of dark red wool with accents of black. According to Donald and Dorothy Cordry, Nahua women achieve these effects by using completely reversible satin stitch, cross and a form of deep looped pile stitch akin to hooked rug work, which reveals a running lozenge design on the reverse side. Very different in style and execution are the *huipiles* worn by Nahua women in Acatlán and Zitlala, Guerrero. Made from *manta* for daily wear and from shiny white rayon for festive occasions, garments are adorned with exotic and

Opposite and above Detail of a Mazahua underskirt border from San Francisco de la Loma, Mexico. Hares are embroidered in running stitch on a detachable band of *cuadrillé*; the reverse side is shown above. When worn, only the horizontal border of the underskirt is visible (see p. 169).

brilliantly coloured flowers. Satin-stitched in artificial silk, these designs have a decidedly non-Indian appearance. Satin techniques were also current among the Nahua of Amatlán de los Reyes in Veracruz: worn up until the 1940s on gala occasions, their splendid *huipiles* of imported linen featured not only the fake seams mentioned earlier but also a squared-off area around the neck incorporating brightly coloured zig-zag patterning worked in imported silk thread. Beside it appeared groupings of eight-petalled, star-shaped flowers, and below these came a mass of more realistically portrayed flowers and leaves, suggestive of modern influence from pattern-sheets. Very much in a native tradition, however, are the predominantly red *huipiles* from Bochil, Chiapas. Embroidered on fine *manta*, their geometric markings reveal an attempt to recreate the brocaded motifs which Tzotzil women in other villages still achieve on the loom.

To the north-east of Chiapas lies Yucatán, where Maya women wear a distinctive costume consisting of a long *huipil* and underskirt. No longer hand-woven, these garments are fashioned from fine white cotton or satin. Distinguishing the *terno de lujo*, or gala costume, are wide, hand-stitched bands of decoration, one along the bottom of the skirt, a second along the bottom of the *huipil*, and a third forming a square collar about the neck opening. Today women concentrate on cross-stitch techniques which come under various local names. In remoter areas it is possible to find bird, flower and geometric motifs, but in acculturated centres such variety has declined in favour of conventionalised floral arrangements which imply a strong outside influence. A change has also occurred in the use of colour, for whereas women traditionally chose a single shade – often red – embroidered areas now resemble luxuriant flower gardens.

Although this style of dress is worn throughout the region by Indian women, it is frequently described as *de mestiza* (for *mestizo* women) because it is much used on festive occasions by non-Indians. The same is true of the Tehuana *costume* from the Isthmus of Oaxaca. Since the decline of weaving at the beginning of this century, Zapotec women in the area have acquired a taste for lavish embroidery. This is particularly evident during *fiestas*, when *huipiles* and gathered skirts of dark sateen or velvet are proudly displayed, replete with large satin-stitched flowers. These brilliantly coloured designs, which rely on artificial and sometimes real silks, are thought to derive from the Manila shawls, or *mantones*, which attained such popularity in nineteenth-century Mexico. To achieve their finest work women tie the stretched cloth on to a horizontal wooden frame and occasionally make use of a special hook. Finished costumes, which are passed down from generation to generation, are often valued at many thousands of *pesos* (see p. 171).

In the Mazatec region of Oaxaca, where weaving skills have been similarly forgotten by most women, the need for decoration is also met with embroidery, combined with an exuberant use of brightly coloured ribbons and sateens. *Huipiles* from Jalapa de Díaz and Huautla de Jiménez present an attractive and immensely striking appearance, yet the workmanship involved is less than that required for almost all other Indian costumes. To fashion these ingenious garments large areas are built up by seaming ribbons and occasionally strips of factory-made lace together. Yokes and other ornamental panels are of white or coloured cotton, and these provide a background for large hand-stitched flowers, parrots and even non-indigenous peacocks. In recent years these colourful designs have conformed more and more to pattern-book stereo-types, and embroideresses have come increasingly to rely on *cuadrillé*. This type of open-meshed cloth is ideally suited to the careful counting of stitches and in particular to cross stitching, which is taking over from satin techniques in many households. Older *huipiles* still feature smaller satin-stitched motifs, however, as do recent examples from San Miguel Soyaltepec. Here embroideresses still achieve a degree of refinement. Motifs are often worked in a single colour as they were traditionally, and the large areas of *manta* which they cover play a negative role in the overall pattern.

Mazatec *huipiles* are popular with tourists, who purchase them from *mestizo* stall-holders in the Oaxaca City market, and the highly ornate *Chiapaneca* costumes from Chiapa de Corzo in Chiapas have found similar favour. Their popularity runs high even in Mexico City, where they are frequently worn to fancy dress parties or displayed by small girls during the festival of Corpus Christi. Relatively inexpensive and quick to embroider, these full-skirted dresses exhibit a profusion of artificial silk flowers, satin-stitched in one or more colours on to black tulle. Given the costume's lack of Indian features, it comes as no surprise to learn that it was created by *mestizas*, who wear it still during local *fiestas*. To cater for this market many women in Chiapa de Corzo devote themselves full time to embroidery, working in addition at dressing dolls and making table-mats for tourists.

Although of European origin, the blouse has been adopted so enthusiastically by Indian women that it now serves as an admirable reflection of native taste. The Nahua of Puebla, have evolved several styles which they wear with their *quechquémitl*, and in highland villages such as Cuetzalán, Zoatecpan, Atla and Huilacapixtla garments are fashioned from white cotton and adorned with embroidered neck and sleeve bands worked in running stitch with mercerised thread. Stylised animals, birds and flowers remain popular motifs, together with some geometric patterning, but whereas earlier garments featured black embroidery, modern examples are more likely to be stitched with red or a combination of differently coloured cottons. Most women take great pride in creating their own blouses, but occasionally embroidered strips are sold in village market-places, enabling women who are less proficient with a needle to save labour.

For a long time the town of Altepexi in the Valley of Puebla was one of a small number of places where blouses were still hand-woven. In recent years, however, younger women have switched their allegiance to commercial cloth, which is profusely embroidered to give an unusually wide yoke, side panels and ornamental sleeves. Negative patterning is featured amidst a wealth of geometric stitching, and embroideresses frequently add their names and perhaps the date. Lettering is popular too with the women of Coacuila, situated near the town of Huauchinango. Here characters are sometimes scattered across the yoke, and even stitched back to front, to spell not only the owner's name but additional words such as *recuerdo* ('in memory'). Designs are chosen with equal eclecticism, and the conventionalised flowers, birds and geometric motifs that decorated earlier blouses have been modernised and joined by others from calendars and advertisements. Mexican horsemen and Virgins surrounded by flowers and cherubs are currently in favour, while a previously popular motif of a man carrying a large fish on his back has been traced by Bodil Christensen to the label on bottles of Scott's Emulsion. The cheerful effect of these blouses is enhanced by the use of a wide range of colours, but increasing reliance among younger women on *cuadrillé*, or squared cloth, threatens to lower the quality of stitching in the village (see p. 170). Today it is rare in Puebla to find examples of *pepenado fruncido*, once a speciality in the region. With this technique running stitches not only serve to create

Otomí blouse yoke from San Juan Ixtenco, Tlaxcala, where *pepenado fruncido* is still a speciality: running stitches form areas of negative patterning while creating minute folds in the cloth. Museum of Mankind, London.

tiny pleats but also form delicately stylised deer, cats, birds, such as eagles, human figures and flowers, many of them appearing in white as a result of negative patterning.

In addition to the Nahua, the Totonac, the Tepehua and the Otomí have also adopted embroidered blouses. Among the most eye-catching are those of San Pablito, where Otomí women employ a combination of cross, long-armed cross, back and running stitches to decorate their blouses with human figures, birds and animals such as deer and two-headed eagles. Across the state boundary the Otomí who inhabit Hidalgo's arid Mezquital Valley were glad to add cotton blouses, which they too embellish with embroidery, to their previously all-wool costumes.

The blouse is not confined to *quechquémitl*-wearing areas, however; since its introduction it has spread into many other regions and displaced the *huipil* in a number of communities. In Oaxaca a range of distinctive blouses has evolved, including those of San Vicente Ejutla which feature geometric and charmingly figurative designs in cross stitch, or San Pablo Tijaltepec which are distinguished by a single band of *pepenado* showing motifs such as deer in negative patterning. In the Valley the Zapotec women of San Antonino Ocotlán have achieved considerable fame with tourists for the beauty of their floral embroidery, and although much of their effort now goes into making dresses, their present technique originated with blouses. When these took over from *huipiles*, they were initially embroidered solely in white, and some women carry on this tradition. In 1928, however, a vogue for using brightly coloured thread was launched by Sabina Sánchez de Mateos, and this style predominates today. Contemporary prices are scaled to accord with the fineness of the satin stitching and the quality of the thread which ranges from pure silk through mercerised cotton to wool. This style of embroidery is also practised in San Juan Chilateca and other neighbouring villages. The irony is that while local women smile to see fair-skinned tourists proudly exhibiting these blouses, they themselves now don them only when photographed or for *fiestas*, preferring Western clothing for everyday wear (see pp. 62–3).

Further south, in Chiapas, the extraordinary versatility of the Mexican blouse is again demonstrated by the Tzeltal women of Aguacatenango, where colourful satin-stitched flowers border the neckline, or by the Tojolobal who inhabit Las Margaritas. Here decorative stitching adorns men's shirts as well as women's blouses and is combined with a multitude of tucks and frills. The role of embroidery is important too in Michoacán. *Huipiles* have been replaced by blouses throughout much of the state, and exuberantly patterned examples have become a conspicuous element of Tarascan costume in villages such as Paracho, Patamban, Tzintzuntzan and Cuanajo. Cross-stitched animals and birds are sometimes in evidence, but preference seems to go to large, brightly coloured pattern-book flowers. Elaborately embroidered European-style aprons are also in favour, and for *fiesta* attire they may be teamed with matching blouses.

When shoulder-bags and *servilletas* are made from commercial cloth, they too offer considerable scope for embroidery, although motifs are generally in keeping with those used by villagers for other garments. The Otomí who inhabit Tenango de Doria in Hidalgo have taken the art to remarkable lengths, however. From satin-stitched *servilletas* they have progressed in the last decade to covering vast expanses of *manta* with a succession of imaginary, rainbow-coloured plants, devils, animals and human figures. The success which these chimerical and ever more ambitious landscapes have gained with tourists has inspired the Otomí of San Pablito in Puebla to launch into a similar style of production.

The willingness shown by many Indian groups to absorb treadle-operated sewing-machines into their material culture has led, in some instances, to ingenious developments in the field of Mexican embroidery. In the highland region which straddles northern Puebla, Veracruz and Hidalgo women in several villages have taken to adorning their wrap-around skirts of *manta* in this way. Totonac and Tepehua examples from Pantepec and Mecapalapa are enlivened along the lower hem by multicoloured bands of undulating lines bordered on each side by straight ones, while Tepehua inhabitants of Huehuetla and Pisaflores specialise in flower and vine motifs. Repeated along the lower edge of the garment, they too are enclosed by line borders. In some of these communities skirts are matched by blouses which feature a combination of hand- and machine-stitching. In the municipality of Acaxochitlán, Hidalgo, the fusion of these two embroidery techniques is responsible for a range of highly ornate blouses, which carry traditionally figurative motifs on the yoke, and whirlpool designs of machine chain stitch across the shoulders, down the sides and along an additional frill (see p. 141).

Machine embroidery is occasionally teamed with hand-stitching by the Zapotec of the Oaxaca Isthmus for their gala costumes, but everyday *huipiles* depend solely on the first method. Photographs taken in 1898 heralded the start of this trend by showing a few garments ornamented with narrow bands of embroidery along the lower edge; by the 1940s, however, *huipiles* had acquired wide bands running parallel with the sides and hem. Their solid appearance was achieved by criss-crossing and superimposing lines of chain stitch done on special Singer sewing-machines, and today this technique still holds good. Although not old, existing designs are known by such names as 'jaguar', 'star' or 'crab-vendor', and new ones are constantly evolving. Colours are generally paired, with lemon yellow and red remaining a popular combination, and when embroidery is finely done it can achieve the delicacy of filigree. The vogue for machine-stitched *huipiles* of factory cloth has spread to the

Opposite Woollen yarns dyed with natural colourants, and the brocaded section of a Tzotzil ceremonial *huipil*. Magdalenas, Chiapas.

near-by Huave community of San Mateo del Mar, where few women now make their own clothing. Most rely instead on their commercially minded neighbours in Juchitán to provide them with specially decorated *huipiles*. These feature a series of narrow bands and are acquired in exchange for fish, maize and other foodstuffs.

A remarkable mastery of machine embroidery is also displayed by the Maya of Yucatán, where hand-stitching has been largely replaced for everyday wear. Although underskirts may remain untrimmed, *huipiles* exhibit decorative and colourful floral borders at the neck and hem. So popular indeed have machine techniques become that an increasingly large number of women now favour them even for the *terno de lujo*, or three-tiered gala costume, which they decorate with a profusion of luxuriant satin-stitched flowers.

Machine embroidery is confined solely to the adornment of factory-made fabrics, but hand embroidery has a far wider application for it is also used on backstrap-woven and treadle-loomed cloth. Within this last category fall the ready-made skirt lengths provided by weaving centres in San Cristóbal de las Casas. When bought by women from the surrounding Indian communities, they are adapted with stitching that is both decorative and functional to distinguish them from those worn in other villages. This is the case in San Andrés Larrainzar, where multicoloured joins secure two loom webs seamed together to form a tube (see p. 166). Of all the wrap-around skirts worn in Chiapas, however, the most eye-catching are without doubt those of Venustiano Carranza. Home-woven webs have been superseded over the last few decades by treadle-loomed cloth, which is seamed with over-and-over stitching in brightly coloured wools. Additional embroidery includes wave-patterned borders and an abundance of fernlike motifs or tendrils, flower forms and birds which cover ever larger areas, in keeping with the taste for increased embellishment (see p. 61).

There are a great many instances in the costume field of weaving communities which supply other communities with backstrap-woven garments. Usually these are patterned in the style traditionally required by the purchasers, but in a few cases cloth is left plain so that wearers can individualise it in their own way. Excellent potters, the Tzeltal women of Amatenango del Valle have long furnished surrounding villages with clay vessels, and as a result have little time left over to devote to costume. Yet although most of their garments are purchased ready-made, they continue to take great pride in embroidering their *huipiles*, which are of white, plain-woven cloth from Venustiano Carranza. Decoration consists of three extremely broad bands, which are satin-stitched in cotton or *artisela* around a squared-off neck opening (see p. 162).

In eastern Oaxaca Chinantec embroideresses from San Lucas Ojitlán occasionally buy *huipil* cloth from backstrap weavers in nearby Analco. Most still prefer, however, to weave their own. For *fiestas* custom demands a predominantly red *huipil* featuring brocading as well as running and cross-stitching. The seams are colourfully disguised by satin-stitched *randas*, or decorative joins. To the eyes of outsiders, however, it is the everyday *huipil* that appears most beautiful. Predominantly white and frequently created from hand-spun cotton, this fine garment combines areas of plain and gauze weaving. Embroidery is carried out at great speed on the reverse side of the cloth, and resulting motifs have a surprising angularity more suggestive of brocading than of needlework. Meticulously worked in horizontal running stitches, designs strike a decidedly pre-Conquest note by featuring long, angular serpents and elegantly stylised birds with long tails and curling plumes. As with the *fiesta huipil*, webs are held together by wide and colourful *randas* (see p. 191).

Tzeltal potter wearing a satin-stitched *huipil*, a tubular two-web wrap-around skirt, and a sash nearly 3 m long. Amatenango del Valle, Chiapas.

Lacandón couple. The woman, who wears a *huipil* and gathered skirt of factory cotton cloth, finger-paints her husband's bark-cloth *xikul* with *achiote*, or annatto. Najá, Chiapas.

Above Trique women wearing brocaded *huipiles* which may be draped over the shoulders for ease of movement. Wool blankets are diagonally patterned. San Andrés Chicahuaxtla. Oaxaca.

Left Otomí family in gala attire. Both types of *quechquémitl* are woven in a curve and richly embroidered. The man wears a hatband of netted beadwork and a shirt sewn with beads. San Pablito, Puebla.

Opposite Tzotzil girls wearing indigo-blue wrap-around cotton skirts, sashes and embroidered everyday *huipiles*. One carries a netted bag. San Andrés Larrainzar, Chiapas.

Right During Easter celebrations Tarahumara men termed *los pintos* paint their faces and bodies. Garments are made from factory cloth. Norogachic, Chihuahua.

Left Tarahumara women wearing brightly coloured clothing which they make from factory cotton cloth. Several skirts are worn at one time. Norogachic, Chihuahua.

Below Mazahua girls with festival hats take the role of *pastoras*, or shepherdesses. The corners of their fringed *quechquémitl* are worn to the front and back, although married women wear them to the sides. Underskirts are edged with bands

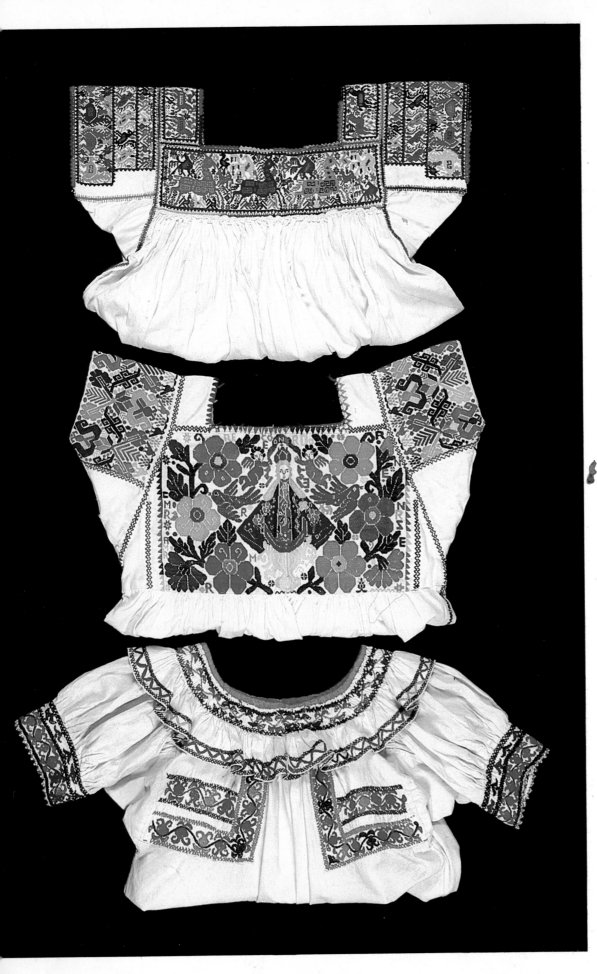

Opposite 1930s Tehuana costume from Oaxaca, worn by collector Elia Gutiérrez. The velvet *huipil* and skirt are hand-embroidered in silk; the flounce is of hand-made lace.

Left Women's acrylic-embroidered blouses with square-cut sleeves: (*top*) Otomí, cross-stitched motifs on *cuadrillé*, San Pablito, Puebla; (*centre*) Nahua, motifs in running stitch on cotton cloth, Coacuila, Puebla; (*bottom*) Tojolabal, motifs on calico worked in chain, long-armed cross and other stitches; cloth is gathered into folds. Las Margaritas, Chiapas.

Opposite Sashes: (*from top to bottom*) 1. Palm-leaf *soyate*, Oaxaca. 2. Tarascan, Cuanajo, Michoacán. w. 1 in (2.5 cm). 3. Otomí, *ikat*-patterned, Tolimán, Querétaro. 4. As 2. 5. Zapotec, Santo Tomás Jalieza, Oaxaca. 6. Nahua, gala, sewn with tufts of wool, lace and sequins, Cuetzalán, Puebla. 7. Tarahumara, Chihuahua. All sashes are female, except 7. Sashes 2, 4, 5 and 7 are warp-patterned.

Above Chinantec *huipil.* Woven on a backstrap loom with plain, gauze and brocade techniques, this three-web, knee-length garment has been partially over-painted with *fuchina*. San Felipe Usila, Oaxaca.

Magnificently attired male dancer wearing a plumed head-dress and a cloak with embroidery and sequins during *La Danza de la Culebra*. Tlaxcala.

Dancer in a wax mask wearing a costly suit embroidered with gold and silver thread during *La Danza de las Cuadrillas*. The leather holster is also embroidered. Los Reyes, state of Mexico.

Above Maya woman from Chichén Itzá, Yucatán. Everyday costume comprises a skirt on a waistband and a machine-embroidered *huipil* with colourful floral motifs. Hand-embroidered 19th-century costumes are shown on pp. 54, 116.

Right Chinantec woman from Valle Nacional, Oaxaca. Colourful cross-stitched motifs pattern her long home-woven cotton *huipil*; web joins are concealed by wide *randas*. A bath-towel covers her head and shoulders.

Opposite Trique woman, from San Andrés Chicahuaxtla, in her fiesta *huipil*, bought from the Trique village of Santa María Yucunicoco, Oaxaca.

In the neighbouring Chinantec community of Valle Nacional traditions are in decline, and few young women now wear Indian dress. The distinctive local *huipil* is still in evidence among older women, however, who create a plain weave background and adorn it with cross-stitched designs. These are freely distributed across the surface of all three webs and include vases of flowers, parrots, peacocks and animals, many copied directly from pattern sheets. Earlier examples, now in museums or private collections, often display areas of gauze, red woven bands, and embroidered geometric motifs. They also confirm that women in the area formerly employed not only running stitch but also plait stitch.

In the coastal region of south-west Oaxaca hand-woven *huipiles* are also embellished with embroidery in a number of Mixtec communities. Particularly fine is the wedding *huipil* from Pinotepa Nacional, which is plain-woven from hand-spun white cotton and bordered at the neck with silk ribbon. This band is then covered with a profusion of minutely chain-stitched fish, crabs, lizards, spiders, scorpions, flowers, rabbits and

Nahua woman embroidering a
wrap-around skirt in Acatlán, Guerrero.

other creatures worked in silk floss of several colours. Outside the ribbon area relatively recent examples display additional chain-stitched decoration in the form of four two-headed birds. This ancient design is also a feature of wedding *huipiles* in Huazolotitlán, where it appears, flanked by two other birds and surrounded by stars and flowers, below a neckline of squared-off geometric motifs. Decorative stitching is employed yet again in Jamiltepec, where colourful lines are worked about the neck with commercial cotton threads and gleaming *artisela*. In this same region live the Tacuate, who belong to the Mixtec family, and the Amuzgo, who also inhabit neighbouring stretches of Guerrero, and although women from both groups concentrate mainly on brocading the patterning of their *huipiles*, occasional motifs may be added in cross stitch to reinforce their decorative appeal.

Embroidery is popular too in a number of Zapotec villages, where women continue to weave their own *huipiles*. Visitors to the annual *Guelaguetza*, or Oaxaca Indian State Fair, are always pleased by the costumes from Yalalag, where gala *huipiles* are adorned with vertical columns of vivid satin-stitched flowers. Worked on four narrow cotton strips to disguise the side and central seams, these were apparently inspired by missionaries and schoolteachers during the early decades of this century, when they took over from the original satin-stitched *randas*. It is also possible at the *Guelaguetza* to see examples of the old *fiesta huipil* from San Pedro Quiatoni, where a colourful arrangement of flowers and tendrils surrounds the silk ribbon which borders the neck. To the south, in the state of Chiapas, embroidery plays a similarly decorative role in villages such as Santo Tomás Oxchuc, where Tzeltal weavers like to add lattices and horizontal lines of stitching to their cotton *huipiles*, or San Juan Chamula where Tzotzil women finish off the arm openings and necklines of their feltlike wool *huipiles* with blanket stitch and rows of multicoloured chain stitching.

Many of the finest examples of contemporary Indian embroidery fall within the category of the *quechquémitl*. Adept at weaving, Otomí women in a number of communities rely also on their skill with a needle. This is particularly evident in San Pablito, Puebla, where garments are shaped on the loom and conform to two styles. Distinguishing the first of these is a narrow purplish band of wool, above which appear embroidered birds and eagles, many double-headed, monkeys, foxes, dogs, prancing horses and people. Highly stylised and worked in red and black commercial cotton, they feature a combination of cross, long-armed cross and outline stitching. These same techniques are employed, also against a background of plain white weave, for *quechquémitl* of the second type. Here motifs are bisymmetric and include large eight-sided, star-shaped flowers together with other flower and stem patterns. Set above an extremely wide curved border of red wool, designs are densely embroidered with black and purplish-red wool (see p. 165).

Also situated in the Puebla highlands are the centres of Pantepec and Mecapalapa, where Totonac women continue to create richly patterned *quechquémitl* of the curved weave variety. Among the most colourful of all Mexican garments, they exhibit only a narrow strip of white along the edge, for the rest of the plain-woven cotton ground is concealed beneath a wealth of designs, worked in vivid re-spun wools. Brocading accounts for a wide outer band of hexagonal spirals and for the dense array of zig-zag lines, birds, calabashes and stylised flowers that it encloses, but embroidery is responsible for a cross-stitched pot of flowers which appears below the neck opening. The combination of brocading and needlework is also a feature of Tepehua *quechquémitl* in several communities in both Puebla and Hidalgo. Huastec garments are today made mostly from factory *manta*, but older examples display a plain-woven background patterned with intricate and colourful cross-stitched motifs. Nahua women in a great many villages have not ceased to weave their *quechquémitl*, however, and in Cuetzalán the corners are often feather-stitched with stemlike patterns.

Wrap-around skirts are rarely as highly decorated as torso-garments, yet those worn in Acatlán and Zitlala, Guerrero, are an impressive exception. Woven and embroidered in the first of these two Nahua villages, they feature plain-woven bands of dark and light blue, the latter covered with fanciful birds, animals and flowers. In the centre of these rainbow landscapes embroideresses even portray Mexico's emblem – an eagle with a serpent in its beak. A recent vogue for lettering has led, in addition, to the stitching of dates, names or patriotic phrases such as *Arriba México*. Stem, fishbone and couching are among the techniques used, but woollen embroidery yarns were long ago replaced by gleaming *artisela*, which is delicate and wears out quickly. For this reason women tend to wear their skirts wrong-side out, reversing them only on Sundays or for festive occasions. Although these lavishly decorated skirts have remained popular, those of the lowland Totonac died out some fifty years ago. Worn in the Papantla area of Veracruz, they were characterised by large flowering trees and birds, which were cross- or satin-stitched in red or blue on to a white plain-woven background. They have been supplanted, like the gauze-woven *quechquémitl* that accompanied them, by machine-embroidered shop-bought organdy.

Although traditional *rebozos* have been replaced in many places by commercial ones, the Nahua of Hueyapan in Puebla have retained their own ornate and highly distinctive version. Unusually wide and plain-woven from black wool, they are almost entirely covered by a profusion of cross-stitched birds, animals and flowers. Of late the strident tones of acrylic yarns have taken over from the subtler and warmer tones of naturally dyed wools, while pattern-book stereotypes have supplanted more traditional designs, but the popularity which this *rebozo* finds with outsiders is ensured by the exuberance of its patterning.

Cotton wrap-around skirt from Acatlán, Guerrero, colourfully embroidered with artificial silks. Museum of Mankind, London.

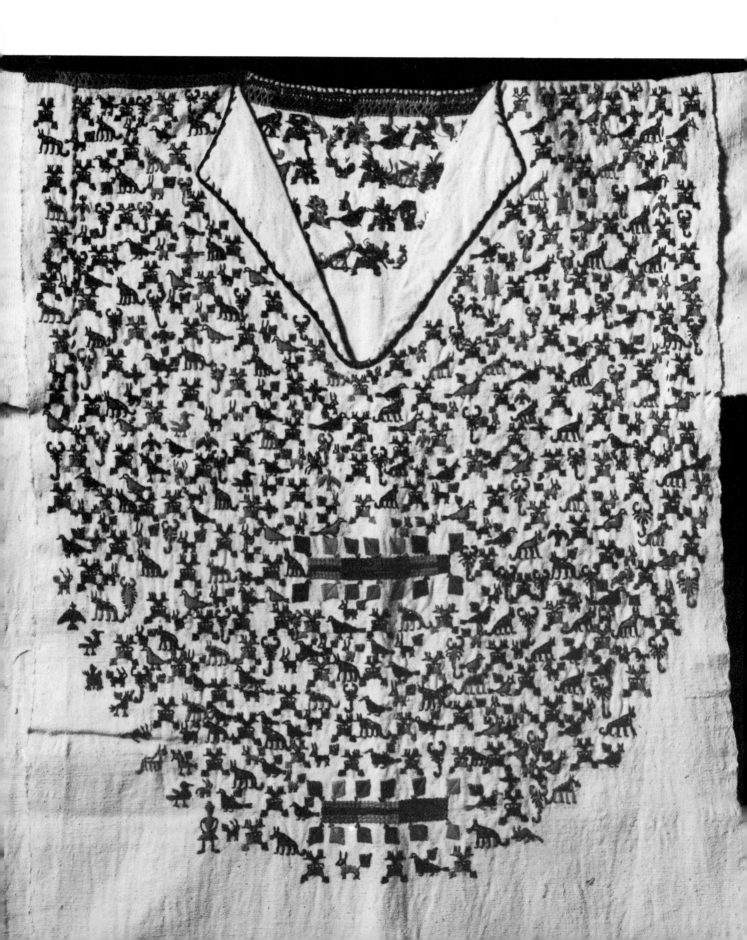

Tacuate man's shirt from Santa María Zacatepec, Oaxaca. Woven from hand-spun cotton on a backstrap loom, it features drawn threadwork and embroidery. Museum of Mankind, London.

Male clothing has long been far plainer and less adorned than that of women, but high on the list of exceptions is the spectacular Tacuate costume from Santa María Zacatepec, Oaxaca. Woven from white or *coyuche* cotton, trousers and shirt both feature numerous rows of minuscule animal, insect and bird motifs. Stylised and multicoloured, they are worked in satin, herringbone, chain and – more frequently in recent years – cross stitch. Very different in style are the delicate, back-stitched designs which embellish the white, home-woven gala shirts of Tzotzil men in Huistán, Chiapas. Worked in black or in subdued colours, they include flowers, vines and, occasionally, crosses. Embroidery may also be used in Hidalgo and the state of Mexico to decorate the *ixtle ayates* of the Otomí with satin-stitched patterning of natural wool. Shoulder-bags constitute an important element of male dress and provide an impressive range of embroidered designs. Among the most handsome are those favoured in a number of Mazahua communities. Plain-woven from white cotton with warp bands of hand-spun wine-coloured wool, they exhibit a densely stitched array of geometric motifs, antlered deer, birds and stylised flowering plants, all worked with wine, red and black wools in cross and long-armed cross.

Embroidery, like weaving, is taught during late childhood, and lessons are taken seriously. According to Nancy Modiano, mothers in the Chiapas highlands may attempt to ensure a daughter's success by pricking her finger with a needle, while among the Huichol divine help is frequently sought by means of prayer arrows and gods' eyes. The beliefs and rituals which attach to this important skill are various, and it has been recorded by Donald and Dorothy Cordry that Huichol women will often leave a design unfinished, with the thread hanging, to symbolise the continuity of life. Another interesting notion, not unlike that of the Huichol regarding woven patterning, is attributed by José Díaz Bolio to the Maya of Yucatán, where it is apparently thought necessary for learners to pass their hands over a rattlesnake if they are to master the intricacies of *xocbichuy*, or carefully counted cross-stitching.

In a great many communities designs are perpetuated by *muestras*, or samplers, which serve not only as a teaching aid but also as a reminder to accomplished embroideresses. Fragments of worn-out garments often play a similar role, and Mazahua women are careful to keep sections from their embroidered skirt bands as models. Indeed, a lack of respect for past work frequently heralds a decline in standards. In the Nahua village of Coacuila, for example, the once fine yokes of tattered blouses are now being used as pillows and dusters in several households, where taste is veering towards more commercial styles of dress. Drawing is looked upon in a number of communities as an additional aid to fine work, and factory cloth is often marked out with a profusion of outline illustrations done in pencil or even ballpoint pen. Women from other villages frequently pride themselves on *not* using drawings to guide them, however. When photographed, a young girl from Huilaca-pixtla, Puebla, asked me to pay particular attention to the freehand patterning of her blouse. In answer to my queries about her skill and patience in counting stitches she, like many others questioned, replied simply: 'But it is my hand which knows how'.

Although the art of embroidery is generally confined to women, men will occasionally practise it as well. Among the Huichol, for example, it is not unusual for boys to learn how to embroider, while in southern Oaxaca woven sashes are habitually finished off with decorative stitching by the male inhabitants of San Pedro Jicayán and other Mixtec villages. I have also been told by a Mexican informant who grew up during the 1940s in Juchitán that small Zapotec boys who exhibited effeminate traits during

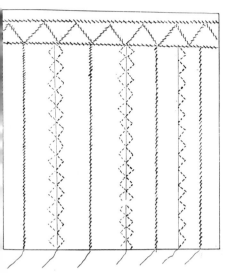

Otomí resist-dyed cloth photographed in the 1930s near Zimapán, Hidalgo, by Elsie McDougal. It was folded and stitched, as shown in the diagram, then dipped in dye.

their early years often turned professionally to embroidery in later life. Encouraged by their mothers and admired for their skill by fellow-villagers, they apparently lived apart from the rest of the community and earned a good living by working on the famous gala costumes of the women. As for the decorative hangings and *servilletas* which are currently produced in Tenango de Doria, Hidalgo, these sometimes represent the joint efforts of an entire Otomí family.

Important though embroidery is, however, it is far from being the sole method employed in Indian communities to embellish already woven cloth. Dyeing procedures, some probably very ancient, account for an interesting range of patterning and include the resist technique known as *plangi*. Within this category fall the tie-dyed wrap-around skirts and *jergas*, or *gabanes*, which were formerly worn in such Otomí centres as Zimapán in Hidalgo, or Vizarrón in Querétaro. In *Design Motifs on Mexican Indian Textiles* Irmgard W. Johnson gives a description of a fine old-style skirt which she acquired in Vizarrón during the 1950s. Plain-woven from wool, its white ground has been tie-dyed with cochineal red and indigo blue to retain a profusion of small white squares with spots of colour in the centre. Viewed overall, this distinctive patterning is seen to consist of a lattice-like series of diamonds and four-petalled flowers, while the lower part of the skirt exhibits a vine motif. This same author has elaborated elsewhere on the methods used in Vizarrón until recently to achieve such effects. Having spread out the woven cloth, women would cover it with a sheet of paper which was already perforated with the outlines of the designs required. Red-ochre earth was then sprinkled through the openings, and the details of motifs were subsequently filled in with a brush dipped in a solution of red ochre and water. To bind the cloth women used *ixtle* cords, and immersion followed in the first dye-bath. If women wished to imbue garments with a third or even a fourth colour, certain white sections were tied and other dyed sections untied, before the cloth was given its second dye-bath.

When stitching is used to reserve areas of patterning, the method is known as *tritik*, and this was the system observed by Elsie McDougall during a visit to Ranchito Guadalupe, near Zimapán, in the 1930s. Here woollen cloth, favoured for its absorbency, was prepared with a succession of running, whipping and overcast or seam stitches. When the gathers had been regulated with a thorn, and the threads pulled tight, the cloth was dipped in dye.

It is usual when describing these dyeing techniques to employ the past tense and to speak of their decline. Research carried out in the late 1970s by Ruth D. Lechuga and Marta Turok in the remoter areas of the Querétaro mountains has yielded some very positive results, however. In a monograph devoted to the study of *plangi* among the Otomí of the region Dr Lechuga relates their productive encounter in Chavarría with a woman who had not practised tie-dyeing in twenty years but who remembered the procedure well enough to make a specimen *jerga* for them to inspect. Its final appearance caused them some surprise for it closely resembled *ikat*-dyed cloth, but the technique proved to be closely related to that of *plangi*. Using a needle, the woman had spent a week winding wet *ixtle* thread round the warp yarns of her twill-woven cloth to reserve them during the garment's subsequent immersion in dye. A second commission resulted in a wrap-around skirt patterned with a garland of flowers. Immersed only once and simpler in style than Irmgard W. Johnson's specimen, it nevertheless constituted an example of true *plangi*. Designs were reserved free-hand, without recourse to guidelines. The long-term effects of these investigations have yet to be seen, but a renewal of interest by local people in tie-dyeing already seems likely. Several villagers have apparently placed orders for *jergas*, and Doña Dolores Aguilar is being officially encouraged to share with younger weavers the skills which she, alone in her village, has preserved.

Although the existence in pre-Conquest Mexico of both *plangi* and *ikat* has yet to be confirmed, the Maya cloth described on p. 29 proves that *batik* was understood. It is ironic, therefore, that this third method of resist-dyeing should today be unknown in Indian Mexico. Other early ways of decorating woven cloth included pattern-stamping and free-hand painting, yet despite their decline a few instances remain. In the Tepehua community of Huehuetla, for example, weavers have a unique form of treatment for their cotton *quechquémitl*. Predominantly white, they are brocaded and embroidered with non-fast woollen yarns to feature floral and geometric motifs, then washed and rinsed. Next they are impregnated yet again with soap and folded with care so that patterned sections press against plain ones. After this, the *quechquémitl* are tightly packed in dried corn husks, and placed for several minutes on a griddle over an open fire. When garments are unwrapped, the colours from the raised designs will be seen to have imprinted themselves on the plain surfaces, thereby providing an additional range of patterning. A second instance of colour-stamping still occurs, albeit rarely, in the Mixtec village of San Sebastián Peñoles. Here bags are woven from white cotton and embellished on the loom with weft stripes of raw *fuchina*-dyed silk, then dampened and folded so as to imprint the ground with purple streaks.

The antiquity of both these decorative techniques is unknown, but the stamping of agave shoulder-bags in Veracruz seems likely to be of more recent origin. Unlike more expensive examples which exhibit finely woven weft stripes, cheaper bags tend to feature uncomplicated motifs, which have been printed in pink and blue on to the finished cloth. Free-hand painting offers a third source of embellishment for *ixtle* bags: in Veracruz they may be adorned with primitively executed birds or flowers, but in Guerrero they often display veritable landscapes created with brilliant aniline colours. Bags of this last type have an undeniable exuberance and charm (see p. 57).

Also included among present-day textile arts is finger-painting. Among the Lacandón of Najá this occurs very occasionally during religious ceremonies, when men ritually spot both their tunics and the objects in the temple with red *achiote*, or annatto, which is carried in small gourds. Two chest decorations, consisting of a circle with a dot in the centre, are the additional prerogative of the group's spiritual leader. According to Roberto D. Bruce, markings are linked with the spots of the jaguar, while the red dye symbolises sacrificial blood (see p. 163). In Ixtayutla Tacuate women also practise finger-painting. Using *fuchina*, which has taken over from the juice of the *pitahaya*, or cactus fruit, they daub not only the plain but also the brocaded areas of garments with their fingers and thumbs.

One of the most remarkable and inexplicable post-weaving procedures of modern Mexico must surely be that employed by the Chinantec who inhabit San Felipe Usila, Oaxaca. Here splendidly ornate *huipiles* are achieved by alternating vivid clusters of narrow weft stripes with magnificent motifs, which are brocaded on to a white ground of plain and gauze weave. Completed garments are then stretched across a framework of wooden poles, enabling weavers to paint over selected areas with *fuchina* and to obliterate their formerly brilliant colours. Only by studying these areas carefully is it possible to discern the intricately woven designs which underly this coat of muted purple (see p. 173). Unique and very beautiful, finished garments often surprise outsiders, but when Carlota Mapelli Mozzi tried to discover the reason for over-painting, she was told it was done 'to stop the sun from eating the colour of the threads'.

Random though these decorative effects may sometimes appear, they are deliberately induced, which is more than can be said for the running of non-fast yarns which so often occurs. Yet, astonishing as it may seem to outsiders, the streaking and merging of colours which affects many garments at the first wash is not only accepted but even admired in many Indian communities. This unusual response has been noted by Donald and Dorothy Cordry in the Mixtec village of San Sebastián Peñoles where the woven surfaces of men's sashes are stained by their stripes of *fuchina*-dyed silk, and in the Nahua village of San José Miahuatlán, where embroidered bands of commercial wool streak the background white of *huipiles*. Examples are many, and although the results are not intentional, they are seen as contributing to the overall appearance of textiles. Responsibility rests not only with the low quality of factory dyes and yarns but also with modern detergents which are now widely available and stocked even in remote village shops. Far gentler but now falling into disuse are traditional washing substances such as *xixi*, which is the pulp which remains after agave spikes have been stripped of their fibres. According to Campbell W. Pennington, the Tarahumara still utilise the crushed roots of yucca, agave, *cucurbita* and other plants. These are soaked and smeared upon blankets and clothing, which are left for several hours in water. A species of red soil, which they term *tecoloac*, is no longer employed, however.

Exposure to sunlight remains the accepted method for whitening cloth, but an interesting custom has been reported by Carlota Mapelli Mozzi for the Maya of Yucatán. There water is boiled with ashes, strained and used to boil clothing. Another procedure, described by this same writer, concerns the Chinantec of Valle Nacional, who dip their *huipiles* in a bath of water and indigo. This treatment, which is apparently repeated after each washing, serves to enhance the white of the background by imparting a pale blue overtone. A not dissimilar effect was also achieved in the past by the Nahua women of Amatlán de los Reyes. According to Donald and Dorothy Cordry, their everyday costume comprised a white *huipil* and wrap-around skirt which had been dipped in blueing.

Additional methods of embellishing finished garments are many and include not only dyeing, painting and stamping but also *appliqué*. In *Design Motifs on Mexican Indian Textiles*, Irmgard W. Johnson has described an old-style gala skirt from the Otomí community of Tolimán. Relying on a background of home-woven, navy-blue woollen cloth, the maker had stitched green or blue silk ribbons on to yellow silk, which she then stitched partially to white cotton cloth and partially to the original backing. Motifs were scalloped to feature the *camarón* (shrimp) and the *medio camarón* (half shrimp). Sadly this particular tradition has died out, but gathered skirts in a number of villages are given wide appliquéd borders along the lower edge. One of the most charming examples is that of Xochistlahuaca in Guerrero, where Amuzgo women select two contrasting cloths of factory cotton and machine-sew the top layer into points. Worn under one arm, these decorative garments are customarily tied over the opposite shoulder and may be used without a torso-garment in the home. The gathered skirts which have been adopted in Santiago Choapan and some other Zapotec villages are worn in less original fashion about the waist, but they too display colourful bands of *appliqué* and combine lines of rickrack braid with rayon ribbon hemmed in points.

In Chiapas, where skirts are predominantly of the traditional wrap-around variety, ribbons are popular with Tzeltal women who inhabit the tropical lowlands. In centres such as Tila, Yajalón and Bachajón they are used to conceal the horizontal seam which joins the two webs of cloth. Positioned just below the hips, their vivid colours contrasting with the sober blue of the background, they may number as few as three or as many as twelve. Blouses, especially in Bachajón where they are made from brightly coloured sateens, frequently display ribbon-trimmed necklines and a wide frill which is oversewn with ribbons.

Although the necklines of gauze-woven white *quechquémitl* in Cuetzalán are occasionally finished off with pink satin ribbon, such adornments are more often favoured for *huipiles*. Where head openings are cut out and not provided for by a selvage split, they may be bound with ribbon as in Venustiano Carranza to prevent fraying, reinforced as in Pinotepa Nacional with embroidered ribbon, or embellished as in Jamiltepec and Metlatonoc with appliquéd ribbon which has been hemmed in points to evoke the sun's rays. Perhaps the widest area of neckline decoration is exhibited by Nahua women in San Francisco Huehuetlán, Oaxaca, where *huipiles* are oversewn with six strips of ruched cloth in two alternating colours (see p. 220). *Appliqué* also occurs in the Huave village of San Mateo del Mar, where vertical bands of ribbon or braid may be used instead of machine embroidery to adorn the dark commercial cloth *huipiles* of older women. A small but significant example of *appliqué* is also customary among the Chinantec women of San Lucas Ojitlán, who decorate their everyday and red *fiesta huipiles* with a small horizontal rectangle of ribbon. Situated some 10 in (25 cm) below the neckline, this addition is closely linked with pre-Hispanic design which often featured a similarly placed rectangular motif (see p. 191).

Ribbons have many uses apart from *appliqué*, however. Once of silk but made today from substitute fibres, they are bought in a range of brilliant colours and represent a considerable expenditure for many women. One popular practice, which in Jamiltepec or Pinotepa Nacional can require as many as 5 yds (4.6 m), is the insertion of ribbon between the webs of *huipiles* to form decorative joins. When seamed together, as in some Mazatec villages, they can provide decorative overhanging frills or fake sleeves, which are then tacked on to the main body of the *huipil* in emulation of European-style blouses. In San Felipe Usila, where sleeves have found equal favour, *huipiles* are capped on each shoulder by a large ribbon rosette (see p. 173). Rosettes are popular too with the *quechquémitl*-wearing women of Cuetzalán (see p. 8).

Widespread use is also made of ribbons to provide *huipiles* with colourful cascades. In Trique villages such as San Andrés Chicahuaxtla, for example, necklines are trimmed at the back with long lengths of ribbon, while Nahua women in San Sebastián Zinacatepec, Puebla, used until recently to integrate a section of ribbon into the embroidered panels that decorated the back and the front of their hand-woven garments. The two long ends of the section were left hanging and occasionally creased when damp by being wrapped round a piece of gourd and pressed with a stone. As Donald and Dorothy Cordry have noted, the peasant costumes of Navalcán in central Spain displayed similarly pleated ribbons. Hats too may benefit from the addition of flowing ribbons, as they do in Zinacantán in Chiapas. In San Juan Copala the sashes of Trique men are often trimmed with ribbons which hang half-way to the knee.

Lace is another factory-made item with a high demand among present-day Indian women. It appeals to the Mazatec of Jalapa de Díaz who *appliqué* it round the neck areas of their *huipiles*, to the Tojolabal who sew lace frills between the horizontal tucks of their gathered *artisela* skirts, and to the Chinantec of San Felipe Usila who use it to trim the sleeves of their *huipiles*. It is popular too with the Maya of Yucatán who employ it to edge the three embroidered panels of their gala costumes, and with the Nahua women of Cuetzalán who incorporate sections of lace into their highly decorative waist-sashes (see p. 172), while in Aguacatenango Tzeltal blouses are sometimes finished off with one or even two overhanging frills.

Flounces are used to great effect along the borders of the full and richly embroidered gala skirts of Tehuantepec, and although these are generally made today from organdy or tulle, expensive modern examples may still feature fine hand-made lace. So too do many of the older skirts which have been passed down from mothers and grandmothers, and which are highly prized for the borders of elaborate ivory-coloured lace displayed (see p. 171). The *huipil grande*, which is the name given to the *huipil*-shaped head-covering worn in Tehuantepec during *fiestas*, veers similarly between factory-produced materials and genuine lace. Whatever the fabric, however, the flounces of both garments require careful laundering, starching and pleating if they are to look their best.

Although the European art of drawn threadwork, or *deshilado*, is less popular than it used to be, it has been preserved in a number of communities where it serves to embellish the neck and sleeve bands of blouses or the edges of *servilletas*. It is also current in Santa María Zacatepec where the shirts of Tacuate men feature a double band of decoration along the shoulder-line and, in some cases, a horizontal rectangle below the front neck opening. Trouser bottoms too may display drawn threadwork. To bind the interconnecting warps women employ vivid embroidery threads and build up small rectangles of different colours.

Crochet, or *tejido de gancho*, is often used by *mestizas* to make *servilletas* and other household articles, but the skill has been adopted by Indian women in many communities. Totonac, Tarascan, Nahua and Popoluca blouses occasionally display crocheted yokes made from white or coloured cotton threads. These are entwined to form a square-meshed ground which is enlivened in some instances by bird, animal or flower motifs. Crochet is also popular in San Lucas Ojitlán, where lace-like frills edge the neck-opening and ribbon sleeves of *fiesta huipiles*, or in San Antonino Ocotlán, where half-inch insets serve to join blouse and dress sections (see pp. 62, 63). Similar joins are achieved in other villages without a hook. A wide, needle-formed band unites *quechquémitl* webs in the Otomí community of Santa Ana Hueytlalpan.

The garments so far mentioned only incorporate crocheted or needle-worked sections, but in Atla and surrounding villages an interesting development has recently taken place. The weaving of figured gauze, once a Nahua speciality, has been largely overtaken by crochet, and many women are now adept at recreating with a hook the animals, birds and flowers which patterned traditionally woven *quechquémitl*. Knitting, on the other hand, has never entered the Indian spectrum. The heavy woollen cardigans which have lately met with such favour in Europe and the USA are fashioned in the states of Mexico and Tlaxcala for sale to tourists and for the export market. In mountain villages such as Tenejapa in Chiapas or San Andrés Chicahuaxtla in Oaxaca some women have recently begun to wear brightly coloured acrylic jumpers beneath their *huipiles*, but these are always factory made.

Fringing, which has a long history in Mexico, remains essential to the completion of many garments, and techniques range from the uncomplicated to the highly elaborate.

Finger-knotting the long warp fringe of an *ikat*-dyed *rebozo* in Santa María del Río, San Luis Potosí.

When weavers sever the warp yarns of two-selvaged textiles, they may simply twist them with their fingers to prevent the cloth from unravelling. *Tortilla* bags, *servilletas* and *sarapes* are frequently finished off in this way; alternatively, the cut warps may be secured with a single row of overhand knots. In a few rare instances, however, warps are left uncut, and the resulting loops knotted. According to Carmen Cook de Leonard, Popoloca *gabanes* in Los Reyes Metzontla, Puebla, display loop-knotted fringes, which Irmgard W. Johnson has compared with a similarly edged pre-Conquest inner mummy blanket from the Tehuacán Valley.

Sashes are completed in a variety of styles by weavers who often wrap, braid or knot warp ends with great skill. In Hidalgo the Otomí, whose double-woven draw-string bags feature an area of highly decorative braiding, often work their sash ends in *macramé* to display a range of geometrical and even figurative motifs. *Macramé* is also used in the Nahua village of Cuetzalán, where men's sashes exhibit delicately patterned fringes and a profusion of tassels (see p. 195). Back in the 1930s these sashes constituted daily wear, and purchasers could buy them unfinished in the market-place to fringe at home, but now they are solely worn during *fiestas* by dancers and older men. In Jamiltepec too the fine Mixtec sashes, which are woven by women but embroidered and knotted by men, seem destined to disappear. Another use for *macramé* has been described by Donald and Dorothy Cordry. While investigating the now extinct male costume of Altepexi, Puebla, they discovered that the bottoms of the hand-loomed, all-white trouser legs were edged with a narrow band of zig-zag patterned *macramé*, then stitched in button-hole. In the 1960s, when the Cordrys made their study, there was just one old man who recalled the technique.

A widespread fondness for fringed *rebozos* ensures the continuity of braiding and finger-knotting techniques in many regions, however. In the villages which surround Chapa de Mota in the state of Mexico *rebozos* are woven with blue and white warp stripes, and embellished by their Otomí wearers to display a criss-cross of warps with solidly blocked areas revealing eagles, dogs and other creatures. In Oaxaca's San Miguel Cajonos Zapotec women specialise in creating four-strand braids, while in near-by Yalalag fringes are tied with overhand knots and carefully spaced to create diamond-shaped openings. Fringes of such complexity can take several days to complete, and in centres such as Santa María del Río or Tenancingo the task is frequently entrusted to outworkers known as *empuntadoras*, who memorise a range of designs with names like *arcos* and *rosas*.

There are, in addition to the types of fringe already described, two unusual methods for decorating *rebozos*: one of these occurs in Altepexi, where Nahua women border each end of their white, treadle-loomed shawls with as many as eighty-six hand-fashioned pom-poms; another interesting technique is that employed in the Paracho region of Michoacán. Here Tarascan weavers incorporate strands of *artisela*, or artificial silk, into the knotted fringes of *rebozos* and occasionally form decorative patterns representing birds and animals. The workmanship struck Frederick Starr in 1897 as 'curious' and caused him to see in it 'a surviving imitation of the ancient feather-work for which the ancient Tarascans were famous'. Although blue and white are the more traditional colours, a recent trend towards a wider spectrum has further intensified the resemblance between these borders and the plumage of exotic birds.

Sometimes *quechquémitl* are adorned with fringes which are made separately and sewn along the outer edge. This is so in Cuetzalán where white cotton is used, and in several Huastec, Otomí and Mazahua villages where colourful fringes are worked in wool. Before the Conquest fringes were sometimes twined, then sewn on to garments. This is proved by the cloth specimen from the *Cenote* at Chichén Itzá, as well as by the two miniature *quechquémitl* and the small *huipil* from the Mixteca Alta. Today *quechquémitl* fringes are similarly twined in various communities including Santa Ana Eyenzú in the state of Mexico's Mazuahua region (see p. 213).

Contemporary *quechquémitl* of this type provide a clear link with the past, but there is no present-day record of a fringed *huipil*. There are, however, instances of tasselled *huipiles*. In San Mateo del Mar the effect is created on the loom by Huave weavers who stop the central stripe some 5 in (13 cm) from the bottom of the garment. The purple threads are then left to hang in a narrow cluster, and white warps used to complete the *huipil*, which is no longer worn locally but sold to collectors and tourists. A similar technique is employed by Mixe weavers in San Pedro Acatlán and San Juan Mazatlán. Today the long *artisela* tassels of Yalalag's Zapotec are generally tacked on to finished *huipiles*, yet formerly they were twined through the warps of the cloth while it was on the loom. In San Juan Chamula, Chiapas, tassels are also popular: there they are formed separately from strands of acrylic or wool. Used to adorn not only the centre of *huipiles* but also the corners of head-cloths, these vivid and bushy tufts contrast flamboyantly with the sombre colouring of the felted woollen ground. As for pom-poms, these provide another striking costume addition by gracing men's hats in Tenejapa, Chiapas, and by embellishing the corners of double-woven bags among the Huichol and the Cora.

Contemporary Indian garments may occasionally incorporate tie-cords, as in Altepexi where the cuffs and collars of men's old-style shirts were drawn together by hand-twisted lengths of cotton ending in round fringe balls, but they almost never rely on European-style fastenings such as buttons or zips. The Tacuate have, however, discovered the decorative value of buttons, and in the remote villages of Carasol and Huamuchi they are aligned below shirt necklines and surrounded with jagged sun-ray embroidery. Unusual though this feature is, it is often accompanied by one still stranger, for among a cluster of brightly coloured cotton tassels many Tacuate like to include the large, silvery chrysalises of butterflies.

Embellishment of a very different kind is provided in several communities through the onlay of sequins. In Acatlán, Guerrero, Nahua women position them haphazardly amidst the rich embroidery of their wrap-around skirts and enjoy the way they glint in the sunlight. *Fiesta huipiles* are often spangled in the Chinantec village of San Lucas Ojitlán, while the Nahua of Cuetzalán use sequins to adorn the embroidered corners of *quechquémitl* and male and female sashes (see pp. 172, 195). Although the nineteenth-century vogue for spangling is still represented by dazzling and expensive recreations of the famous *china poblana* skirts, these garments have no place in Indian life but may be seen only at costume balls or in stage shows.

Beadwork also achieved great popularity during the course of the nineteenth century. Today it retains its attraction in many regions, although rising prices are pushing this costly form of decoration beyond the reach of many people. In the Puebla highlands colourfully beaded blouses are still worn for *fiestas* by a few Otomí and Nahua women, who create animal and flower motifs on yokes and sleeve bands by sewing the beads to flat or gathered cloth (see p. 60), or alternatively by incorporating them into areas of crochet. In Guerrero beaded blouses have lost the appeal they once had for the Nahua in villages such as Atzacoaloya, but they are still occasionally worn during festivities by mulatto and *mestizo* women in parts of Guerrero and Oaxaca.

The beading of men's gala shirts has virtually died out, yet in the Otomí village of San Pablito a few examples may still be seen, with hat-bands of netted beadwork (see p. 165). This last technique is also a speciality in Huichol communities, where male sashes, hat-bands and bags of netted beadwork are highly prized. Featuring brilliantly coloured butterflies, deer, double-headed eagles and flowers, they are worn with armlets and pectorals which depend upon agave or, more recently nylon, thread (see p. 64). Outside the costume field, a further instance of beading is provided by Tarascan *servilletas* in Pichátaro and Uricho, Michoacán. Woven from white cotton, they are decorated along one side by a wide fringe worked with a multitude of beads depicting animals, flowers and geometrical designs.

Pleating is an important skill in Michoacán, where many Tarascan women continue to wear unique and eye-catching skirts of blue-black or red wool. A description from the turn of the century by Frederick Starr recorded one as comprising fourteen webs of cloth: sewn vertically side by side, these formed a pleated tube with a circumference of 22 ft (6.7 m). Today measurements are rarely so extreme; skirts are produced on a treadle loom instead of a backstrap loom, yet they remain heavy and require numerous woven sashes to keep them in position. High-backed and worn over a white embroidered underskirt, these magnificent wrap-around garments lie flat at the front but display a profusion of thick European-style pleats at the back. According to Isabel Marín de Paalen, this effect is created by folding the cloth when damp, then leaving it for several days under a *metate*, or grinding-stone. In the past women arranged the skirt about their bodies each time they dressed, but there is a growing trend towards securing the pleats permanently on a waistband. Pleats are popular too with the Nahua of San Sebastián Zinacatepec, Puebla, where skirts are made from dark blue cotton cloth that has been treadle-loomed in or near Oaxaca City. When Donald and Dorothy Cordry visited the village in the 1960s trade was controlled by a single woman who fetched the cloth, prepared the skirts in two sections, farmed them out for pleating to local families, and then finished them off by hand. Gathered on to a waistband and featuring an upper section of *manta*, skirts are worn in unusual fashion by tying above the breast.

Ruffles, frills, tucks and other tailored embellishments are generally confined to European-style garments such as blouses and gathered skirts. Often these are teamed with indigenous garments as in Metlatonoc, Guerrero, where beautifully brocaded *huipiles* are worn over flounced, ankle-length skirts on waistbands. The costume used by Seri women is wholly indicative of foreign influence, however: adopted towards the end of the last century as a result of missionary teachings, it is semi-Victorian in appearance and features a high-necked, long-sleeved bodice with buttons down the front and a frill which hangs below the waist. Skirts are long, gathered, and likewise hand-sewn from factory materials. In general men's clothing is less ornate than that of their womenfolk, but there are a few instances where shirts have benefited from skilful trimming. In the Tojolabal region of Las Margaritas, Chiapas, shirts are characterised by a profusion of vertical tucks which cover the chest. When giving each tuck its distinctively serrated edge women habitually resort to using their teeth before hemming it by hand. Cuffs are elegantly adorned to match. *Guayabera* is the name given to the gala shirts of Yucatán. Distinguished by narrow pleats which run from shoulder to hemline, they are however worn almost solely by *mestizos*.

Although many garments – European-influenced as well as traditional – are still assembled by hand, there is a growing acceptance of sewing-machines. Even in

Chinantec everyday cotton *huipil* from San Lucas Ojitlán, Oaxaca. Plain- and gauze-woven on a backstrap loom and assembled with the aid of a sewing-machine, it features embroidered motifs and trimmings of crocheted lace and ribbon. w. 31 in (78.7 cm); L. 35½ in (90.2 cm). Museum of Mankind, London.

comparatively remote villages it is possible today to find a treadle-operated machine ensconced on the dirt floor of a one-roomed house, enabling the proud owner to save time on her own sewing, and also to earn a regular income by seaming or trimming the garments of less fortunate neighbours. The appliquéd skirts of the Amuzgo in Xochistlahuaca, blouses in a number of communities and the *huipiles* of the Mazatec are among the many garments sewn in this way. Even the Chinantec of San Felipe Usila have taken to machine-finishing their carefully woven and over-dyed *huipiles*. Yet, at the other end of the scale, it is also possible to meet with traditionalism and self-sufficiency. An anecdote by Carlota Mapelli Mozzi well illustrates this point for while in the arid Mezquital Valley she saw an Otomí man tear his *manta* trousers. Seeking out a *maguey*, he broke off a spike but left a long fibre trailing. He then proceeded to squeeze the moisture out of the fibre, to twist it with his fingers, and to repair his trousers with this makeshift needle and thread in the manner of his ancestors.

It is this mixture of ancient and modern, of tradition and innovation, which lends such richness and vitality to Mexico's wide range of costumes. In some villages caution and conservatism have favoured natural dyeing methods and preserved the intricacy of native weaving techniques. In other more fashion-conscious communities women have adopted European skills with imagination and ingenuity, welcoming the availability of embroidery threads, colourful ribbons and the other decorative trimmings produced by an industrialised society

Lacandón father and son at Najá, Chiapas; each wears a *xikul*, or male tunic, of industrial cotton cloth. The bark-cloth *xikul*, abandoned in recent decades, is now made for sale to outsiders (see p. 163).

7 Contemporary male dress

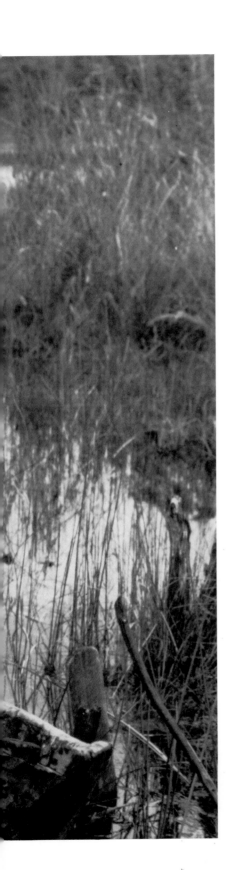

Indian garments, like textile techniques, represent a wide spectrum of styles and influences, ancient as well as modern. Affected more profoundly than female dress by the vicissitudes of Mexican history, male costume continues to offer some remarkable survivals, yet generally combines them with Colonial or even twentieth-century additions. Pressurised after the Conquest to cover their nakedness and to conform to European notions of modesty, Indian men have gained a reputation for being less conservative in their dress than women, and this receptiveness to change has intensified still further over recent decades. One reason for this trend is the fact that men travel further from their communities than women, often seeking work in other states or even in the USA, where village costumes would prove a source of embarrassment and alienation. Shop-bought shirts, trousers and denim jackets are now routinely worn by vast numbers of Indians, whose wives and daughters retain a largely pre-Conquest style of dress, and in many cases it is only the use of sandals or a shoulder-bag that points to a man's heritage and distinguishes him from his *mestizo* neighbours. The last thirty years have seen the demise of several fine costumes, so the tenacity shown by non-acculturated groups is all the more to be admired.

Many striking examples of male dress are to be seen in the Chiapas highlands, where numerous Tzotzil and Tzeltal communities preserve distinctive and instantly recognisable styles which unite villagers and indicate status. Frequent contact with non-Indians during buying and selling expeditions to the town of San Cristóbal has done little to weaken their resolve to retain a separate identity. Many men even make yearly trips lasting several months to the coffee plantations where they adopt modern dress, yet when they return home they revert to their own costume traditions. Equal pride is to be found among Huichol men, who wear their uniquely decorative clothing at all times, even during visits to Mexico City, and who still dress more elaborately than their womenfolk. Geographic isolation has also favoured the Lacandón of Najá, where *huipiles* are worn by men as well as women, and the Tarahumara, whose male garments maintain similarly close links with the past. In Oaxaca handsome hand-woven shirts and trousers are still preferred to shop-bought substitutes by many Amuzgo and Mixtec villagers, who combine them with indigenous elements such as waist-sashes, while in the remoter areas of Puebla and Veracruz men's uniformly white *manta* clothing continues to conform to Indian notions of propriety instilled in earlier times by Spanish missionaries.

Given the pious and overriding concern with male modesty which characterised the Conquest, it is particularly surprising that garments as ancient as the loincloth and the hip-cloth should have survived to the present century and even, in some cases, to the present day. According to Alfonso Villa Rojas, the Maya *ex* persisted in isolated areas of eastern Yucatán until a generation ago, while the Cordrys report seeing several Huichol in the 1930s dressed in shirts and loincloths. The Huave of the Oaxaca coast, the Mayo of Sonora and the Cora of Nayarit were also extremely late in exchanging their breechclouts for trousers – indeed, they are worn even now by small boys from the third group, as well as by conservative adults among the Northern Tepehuan of Chihuahua. Retention of the loincloth has occurred most extensively in modern times within Tarahumara territories, however. Lumholtz, who visited the region in the 1890s, described and photographed many Indians 'whose entire clothing consisted of a breech-cloth'. Fashioned initially from skins or *pita* fibre, and in Lumholtz's time from 'coarse, home-spun woollen material', the *tagora* is made today from commercial white *manta* and frequently worn during the summer months with just a sash for support. According to Fructuoso Irigoyen, who has worked as a doctor among the Tarahumara, a *tagora* can be formed in different ways (see p. 206). Most commonly it is made from a single square of cloth and folded diagonally to create two layers. When the *tagora* is tied round the waist, two corners cross the abdomen, while the third corner of the lower layer is pulled diaper-fashion between the legs and tucked into the sash. The top layer is then left to hang down behind in the manner of a hip-cloth. Carlota Mapelli Mozzi reports that this style is likened by local *mestizos* to a 'pig's ear'. In the region of Norogachic, however, the cloth is folded to form rectangular layers. The lower layer, which is often secured with safety-pins as well as the sash, resembles drawers, while the top layer gives the appearance of a back-skirt. A third widespread alternative features two triangularly folded cloths: one serves as a loin-cloth, the other as a hip-cloth. Embroidered motifs, which include flowers, crosses and solar disks, sometimes pattern the top layer of the *tagora*.

Even the inevitable spread of trousers among the Tarahumara has not negated this important link with the past, for although increasing numbers of men now wear the newer garment, many continue to demonstrate their loyalty to the *tagora* by displaying it like a triangular hip-cloth over the top. This custom, which is shared by some Cora and some Northern Tepehuan, was documented at the end of the last century by Lumholtz, whose photographs show men from this last group and also a Pima and a Tubar Indian dressed in this manner. In central Mexico too a hip-cloth was retained until about 1900 by the Nahua of Altepexi. Triangularly folded over trousers and knotted low down in front, it was recently recreated for – and photographed by – the Cordrys. Rectangular cloths, worn like kilts over trousers and tied on one hip, appear in several turn-of-the-century photographs from Oaxaca, while on the coast of Sonora many Seri men continue to wear equivalent garments with their shop-bought and otherwise conventional clothing. Reaching to the knee, these wrap-around rectangles of coloured cotton closely recall the skirts made from skins which were once worn by both sexes within the group.

Despite the growing popularity of factory-produced belts of leather and plastic, Mexico still boasts an impressive range of woven male sashes. These functional and often decorative garments may have received a degree of inspiration from the broad waist-cloths worn in many regions of Spain, yet their origins undoubtedly lie with the sashes and breechclouts of pre-Conquest times. Dimensions and styles of embellishment are as varied as the methods used to secure them. Tzotzil men from Magdalenas and San Andrés Larrainzar in Chiapas wrap their handsomely woven sashes twice round the waist before knotting them in front with the ends dangling (see pp. 118–19). In Huistán they follow a different custom: frequently measuring an astonishing 15 ft × 20 in (4.6 m × 51 cm), their unusually large sashes are twisted several times around the body; the fringed ends are then looped up and left to hang down on either side of the wearer. A third alternative is demonstrated by the Tacuate of Ixtayutla, whose dark blue everyday belts are tied behind to show a cascade of fringing, and a fourth by the Nahua of Cuetzalán, whose elaborately finished sash ends are knotted on one side and left hanging. As for the Huichol, they secure the plaited fringes of belts by tucking them in. Justly famed for their weaving skills, women from this last group provide their menfolk with a profusion of richly patterned double-woven sashes which are proudly worn one on top of the other, and sometimes accompanied during festivals by colourful belts of netted beadwork (see pp. 58, 59, 205).

Although Tarahumara sashes still support breech-cloths, the majority are now

Section of a Nahua man's plain-woven cotton waist-sash from Cuetzalán, Puebla. Both ends have *macramé* fringes worked with needles, tassels, sequins and wool-embroidered birds and zig-zag lines. w. 6½ in (16.5 cm); total L. 36 in (91.4 cm).

Nahua man from outside Huejutla de Reyes, Hidalgo, wearing clothing of industrial cotton cloth. His *calzón* recalls the homespun garments once worn by Spanish peasants.

worn with European-style trousers. These have been interpreted by Indians in a variety of ways. In many regions the prevailing style is still that of the *calzoncillo*, or long drawers, described and illustrated by many nineteenth-century observers. Over-trousers, which were frequently of leather with vertical leg openings, have been abandoned for everyday wear, although contemporary versions survive as *fiesta* attire in a few villages. Particularly decorative are the *manta* trousers of the Huichol: un-adorned and worn only by a minority in Lumholtz's time, these wide and straight-cut garments have since gained general acceptance and attracted a quantity of embroidered designs along their bottom edges. Huichol trousers incorporate an inset along the crutch, but many garments lack this feature. In Amatenango del Valle, for example, the knee-length *manta* drawers worn by older Tzeltal men are fashioned from two rectangles of cloth. So too are the white cotton trousers favoured near Papantla by the Totonac who emphasise their fullness by tying them in at the ankle. The length of these simple and largely untailored garments is highly variable, ranging from around 36 in (90 cm) in the case of this last group to less than 20 in (51 cm) among some Huave or in parts of Yucatán and Chiapas. Among the shortest are those of Zinacantán which barely reach to mid-thigh, and those of Oxchuc which are totally covered by the overhanging shirts of their Tzeltal wearers. In some Maya villages trousers which are longer when measured are worn rolled up as in San Juan Chamula or Magdalenas (see pp. 118–19). Occasionally, as in Papantla, garments are gathered at the waist with a draw-string, but generally the surplus material is folded across the stomach and secured by a sash.

Many of the trousers just mentioned are assembled from bought cloth, but a few curious and ornate examples are still created on the backstrap loom. One *calzón* which fully deserves both adjectives is that woven in Santa María Zacatepec by the Tacuate, whose embroidery skills have already been mentioned. Embellished along the lower edges by a multitude of colourful motifs and by a border of drawn threadwork, these remarkable trousers are also distinguished by their enormous dimensions which derive

Opposite Tacuate villagers from Santa
María Zacatepec, Oaxaca, *c.* 1900.
Contemporary male garments are more
decorated (see p. 180), but their
construction is unchanged.

from the use of four webs, each measuring approximately 15 × 43 in (38 × 109 cm).
When rolled over at the waist, however, and secured both by a tie-cord and by an
unusually long sash, garments reach only to mid-thigh where they give the appearance of flared and richly decorated shorts. The trousers worn by the Tacuate in
Ixtayutla and other neighbouring villages are similarly fashioned from four webs,
each one measuring 14 × 38 in (35.6 × 96.5 cm), but the legs feature a brocaded
border and are designed to reach to mid-calf, where they end in a tight roll.

Chiapas, like Oaxaca, has retained several home-woven styles, one of the most
notable being that of Tenejapa. There Tzeltal weavers decorate the short four-web
trousers of their menfolk with a final band of predominantly red woollen brocading,
which is almost totally concealed by their woollen over-garments. Weaving is also a
speciality in Venustiano Carranza, where Tzotzil men wear long white cotton trousers
which are brocaded for *fiestas* with red figures of eight. Gathered in at the waist with
the aid of a fine sash and fitting tightly about the ankles, they balloon out over the hips
in a curiously Oriental way. Stranger by far, however, are the Tzotzil trousers of
Huistán: described rather disparagingly by local *mestizos* as a *calzón pañal* ('diaper-like
drawers') they comprise four webs of plain-woven white cotton cloth which are hand-
seamed to create two gigantic trouser legs, each with a circumference of 60 in (152.4 cm)
and a length of 35 in (89 cm). When in use, the great width of both legs is pulled up in
front to reveal the wearer's thighs, while the backs and sides remain covered. The
voluminous folds of cloth are then secured at the waist by a tie-cord and by the
necessarily long sashes described above.

Missionary zeal during Colonial times was also responsible for the introduction of
shirts. The Huichol, who came briefly under Franciscan influence, adopted hand-
woven shirts of dark brown wool with their loincloths. Largely unadorned and open-
sided, they were succeeded at the turn of this century by the *manta* shirts which have
become such a decorative element of contemporary male costume. The ingenuity
with which many groups interpreted alien garments such as shirts and trousers is
much to be admired, and Lumholtz was greatly struck by the skill of the Papago of
Sonora. In *New Trails in Mexico* he noted: 'The women are clever in adapting themselves to the new conditions. I know of an instance where the wife made a shirt for her
husband without ever having learned how to cut it out, and the garment, when
finished, was very creditably done.'

Most shirts are today made from *manta* and other bought cloths. Styles and proportions vary from village to village, but the majority are loose-fitting, buttonless, and
worn outside the trousers, thereby concealing the sash or belt. The tucks and pleats
favoured in Tojolabal communities and in parts of Yucatán have already been mentioned, as have the brilliant colours of many Trique shirts. Other variations include
the embroidered *manta* shirts of the Mazahua, with animal motifs across the chest,
and the gleaming white poplin shirts of Papantla's Totonac. Elegantly finished with
large square collars, pockets and cuffs, these last are thought – like the distinctively
shaped trousers that accompany them – to have evolved after contact with French
sailors. Also interesting are the shirts adopted by many Tarahumara. Made from
manta, or alternatively from red or flowered cotton, they carry a pleated front panel,
gathered sleeves and narrow cuffs.

Home-woven shirts, like trousers, are generally fashioned from rectangular webs
of cloth. Brocading occurs in some Amuzgo villages, while in Jamiltepec, Pinotepa
Nacional and other Mixtec centres many weavers still use either *coyuche* or hand-

spun white cotton which they occasionally combine with *caracol*-dyed thread to create warp stripes. In Santa María Zacatepec the body of the shirt is provided by a single web of cloth which is folded and cut to make an opening for the head. What is remarkable, however, is the length of the web which averages 110 in (280 cm). Totally unsewn at the sides and featuring two rectangular sleeves which are joined only at the wrist, this unique garment resembles a gigantic T. The method of wearing is equally spectacular, for both the front and the slightly longer back-section are gathered up and looped over the sash, with the foremost fold providing a useful pouch for possessions. According to Carlota Mapelli Mozzi, the back length was formerly left trailing, thereby earning Tacuate villagers the name of *coludos*, or 'tailed-ones', among their *mestizo* neighbours.

In Chiapas hand-woven shirts have been retained by a number of Tzotzil and Tzeltal communities. Venustiano Carranza is characterised by the variety of brocaded motifs that embellish not only *huipiles* but also men's single-web shirts. Rectangular sleeves and a collar formed from an additional strip of cloth complete these unusually short garments which often stop high above the waist. Not one but two main webs are used in the Tzotzil villages of Huistán, Santa Catarina Pantelhó, San Miguel Mitontic and San Pedro Chenalhó. Woven from white cotton and seamed down the middle to leave an opening for the head, they have a narrow strip of cloth at the back of the neck which creates a collar while gathering the folds of cloth. Sides are left unsewn, and the rectangular sleeves are joined only at their extremities. Whereas shirts from the last two villages are knee-length, with a band of woollen brocading on the forearm to distinguish villagers from Mitontic, those from Huistán are worn tucked in and are embellished with embroidery for *fiestas*. In Pantelhó, however, garments are often folded unevenly, making them substantially longer at the back than at the front, and patterned with a profusion of brocaded motifs or with a series of *coyuche*-brown warp stripes. In Tzeltal communities such as Oxchuc and Cancuc shirts feature four webs which meet down the centre and along the shoulder-line. Seams are decorative and sides are closed, except for a gap of about 10 in (25 cm) below the armpit. In Oxchuc woollen brocading adorns the chest area and the sleeves, which are so exceptionally narrow that wearers often prefer to leave them empty and to put their arms through the space below.

The form taken by many of these tunic-like shirts is very similar to that of a *huipil* with additional sleeves. In the rain-forests of Chiapas, however, true *huipiles* are still worn by the Lacandón men of Najá. Formerly the *xikul*, which derives its name from the Aztec word *xicolli*, was made from bark cloth, but since the 1940s this ancient material has been totally superseded by cotton. Today only a few older men favour home-woven garments, which are assembled from two centrally seamed webs. Younger members of the group prefer shop-bought *manta*, which they say is lighter, cooler and smoother in texture. Their labour-saving *huipiles* are therefore fashioned from a single width, which is folded to knee-length and cut to provide an opening for the head. Despite greatly increased contact with the outside world, men at Najá show no desire to abandon their highly distinctive form of dress, because they find it practical and well suited to forest life. The *xikul* offers them freedom of movement while they hunt, work their land or manoeuvre their great dug-out canoes across the lake, and when they squat down on their haunches to rest it can also afford tent-like protection against flies or the coolness of a winter evening (see p. 192).

The front-opening *xicolli*, portrayed in ancient times and likened by chroniclers to 'a jacket with two flaps', is paralleled today by the *cotorina*. This waist-length, sleeve-less over-garment, woven from wool and fringed, is worn in several villages in the states of Mexico, Tlaxcala and Hidalgo. Close similarity with the early *xicolli* would seem to be fortuitous, however, because according to Ruth D. Lechuga the *cotorina* is a recent innovation emanating from commercial treadle-loom centres. For most Indians it is the *sarape* and its many variations that provide covering during cold weather: extremely versatile and often very decorative, a man's *sarape* is a treasured possession which lasts him for many years and may even accompany him to the grave. As Sartorius noted in the last century, 'it is a symbol of his dignity, which goes with him to market or to church and which he only leaves off at home, or while working'.

Despite rising sales of acrylic factory-made blankets, treadle-loom workshops exist in numerous centres throughout Mexico to meet the demand for durable wool-woven *sarapes*. Saltillo and San Miguel de Allende, which rose to fame during the Colonial period, continue production using old as well as new designs. The use of gold and silver thread, or silk, has long since died out, however. Equally celebrated in recent times is San Francisco Xonacatlán in the state of Mexico. Here undyed wools are hand-spun, then tapestry-woven to create elaborate landscapes featuring flowers, birds, horses, dogs and elegant step-fret borders. Slow to complete, a single *sarape* can remain on the loom for up to six weeks. Also distinctive are weavings from Coatepec Harinas and San Miguel Chiconcuac (see p. 128). Characterised by the intricacy and boldness of their geometric markings, they are widely sold in market-places in the state of Mexico. The retention of natural colourants by many weavers in Santa Ana del Valle, Oaxaca, has already been mentioned, while *sarapes* from near-by Teotitlán del Valle are frequently distinguished by a large, centrally positioned red rose with rounded petals. Additional to the regional designs, faithfully adhered to in these and other centres, are the borrowings which often occur: commercially minded weavers in San Bernardino Contla, for example, have mastered a broad range of patterns inspired variously by Oaxacan and Tarascan weavings, by popular interpretations of pre-Conquest idols, plumed warriors and step-fret motifs, and even by cross-stitch pattern-books.

Although the term *sarape* applies to all treadle-loomed blankets, whether or not they have openings for the head, there are a number of other names to describe similar but usually smaller garments. The *gabán* and the *jorongo* have head openings and are still woven on a backstrap loom in many places. Fine examples, which rely on the natural colours of the wool for patterning, are woven in Hueyapan in Morelos, in parts of Hidalgo and Puebla, and in the Chiapas highlands where the term *chamarro* has gained currency. Shaped like an open-sided *huipil*, these highly practical garments often feature two webs which are joined as in Hueyapan to leave an opening for the head. Alternatively, they may consist of a single web which has been woven with a *kelim* slot, or cut as in most Chiapas villages to give a square or rounded neckline which is reinforced with tape and stitched.

The women of San Juan Chamula remain prolific weavers and furnish surrounding villages with *chamarros* of different designs. Among their many clients are the Tzeltal of Tenejapa, who have only recently begun to use factory-made shirts beneath their black and white striped top-garments, and the Tzotzil of San Andrés Larrainzar. As for the men of Chamula, they favour fringed garments of white wool for everyday wear but adopt black ones on ceremonial occasions if their status demands it. Their thick and felt-like texture, arrived at by washing, beating and shrinking the cloth after it has left the loom, makes these *chamarros* not only extremely warm but also virtually rainproof (see pp. 120, 207).

Not wool but cotton is used in Zinacantán, where men wear a two-web over-garment called a *colera*. Woven with red and white warps, it has a candy-striped appearance, a colourful line of embroidery above the final fringe, and tasselled cords which serve as fastenings at the sides. A similar garment has been retained by the Tarahumara of Chihuahua. Used by small boys and by some men, it is a single open-sided width of cotton cloth which is generally worn over a shirt. According to Campbell W. Pennington, this may derive from *pita* garments found in local Basketmaker sites, and from later woollen garments likened in 1682 by a Jesuit priest to a 'dalmatic without sleeves' (see p. 167).

The term *cotón*, which applies to many of the rectangular shirts mentioned earlier, also describes similar garments of wool. Popular with the Nahua of Puebla, the woollen *cotón* remained the only torso-garment in many villages until the end of the nineteenth century. In the Cuetzalán region it is backstrap-woven and generally black, with sleeves which are too narrow for use. Regarded as a decorative feature, they are left to hang loosely over the wearer's arms which protrude through the *cotón*'s unsewn sides. Sleeved garments of black wool are also woven in Chiapas by the Tzotzil weavers of San Juan Chamula. Heavily felted and fashioned principally from a single web like other *chamarros*, these splendid garments are partially seamed at the sides and are reserved for men of high authority. The Tzeltal of Amatenango del Valle and Agua-catenango also wear dark woollen *cotones*, but theirs come from Guatemala where they are decoratively machine-stitched along the neck opening. Sleeves are wide, but are often left empty.

Although men from most groups favour woollen garments which slip over the head, there are still communities where blankets are used without this opening. One of these is Huistán, where striped black and white rectangles of cloth are carried over one shoulder until needed. Ceremonial all-black blankets are sometimes used as capes by Tzotzil dignitaries in villages such as Zinacantán, while across the state boundary in Oaxaca the Mixtec inhabitants of San Sebastián Peñoles derive considerable warmth from thick two-web twilled blankets.

Tarahumara blankets, which recall early *pita* examples, are wrapped Navajo-style about the body to protect wearers from the chill of winter. Lumholtz, who visited this hardy people at the end of the last century, noted with amazement: 'The Tarahumara endures cold unflinchingly. On an icy winter morning, when there are six inches of snow on the ground, many a man may be seen with nothing on but his blanket fastened round his waist, pursuing rabbits'. Other novel uses apparently included fishing, when several blankets were knotted together to form a 'large and serviceable net', and marriage ceremonies during which the bridal couple was covered with blankets. Today weaving is still considered a wifely duty, although blankets do not always carry the 'admirable designs' common in Lumholtz's time. Nor are they always destined to be worn by the weaver's family, being often intended for barter with *mestizo* pedlars or for use as wagers during highly competitive foot-races. Successful gamblers may take possession of numerous weavings after these events, leaving less fortunate Tarahumara to manage as best they can with the ragged remains of cheap factory blankets. Life among the largely acculturated Mayo is very different: close proximity with non-Indians has eroded their costume traditions, and today their clothing is virtually indistinguishable from that of their neighbours. In some con-

servative families, however, ring-woven blankets remain an important symbol of Mayo identity. Among the finest in Mexico, they are used as coverings at night and occasionally sold to collectors at high prices.

The pre-Conquest *tilmatli*, or rectangular cloak, identified by many as a possible precursor to the *sarape*, survives today among many Otomí in the states of Mexico and Hidalgo. Woven from *ixtle*, as were low-class garments within the Aztec empire, contemporary *ayates* are fashioned from two webs and used as carrying-cloths. Finely textured examples, which occasionally display brocaded or embroidered motifs in wool, are presented as gifts during weddings and other ceremonial events. Cotton *ayates* are also woven in a few villages. Bodil Christensen has reported seeing white festival *ayates* with cross-stitched corners in San Pablito, while in San Miguel Ameyalco in the state of Mexico girls traditionally weave colourfully brocaded *ayates* for their sweethearts.

To supplement the lack of pockets in Indian dress men from all regions carry distinctive shoulder-bags, or *morrales*, which often combine utility with great beauty (see pp. 57, 59). The widespread use of vegetable fibres, whether netted or woven, has already been described, together with the decorative methods employed. Woven *morrales* of cotton or wool also occur in many areas, generally with richly patterned shoulder-straps. Although owners take great pride in their bags, enthusiasm rarely equals that of Huichol men who generally display at least two. Arranged to cross from opposite shoulders, these are accompanied during festivals by a number of others which may be double-woven, beaded or fashioned from exquisitely embroidered *manta*. The Huichol predilection for bags is further reinforced by a succession of miniature examples which are fastened together with twisted tie-cords and worn about the waist. Despite their obvious uses, *morrales* and sashes in such quantity are worn, as the anthropologist Robert M. Zingg noted in 1938, 'for pure swank'. In Chiapas leather constitutes the substance of many shoulder-bags: although skins are home-cured by some Indians, men from Zinacantán and a few other communities prefer to buy their *morrales* in San Cristóbal from *mestizo* craftsmen, who not only tool and fringe the leather to their taste but also add tufts of red and black wool to bags which are intended for ceremonial use (see p. 120). Throughout the highlands many men also carry small money purses which may be netted, made from suede or woven.

Countless Indians in Chiapas and other regions continue to go barefoot, except during *fiestas* or when visiting local towns. For the majority, however, sandals, or *huaraches*, are an essential feature symbolising Indian culture as apart from *mestizo* shoe culture, and it is significant that national census forms should include questions dealing not only with language and literacy but also with footwear. Techniques for plaiting sandals from strips of yucca and palm have been mentioned earlier: Lumholtz mourned the decline of palm sandals among the Huichol, noting that the style was 'not only better looking, but also less slippery and therefore more serviceable' than the rawhide variety, which also has a long tradition in Mexico and which predominates today. Among the Nahua of Cuetzalán, as among many other groups, the leather sole is attached to the foot by a front thong which separates the big toe from the rest, and by strands which pass across the instep and behind the heel. For ceremonial wear in the Chiapas highlands many Indians have retained the high-backed *caites* of ancient times. Made in San Juan Chamula, these feature unusually thick and inflexible soles composed of several layers of leather which are nailed together. Heel supports are rigid and painted black, and their height ranges from around $3\frac{1}{2}$ in (9 cm) in Chamula to a maximum of 10 in (25.4 cm) in Huistán. Although these remarkable sandals are tied so as to give the feet freedom of movement, calves are sometimes chafed by taller versions.

As an alternative to conservative village-made styles, most markets offer more modern sandals with leather straps which cross the toes and car-tyre soles which are becoming increasingly popular because of their durability. Even the Huichol have begun to use rubber soles, but they are careful, according to Fernando Benítez, never to bury their fully costumed dead with sandals of this type lest the car-tyres reinflate in the afterlife. Modern technology has also provided the traditionally barefoot Lacandón with rubber boots. Gratefully adopted by the young, because they furnish protection from marshy ground and more importantly from venomous snakes, they are worn with no apparent sense of incongruity under their white *huipiles*.

Palm hats are widely worn by rural workers throughout Mexico, yet they also constitute an essential costume element for most Indians, who would never think of appearing bareheaded outside the home. Looked on like the *sarape* as a symbol of male dignity, the *sombrero* provides shelter from rain as well as sun, if as in many regions it is fitted with a polythene cover. Even with shop or market-bought hats it is generally possible to tell at a glance where a man is from, since most states have evolved a particular style. Designs are less extreme than formerly, however, with lower crowns and more modest brims. Hats are often trimmed with strips of leather or *henequén* cord, but occasionally Indians add their own decorations for *fiestas*. Near Papantla, for example, Totonac hats are sometimes embellished at the brim with fresh or plastic flowers, while Mayo musicians often use paper ones.

Predictably the greatest diversity is to be found with home-made hats. The exquisitely beaded hatbands of San Pablito's Otomí have already been mentioned, and the custom also persists among the Huichol who occasionally use them instead of double-woven ribbons. Other Huichol decorations include bindings and crosses of flannel, clusters of iridescent plumes, bead droplets, colourful woollen pom-poms, seed-pods, *madroño* leaves, squirrel tails, deer hooves and even metal rings from the lids of beer cans. Although a wide array of trimmings is worn during local *fiestas*, the full complement is generally the prerogative of pilgrims who make the long and arduous journey to gather *peyote* – the hallucinatory cactus known to botanists as *Lophophora williamsii*. Such is the elegance and splendour of Huichol hats that only those from the Chiapas highlands can rival them. Delicately patterned by a combination of natural and black-dyed palm strands, these remarkable creations conform to a variety of shapes. Instantly recognisable are the hats of Huistán with their flat brims and small, low crowns surrounded by a length of woven red wool, or the hats of Tenejapa with their concave brims and peaked crowns decorated with four bunches of brilliantly coloured ribbons and a red tassel. It is not difficult to see parallels between these fanciful *sombreros* and the glorious head-dresses and hats of the ancient Maya, or to identify the streaming ribbons of Zinacantán with the towering plumes of the past.

Waterproof black felt, impregnated with tar or wax, has long provided Indians with an alternative material for hat-making, and styles closely recall those of Spain. Hard, with a rounded crown and a straight brim, they are still occasionally worn in parts of Oaxaca, although their use is becoming increasingly rare. Unusually lavish examples, with silver cords and embroidered lettering, were once worn in Tehuantepec during *fiestas*, but these have all but disappeared, as have the beribboned hats favoured until recently by Tacuate dignitaries in Santa María Zacatepec. Ceremonial use continues in the highlands of Chiapas, however. There black felt hats serve as symbols of authority, and in Zinacantán these are often distinguished by ribbons or by a feather. Throughout this region hats of both felt and palm may be worn during *fiestas* over head-cloths of differing styles and colours (see p. 207). On pictorial evidence similar combinations were popular during the nineteenth century with Creoles (see p. 53).

The wearing of head-cloths without hats also continues in some Chiapas villages, although the custom has now disappeared among Oaxaca's Chinantec. In Venustiano Carranza Tzotzil men complete their striking gala costumes with richly brocaded red cotton kerchiefs, which they wrap pirate style about their heads. The *poc* is a square cloth of chequered design which is treadle-loomed in San Cristóbal for the men of Zinacantán. Trimmed with pink woollen tassels, it is generally worn as a triangular shoulder-cape, but it can also be used on the head, with or without a hat, as a protection against cold or heat. Factory-made bandanna handkerchiefs known as *paliacates* may occasionally serve as head-cloths among old men from Amatenango del Valle or from Zoque villages, but elsewhere in Mexico they are widely used as neckcloths. Predominantly red and gaily patterned, they are sold in every market and worn even in remote communities. Among the Totonac of Papantla, however, distinctive neckcloths of brightly coloured *artisela* or nylon are preferred for festive wear with embroidered borders and floral motifs in one corner.

Hair adornments are rare among male Indians, who mostly follow the Western lead and opt for 'civilised' haircuts, especially during festivities. To show respect for the saint whose day is to be celebrated men in the Puebla highlands and elsewhere generally visit the villager whose role is that of barber and receive a 'short back and sides' in his front yard or in the main square. There are exceptions among the Huichol, however, many of whom wear a pudding-bowl style with a fringe, or else allow it to grow long and restrain it with a woven headband or plait it with tapes. Conservative Tarahumara also eschew short hair, preferring a pageboy bob which is held in place by a *coyera*, or headband, of bought cotton cloth. Narrowly folded and wrapped about the head, it is secured with the ends trailing, and is often decoratively wound with narrow ribbons or ornamented with safety-pins (see pp. 201, 206). Very occasionally hats are worn over these headbands, which are paralleled by early *pita* examples.

On ceremonial occasions Tzotzil dignitaries from Huistán also adopt headbands, but theirs are home-woven, extremely stiff, and worn perched far back on their closely shorn heads. In the forests of Chiapas, however, long hair is still favoured by the Lacandón of Najá who wear it unconfined, with a fringe to distinguish them from their womenfolk. Ironically, when they visit San Cristóbal, any mockery inspired by their flowing locks and long *huipiles* is generally levelled by other Indians, who taunt them with their feminine appearance. Among the Seri of Sonora long hair and retention of the hip-cloth seem to be linked. Those who adhere to tradition wear their hair loose or in a single plait, but those who abandon the hip-cloth prefer to cut it short. Reports by Frederick Starr on the Huave and the Otomí indicate that male hair-styles were more varied at the end of the last century. Facial hair, once so disliked by the Maya, is not generally popular with Indians, although a small minority do achieve sparse beards and moustaches. Few contemporary groups can equal the aversion felt by the Tarahumara to facial hair, however. According to Lumholtz, it reminded them of 'the fur on a bear', and they refused to smoke the tobacco proferred by white men for fear of getting their beards.

One of the most significant changes to occur since the Conquest has been the

Huichol man from San Andrés Cohamiata, Jalisco, painting his face for a festival. He wears a pectoral and bracelet of netted beadwork, woven sashes, a *paliacate*, and a richly embroidered shirt and shoulder-bag.

Illustration by Carl Lumholtz showing facial painting by Huichol *peyote*-pilgrims. Motifs represent clouds, maize, *peyote* and coiled serpents, symbols of rain.

almost total abandonment of male jewellery. Of the magnificent pectorals of gold and silver, the flaring jade ear-plugs and the anklets nothing today remains. The Maya custom of piercing the septum of the nose persisted among the Lacandón, who sometimes inserted feathers, but even this has been discontinued since the 1940s. Only the Huichol continue to make regular use of male adornments. Inspired by the introduction of *chaquira*, or small glass beads, which doubtless replaced seeds and berries, the Huichol have long been adept at netting the colourful and figuratively decorated pectorals, bracelets and earrings worn in such profusion (see p. 64). Strings of beans, seeds and wooden beads are also worn by some Tarahumara, who add a modestly carved cross in memory of Jesuit teachings. Ornaments are rarely found outside these two groups, however, except in cases of illness or misfortune when a man might adopt a talisman, or during *fiestas* when, as in Tenejapa, dignitaries are distinguished by long rosaries hung with medallions and a cross. Altogether more modern are the sunglasses anachronistically displayed by some Huichol during recent festivities, or the large and newly acquired watches enjoyed and ceaselessly consulted by younger Lacandón men.

Face and body painting, which Spanish missionaries tried with great zeal to suppress, is still practised by some Indians. During very important Lacandón ceremonies both men and women are daubed with annatto on their foreheads, cheeks, chins, wrists and ankles. Among the Huichol facial decoration is also shared by both sexes during *fiestas*, although male designs are often more elaborate. During the events of Holy Week male participants from Tarahumara and Cora communities paint not only their faces but also their bodies for rituals and dances which combine Christian elements with pagan traditions (see pp. 167, 206).

As in ancient times *fiestas* mark the high point of village life, with the whole com-

205

munity sharing in the often costly preparations. Costume is an important aspect, and even the poorest villager contrives to keep a change of clothing for festive occasions, while weavers in some groups like to equip themselves and their menfolk with new garments. Cleanliness and neatness are a constant preoccupation with most Indians, but during *fiestas* they are of paramount importance. Some gala additions have already been mentioned, such as the flower-trimmed hats and colourful kerchiefs of the lowland Totonac; in addition, the status of those in authority is symbolised within most communities by special items of dress which are denied to the rank and file. In the Chiapas highlands, where hierarchies of native officials, or *alféreces*, still wield great power, ceremonial attributes abound and include the hats, head-cloths, headbands, waist-sashes, rosaries, high-backed sandals, black *chamarros* and capes which have been described.

Some idea of the significance attaching to such garments can be gauged from the writings of Frank Cancian, who reports that one informant in Zinacantán contracted for the weaving of his ceremonial robe while still six years from office. Information is also provided by Marta Turok, who notes that in Magdalenas ceremonial garments

Male Tarahumara with face and body painting during Easter celebrations in Norogachic, Chihuahua. They wear cotton loincloths, wool sashes, sandals, headbands and feather head-dresses. Voluminous cotton sashes may be used to carry possessions.

Tzotzil dignitaries in San Juan Chamula, Chiapas. They wear head-cloths, hats with ribbons and a tassel, wool *chamarros* and suede sashes. Sandals are from San Cristóbal de las Casas.

are hired out to dignitaries, and woven only by a few privileged weavers. Additional symbols take in the silver-topped staffs of authority which are passed on to new incumbents, the necklaces of ribbons which are worn in some communities, and the exquisitely brocaded sashes which are displayed about the neck in Tenejapa. For sheer dignity few can equal these magnificently attired officials as they preside over festivals, meet to settle local disputes, or keep order in the village market-place. During weddings some of this splendour is also accorded to bridegrooms, especially in Zinacantán where several layers of clothing are required. Garments combine native and Spanish influences by including high-backed sandals, a cape, an unusually long head-cloth, a black felt hat and bottle-green velvet breeches to the knee.

Outside Chiapas ceremonial garments are fewer but they are often very fine. In Ixtayutla, for example, handsome sashes featuring weft bands of cochineal-dyed silk are handed down by each Tacuate dignitary to his successor and replaced only when they become ragged. During festivals most Huichol men contrive to deck themselves out in richly embroidered clothing, with an array of bags, sashes and beadwork. Some also adopt elegant shoulder-capes triangularly folded and edged along the upper layer with cross-stitching and red flannel (see p. 59). The greatest splendour, however, is achieved by *peyote* pilgrims who are under a spiritual obligation to wear their best costumes for the journey. As for the *mará'akáme*, or shaman, who accompanies them and who guides community members through the various rituals which punctuate the Huichol year, he may choose to dress modestly and show his disregard for material possessions, or he may prefer to underline his powers by the magnificence of his attire.

Dances are an essential feature of most festivals and are often performed by villagers long after the disappearance of other cultural traits such as language and costume. Those who participate take their roles seriously, for dancing is traditionally seen as a way of praying and of serving the community. The necessary regalia, which are often extremely costly, are paid for by performers and their families, and the various elements show a wide range of influences. Numerous villages are committed to the re-enactment of biblical themes, with participants adopting fanciful, hybrid costumes to play the parts of Pharisees, devils, shepherds and angels. Alternatively, dances recount the defeat of exotically garbed Moors by the Christians of Spain, or the subsequent Conquest of Mexico, and great initiative goes into the making of armour, helmets and velvet breeches.

European influence is also evident in other areas. In Zinacantán, during the festival of San Sebastián, male dignitaries dress up as *Caballeros Españoles* and *Damas Españolas* (Spanish Gentlemen and Gentlewomen), while in Tenejapa the red cloth jackets and side-buttoning breeches worn during *Carnaval* are a reminder of nineteenth-century fashions. So too are the beautifully appliquéd over-trousers of leather, with buttons made from Mexican and Guatemalan coins, adopted by Zoque men during *fiestas* (see p. 100). Elsewhere the legacies of Spanish rule are demonstrated by dazzling examples of gold and silver embroidery and exquisite displays of sequins (see pp. 174, 175).

By contrast the frequent use of animal disguises provides continuity with pre-Conquest traditions, although attempts to portray the warriors and emperors of ancient Mexico produce costumes as hybrid as those which apply to the Spaniards. Nevertheless, despite the passage of time, a few dances do retain vestiges of ancient splendour. One such is the *Danza de los Quetzales*, for although performers now wear fringed trousers and satin capes, their immense and colourful head-dresses offer a vision of male glory which has all but vanished from the modern world.

8   Contemporary female dress

Tzotzil weaver in Magdalenas, Chiapas, winding weft yarn on to a cane bobbin. Her brocaded *huipil* is only partially tucked into her two-web indigo-dyed *enredo*; the wide woollen sash is from San Juan Chamula.

Although women's costumes may also incorporate garments of foreign inspiration, they generally reflect a far greater continuity with native styles than those of their menfolk. Freed after the Conquest from the sumptuary laws which had restricted their dress, the rank and file were able to take on – albeit in a modified form – the raiment of the old ruling class. Missionaries' concern with modesty brought about certain changes, it is true, yet despite their teachings even the custom of going topless was retained by many women in remoter areas. An 1828 illustration by Linati showed a Zapotec girl from Tehuantepec with just the flounce of her head-dress to conceal her breasts (see p. 98), while Lumholtz noted in 1902 that Tarahumara women donned a tunic only when away from home. In several unacculturated Maya and Zoque villages, in Quintana Roo and Chiapas respectively, toplessness in the home remained usual among older women right up until the 1940s, and the practice endures to this day in several Nahua and Popoluca communities in southern Veracruz, as well as in Pinotepa de Don Luis and surrounding Mixtec settlements.

Enredos, or wrap-around skirts, whether worn on their own or accompanied by a torso-garment, are assembled and arranged in a variety of ways, and are known by a number of other names both Spanish and Indian. Elegant and often distinctively patterned, they are still backstrap-woven in many communities and sometimes consist of just a single web. In San Andrés Chicahuaxtla striped cotton rectangles are wrapped sarong-style about their Trique wearers to form unusually short knee-length skirts (see p. 164), while in Santa Ana Hueytlalpan Otomí weavers seam wider lengths of *añil*-dyed blue or black woollen cloth to make tubes. These heavy skirts, which weigh up to $6\frac{1}{2}$ lb (3 kg), are folded to give three layers at the back and a series of deep pleats on the wearer's left hip. Occasionally, as among the Otomí of Santiago Temoaya, a section of *manta* may be sewn along the top of a one-web skirt to give additional length. Far more usual are the two-web skirts which are to be found in villages such as Hueyapan in Morelos, where they are woollen and tubular in shape, or Yalalag in Oaxaca, where they are open-ended and woven from cotton. In the Mixtec villages surrounding Pinotepa Nacional skirts are similarly open-ended but fashioned from three webs which are wrapped about the limbs without fullness or pleats. In San Pablito Otomí weavers employ six horizontal webs for their tubular garments – a number only exceeded in the past by the backstrap-woven skirts of Michoacán. Treadle-loomed lengths known as *cortes* and factory-made cloth also provide villagers in many regions with wrap-around styles, open-ended as well as closed-sewn.

In the vast majority of cases waist-sashes play a vital role by securing the often voluminous folds of cloth. When arranging them anew each morning, wearers generally pull skirt tops high above the waistline before turning them down inside or outside over the sash. More rarely they are left as in San José Miahuatlán to stand up like a ruff in front, or as in Michoacán to form an immensely high back termed a *rollo*, which is suitable for carrying a child or a bulky load. Although women's sashes are identical with those of their menfolk in a few villages such as Huamelula, designs and measurements usually differ widely. The narrowest belts in existence must surely be those of Cuanajo, which sometimes measure just 1 in (2.54 cm) across, and the broadest those of Santo Tomás Mazaltepec, which have an average width of 17 in (43 cm) and a length of 130 in (330 cm). Worn in pairs with a *soyate*, or palm tube, for additional support, these form a tyre about the wearer's waist. Because they are flexible yet have a rough surface which adheres well to cloth, *soyates* are favoured in a number of other Oaxacan villages as well as in some areas of Puebla, where they are concealed by the generally single sashes to which they are attached. In regions such as Chiapas where palm extensions are not used, however, sashes are woven with sufficient length to encircle the waist at least twice. The pairing of belts without a *soyate* also occurs in Tenejapa, Jamiltepec, Tetelcingo and in some parts of Michoacán.

Sashes are prized in most communities not only for their utility but also for their decorative value. Costumes which are predominantly white or sombre in colour benefit from the addition of a bright sash, while vivid ensembles are further enhanced. Even when concealed from view by long *huipiles*, sashes often demonstrate considerable workmanship, yet not all are woven in the villages where they are worn. In Chiapas, for example, many originate in San Juan Chamula where they are patterned for sale to surrounding communities. As for the Zapotec sashes of Santo Tomás Jalieza, these are sought after in many Mixtec communities, and it has even been reported by Lilly de Jongh Osborne that Pokoman women in Mixco, Guatemala, 'would not consider wearing any other kind of belt but these'. Given the long trade routes still followed by many pedlars, it is not surprising that wearers should often be unable to say where their sashes are made, but know only that they come periodically 'from somewhere far away'.

Reinforcing the importance of women's sashes within many Indian groups is a strong belief in their medical value. Binding is thought to give valuable support to the stomach, especially during pregnancy, while the woven designs of sashes are believed by the coastal Mixtec to help the Rainbow of the West ward off the Rainbow of the East which might harm the unborn child. Even outwardly acculturated women often continue to use short sashes under Western-style clothing for what they say is the 'good of their health'. It is all the more interesting, therefore, that in Venustiano Carranza tubular wrap-around skirts should be secured not by sashes but by twisting the excess cloth and tucking it in at the waist (see p. 61). Photographs taken during the 1940s by Donald Cordry show that today's richly embroidered garments are narrower and shorter than formerly, yet the folds still provide Tzotzil wearers with a *bolsa*, or bag, on the right-hand side. This style has died out in recent decades among the Zoque, but when the Cordrys visited the region it was still in evidence among older women, whose extraordinarily voluminous skirts frequently required the assistance of a second person before they could be properly secured.

European-inspired skirts, or *enaguas*, which are gathered on to a waistband, have been adopted in many communities during recent decades because they are lighter and require no effort in their arrangement. Older women often deplore this trend, but younger relatives tend to look on the old-style skirts as less 'civilised'. Fabrics are rarely home-woven, and styles have evolved to include flounces, lace trimmings, appliquéd ribbons and embroidery as already described, while methods for fitting them to the waist include tie-cords and elastic. A taste for wearing two or more skirts is shared by the Tarahumara and the Mazahua. Within this first group colourful cretonne garments are fully gathered and may number three or four in winter, while many women from the second group favour one, two and even three *enaguas* of *manta* which they top with a skirt and an apron of brilliantly coloured *artisela*. Both continue to employ woven sashes to position their several layers (see pp. 168, 169).

Aprons were once an important accessory in country areas of Spain but in Mexico they seem to be a twentieth-century addition. In recent decades they have caught on not just with the Mazahua but with women from many other groups as well. The decorative value of Tarascan aprons has already been touched upon, but the effect is not always so pleasing when cheap factory-made articles are worn over fine hand-woven costumes. Sadly this is increasingly the case in Pinotepa de Don Luis and surrounding Mixtec villages, where women are adopting bibbed aprons to cover their naked breasts (see p. 142). The sight of European-style aprons in earlier times may, however, have inspired a delightful and curious costume which is worn by the Zapotec of Santo Tomás Mazaltepec. Here women delight, like the Tarahumara and the Mazahua, in presenting a many-layered appearance, and this they achieve with a series of half-skirts, some covering the front and some the back, which they team with full ones.

Upper garments are similarly divided between native and European styles. The blouse has proved without doubt to be Spain's most significant contribution to female dress, and Indian ingenuity has resulted in a wide range of decoration (see p. 170). One feature, which is particularly characteristic of blouses from the Valley of Mexico and the state of Puebla, is the angularity of design. Box-cut and totally unfitted, they are fashioned from straight panels of cloth and feature square necklines. Sleeves are nearly always short, although exceptions to this rule are provided by the Huichol, the Seri, the Tarahumara and the Mazahua. As with their skirts, women from this last group like to wear more than one. Over a blouse of *manta* they frequently display a

Nahua woman from Atla, Puebla. Her blouse, embroidered in running stitch, has square-cut sleeves.

second and possibly a third of *artisela*, and this custom is shared by some Tarascan women who live near Lake Pátzcuaro.

Blouses were introduced into many communities by missionaries who were concerned about the immodesty of the *quechquémitl* when worn on its own, and today this ancient garment, which has existed in Mexico for over fifteen centuries, maintains its popularity in many central and northern territories. Deprived by the Conquest of its noble and ceremonial status, it is today widely used by the Huichol, the Huastec, the Mazahua, the Tepehua, the Totonac, the Otomí and the Nahua, who together employ an astonishing variety of weaving, embroidery and other decorative techniques. Although it is still possible to find older women from the last three groups whose *quechquémitl* are worn without blouses, this is becoming increasingly rare. By contrast, younger women often prefer to wear just their blouses in warm weather, and to don their *quechquémitl* during cold spells and *fiestas*. It is also true that increased embellishment of blouses has led in many villages to a marked decrease in the size of the *quechquémitl* which cover them. Few, however, approach the diminutive proportions of the collar-like garments worn by Nahua women in Sasaltitla, Veracruz.

Although various pre-Conquest styles of *quechquémitl* have died out, three basic methods of construction are practised today. The simplest of these, which is called Type 1 in the accompanying diagram, is used in San Luis Potosí by Nahua and Huastec women in Cuatlamayán and Aquismón respectively, in Puebla by the Nahua of Zacatlán, and by Huichol women who use either *manta* or colourful bandanna handkerchiefs. Points fall to the front and back, and dimensions are generally larger than they are for Type 2, which has a far wider distribution. *Quechquémitl* within this second category are often hand-woven, with points falling either to the front and back as in Cuetzalán or to the sides as in San Pablito. Great ingenuity was required for garments of Type 3, which existed in the Puebla highlands but which have virtually disappeared in recent decades. It is interesting to note that ways in which *quechquémitl* are worn can often vary within a single linguistic group. Among the Otomí points are distributed in both fashions, while many Totonac women near Papantla differ from their counterparts in Puebla by displaying their organdy garments like capes about

Quechquémitl constructions.
After Donald Cordry.

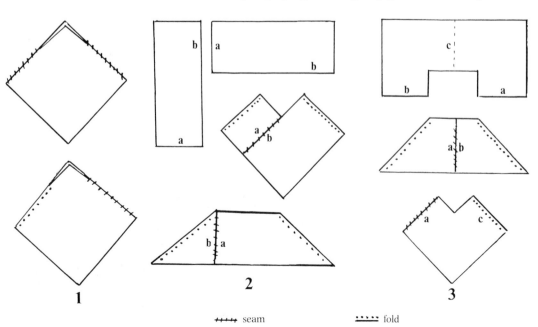

1   **2**   **3**

++++ seam   ····· fold

their shoulders. Another custom, recorded by Carlota Mapelli Mozzi in Veracruz, concerns the elderly Nahua inhabitants of Chicontepec, who rarely wear blouses and who slip one arm through the neck opening of their *quechquémitl* while in the home. Unusual too are the Nahua women of Atla, who not only retain four different kinds of *quechquémitl* but also wear the points in both styles. Given the strong attachment which conservative women still feel for these elegant and adaptable garments, it seems likely that they will endure in many villages for some time to come, despite the secondary role they now play.

Rather stronger is the threat posed by the blouse to the *huipil*. The later garment has replaced the earlier in a number of communities, while in others European influence is indicated by the addition of sleeves or by shrinking dimensions. Fortunately women from a great many groups have withstood the lure of the blouse, and Mexico continues to boast a wide range of *huipiles* which are either woven traditionally or created with bought cloth. Before the Conquest *huipiles* and *quechquémitl* often existed simultaneously and were on occasion worn together. Today in Angahuan, Michoacán, Tarascan women ceremonially don *quechquémitl* over their small *huipiles* when performing a certain dance. This is altogether exceptional, however, as in other communities the two garments never now coincide. Largely confined to areas of Morelos, Michoacán, Guerrero, Oaxaca, Chiapas and the Yucatán Peninsula, the *huipil* is also to be found in isolated Nahua villages in Jalisco, Veracruz and south-east Puebla, as well as among the Otomí of Santiago Temoaya in Hidalgo.

Construction methods vary widely and demand between one and four webs. *Huipiles* belonging to the first category are worn in Venustiano Carranza, where a single length is folded transversely and cut to provide a neck opening. In Jalisco the Nahua inhabitants of Tuxpan employ a very unusual technique which requires the web of cloth to be folded horizontally. When two strips are joined lengthwise as in Yalalag, a section is simply left unsewn for the head, although Zoque weavers prefer to enlarge the opening with scissors. Three-web *huipiles* are the most prevalent type, however. The middle strip, which is sometimes the widest, displays either a square-cut neckline, a rounded one, or a vertical slit which stretches to a v-shape when worn. Only rarely,

Below left Huichol *quechquémitl* (construction 1) from Jalisco of *manta* embroidered with cross and long-armed cross stitches. 23½ in (59.7 cm) square. *Far right* Nahua *quechquémitl* (construction 2) from Sasaltitla, Veracruz; the loosely woven surface is covered with looped stitches of coloured wool; edges are bound with red cloth. Strips are 6 in (15.2 cm) wide. *Centre* Mazahua fringed *quechquémitl* (construction 2) from Santa Ana Eyenzú, Mexico, with cross-stitched motifs on a woven ground. Strips are 10½ in (26.7 cm) wide with needle-formed joins.

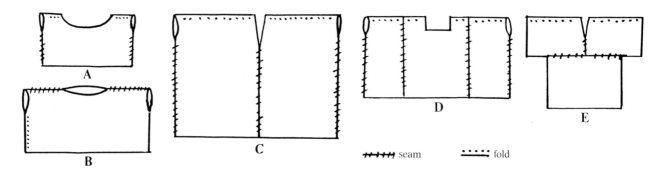

++++++ seam   ····· fold

Huipil constructions: A. One web, Venustiano Carranza, Chiapas (see p. 61); B. One web, Tuxpan, Jalisco, after Johnson, Johnson and Beardsley; C. Two webs, Yalalag, Oaxaca (see p. 219); D. Three webs, San Andrés Larrainzar, Chiapas; E. Four webs, Santiago Temoaya, Mexico.

as in the Mixtec village of Santiago Nuyóo, do weavers furnish their *huipiles* with *kelim* openings in the manner of archaeological examples from the Mixteca Alta. Four-web garments are found solely among the Otomí of Santiago Temoaya, whose method of construction is thought to be unique. Non-selvage necklines are reinforced with ribbon bindings or stitching, which provide everyday *huipiles* in some villages with their only form of decoration. Web joins often afford similar embellishment.

Proportions and styles of wearing are equally variable. Some garments are wider than they are long, many are longer than they are wide, and a few are virtually square. Shorter examples are generally tucked inside the skirt, as they are in San Juan Chamula and the majority of other highland villages in Chiapas, but longer ones are left to hang freely. In San Pedro Amuzgos, Oaxaca, women tend to go skirtless, only adopting *enredos* beneath their calf-length *huipiles* for *fiestas*. Nahua and Tzotzil inhabitants of San José Miahuatlán in Puebla and Magdalenas in Chiapas combine both styles, however, by tucking their *huipiles* in at the front while leaving them to hang down behind. Further variations are demonstrated by the Trique women of San Andrés Chicahuaxtla, whose ankle-length *huipiles* are often gathered up about the waist to provide greater freedom of movement. Sometimes possessions may even be transported in the folds of the cloth. Their *huipiles* may also be pulled over the shoulders or the head to offer protection from sun or rain. In Trique villages sides are left unsewn except for a few stitches at the bottom (see p. 164). Tzotzil *huipiles* in Santa Catarina Pantelhó receive, in contrast, just a few stitches below the armpit, while in neighbouring San Miguel Mitontic the sides are left totally open, and the same is true of Tetelcingo in Morelos. Nursing mothers are thereby enabled to suckle their babies with even greater ease than is usual with other *huipiles*.

Although narrow examples may barely cap the wearers' shoulders, many garments are broad enough to overhang the arms to the elbow and beyond. Before the blouse took over from the *huipil* in many Zapotec villages, inhabitants used to rely on narrow sashes to hold back these 'sleeves' while working. Doña Sabina Sánchez de Mateos from San Antonino Ocotlán recalls this custom from her youth. Some fifty years ago, according to her, poorer women still wore *manta huipiles* and acquired finely woven, *caracol*-dyed bands from Santo Tomás Jalieza. These were positioned about the neck, over the shoulders, through the sleeves, and then knotted across the chest below the *huipil*. Two other tying methods which were current in the area have been documented by Anita Jones and illustrated by Donald Cordry in *Mexican Indian Costumes*.

Fiesta huipiles are generally more complex and costly to produce than everyday ones, although styles do not always differ greatly. In San Lucas Ojitlán, however, Chinantec women favour two widely divergent garments. Both have already been described, as have the variations enjoyed by Zapotec women in Yalalag and Tehuantepec.

In Chiapas fine gala *huipiles* are woven in the Tzotzil communities of Magdalenas and San Andrés Larrainzar. As for the Mixtec women of Santa María Cuquila, they make everyday *huipiles* in two webs from wool but gala ones in three webs from cotton. When studying the Nahua costume of Amatlán de los Reyes in Veracruz, the Cordrys noted that in wealthier days women used to delight in enlarging their store of *huipiles* by buying examples which came across the Oaxacan border from Chinantec and other villages. Such eclecticism is most unusual today, yet when I recently visited a proficient weaver in the Trique village of San Andrés Chicahuaxtla, she was anxious to be photographed in her new *huipil* which she had acquired for gala wear from the Trique village of Santa María Yucunicoco (see p. 176). It was stated by the Anonymous Conqueror that women wore 'two, three and four shirts, all different and some longer than others so as to show beneath'. This custom, which was seen as a mark of nobility, continues in some Trique and highland Mixtec villages, where the use during *fiestas* of two and even three *huipiles* confers prestige upon the wearer.

One of Mexico's finest remaining gala garments is undoubtedly the feather-embellished *huipil* which is worn during weddings in Zinacantán, Chiapas. Sadly ceremonial *huipiles*

Three-web ceremonial Mixtec *huipil* from San Pedro Jicayán, Oaxaca, of white and shellfish-dyed cotton and *hiladillo*, or cochineal-dyed silk. Motifs are brocaded. Museum of Mankind, London.

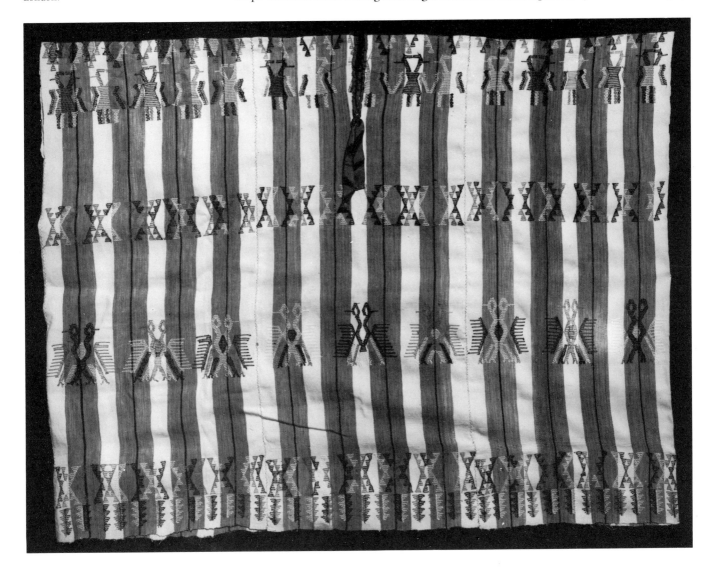

are fast disappearing from many villages in south-east Oaxaca, together with some unusual ways of wearing them. The photograph shows a splendid wedding *huipil* from the Mixtec community of San Pedro Jicayán where it is left to hang freely over the accompanying *enredo*. Wedding *huipiles* in Pinotepa Nacional, however, are worn by Mixtec brides who put their heads through the opening but avoid using the armholes. Garments are then turned sideways with the 'sleeves' facing to front and back, or conventionally positioned with the sides pulled up over the shoulders. If this interesting custom could be traced to pre-Conquest times, then it seems likely that some early representations of shoulder-garments might portray similarly worn *huipiles* rather than *quechquémitl*. In Pinotepa Nacional and a few other local villages such as Pinotepa de Don Luis marriage *huipiles* are stored away after use. Only in death are they worn again, but then the owner's arms are permitted to enter the armholes. In Jamiltepec women observe this same procedure for both weddings and burials, yet *huipiles* may also be worn everyday so long as they are distributed like capes about the shoulders or arranged to cover the head as well.

Although Mixtec women in the Pinotepa region are accustomed to going bare-breasted in and around the home, they tend on public occasions to adopt a modesty garment known either as a *tralla* or, rather confusingly, as a *huipil*. This is a square or rectangular cloth which is made from two webs and covers the breasts in the same way that real *huipiles* do in Jamiltepec. Some examples, like those of Ixtayutla and Mechoacán, are handsomely woven with brocading in the first village and widely spaced weft stripes in the second; other examples, like those of Huaxpaltepec and Huazolotitlán, are simply made from white *manta*. Women in Santiago Tetepec have evolved a uniquely complicated *tralla*, however. Rectangular in shape and woven in one piece, it is folded along the shorter side and stitched along one of the longer sides to leave an opening for the right arm. The garment is then pulled across the back and held over the chest with the left arm. Across the border in Veracruz Nahua women in Cosoleacaque also wear a modesty cloth, but theirs is of the simpler variety and made from *artisela*.

A further range of coverings is used over the *huipil* by women who inhabit the Chiapas highlands. Cape-like in appearance, they recall ancient Máya garments, although shapes today are rectangular. Wearers include the Tzotzil of Chenalhó, Mitontic and Huistán, who knot the two top corners across the chest. Woven backgrounds are white and embellished with brocaded motifs in the first two villages, but with embroidery in the third. Cotton is also used in Zinacantán to weave candy-striped shoulder-cloths which are tied with tasselled cords and worn in pairs during cold weather. Alternatively grey, diagonally woven capes of wool may be adopted for greater warmth, while in San Juan Chamula protection is afforded by thick cloths of felted black wool. Tzeltal women in Tenejapa rely on similar garments woven from either cotton or wool. Although many of these capes double as carrying-cloths for loads and babies, weavers in some villages employ a second cloth which is differently patterned and intended solely for babies. This top cape may then be arranged like a protective tent over mother and child.

Chill and misty conditions in the Oaxaca highlands cause Trique women in San Andrés Chicahuaxtla to adopt two-web woollen blankets, which are woven with diagonal patterning by Mixtec weavers. These are generally worn doubled to the width of a single web and wrapped about the body (see p. 164). In extremely cold weather Tarahumara women also don blankets which are smaller than those of their menfolk. At other times they rely on their several blouses and skirts for warmth, and use cotton shoulder-cloths to carry burdens and children (see p. 168). In the arid Mezquital Valley *ixtle ayates* play an equally important role. When Otomí women require shelter from the sun, they knot two ends across the forehead, leaving the rest of the cloth to cover the back and shoulders, and this arrangement also enables them to carry loads as by tump-line (see p. 131). On the day of their baptism babies may be carried to church in especially fine *ayates*, while on other occasions these versatile cloths serve as cradles which are suspended from house beams or tree branches. In the neighbouring state of Puebla striped *mamales*, or baby-slings, are woven from white and *coyuche* cotton, although some mothers prefer to transport their offspring in netted baskets (see p. 8). Across the border in Oaxaca many Chinantec and Mixe women continue to weave multi-purpose cloths which are highly decorative as well as functional. In Ojitlán these coverings provide an added touch of colour to costumes. When worn traditionally, they are knotted across the forehead and arranged in the style of Otomí *ayates*. In Usila and Cotzocón, however, garments are draped like shawls over the head and shoulders when they are not being used as carrying-cloths. Mazatec women often employ lengths of *manta* in a similar fashion.

Smaller cloths, suitable only as head-coverings, are also worn in a number of villages. One of these is San Juan Chamula, where Tzotzil women sew bright woollen tassels to the corners and fold cloths so that they lie flat. Another is Santiago Choapan, where cloths are predominantly red. According to the Cordrys, Zapotec women in this village used, long ago, to secure them at the front with ornamental pins of silver. In Venustiano Carranza a brocaded *servilleta* or a second neatly folded *huipil* is placed on the head for ceremonial occasions. An alternative form of protection is afforded by the *quechquémitl*. During hot weather Nahua women in Atla and Xolotla drape this garment over the head, and this practice is also shared by the Otomí of Tolimán, San Pablito and Santa Ana Hueytlalpan. In this last village the *quechquémitl* may be folded instead to give a peaked cap. The Tepehua of Huehuetla prefer to wrap theirs pirate-fashion about the head, while Huichol women favour yet another style (see p. 59).

Of all the head-dresses worn in Mexico the *huipil grande* is among the strangest and the most spectacular. It is, as its name suggests, a large and glorified *huipil* and is displayed during *fiestas* by the Zapotec women of Tehuantepec. The bodice is adorned at the neck and along the lower edge with flounces of lace, which also form sleeves too narrow for actual use. When in church, women frame their faces with the frill of the neck opening but allow the rest of the garment to cover their chest and shoulders like a cape, while the lacework of the sleeves falls to the front and the back. During all other festive events Tehuanas cover their heads with the lower flounce and leave the collar and sleeves to hang down behind. Linati's lithograph from 1828 featured this as sole top-garment and illustrated the first method of arrangement, although the bottom ruffle was absent at this early stage (see p. 98). Subsequently a conventional *huipil* was adopted.

According to Carlota Mapelli Mozzi, a few gala *huipiles* from the turn of the century still remain in Tehuantepec. Exquisitely trimmed, they are apparently worn during weddings with the sleeves pushed to the front and back as in Pinotepa Nacional. It is possible, therefore, that the origin of the mysterious *huipil grande* may lie with this Oaxacan custom. The popular explanation, which seems a good deal less plausible, concerns a shipwrecked alb or alternatively a christening robe, and suggests that local women misconstrued its purpose and imitated it, thinking it to be a cape. Sadly the disappearance of the old Zoque costume has entailed the near loss of a similar garment, known as a *huipil de tapar*. This beautiful garment was elaborately woven in three strips, then given sleeves and a neck-frill of lace. The few old women who retain such a garment today wear it folded on top of the head, or arrange it during *fiestas* so that the neck-frill frames the forehead while the sleeves hang down on to the shoulders.

Far less decorative are the kerchiefs that are worn in some communities. To protect themselves from the sun Huave women sometimes tie a square of commercial white cloth pirate-style about their heads, while Seri women have acquired a taste for patterned factory scarves which they knot under the chin. Commercial bath towels have also gained a place in the Mexican costume field, for they are sometimes used as turbans in Huehuetla, Hidalgo; more commonly they are worn draped over the head and shoulders (see p. 177). Yet another type of covering is to be found in Amatenango, where Tzeltal potters have taken to wrapping their heads in factory-produced checked aprons. Although a few hats were shown on pre-Conquest female figurines from Jaina, those worn today are merely borrowed from contemporary male costume. Otomí, Nahua and Trique women are occasionally to be seen with conventionally shaped palm hats. Half-gourds provide members from this third group with an alternative and more traditional form of protection, and the custom persists throughout the Mixteca Alta, although it is no longer shared by men. Generally plain but sometimes decorated, these close-fitting 'hats' double usefully as drinking-vessels.

Despite the wide range of coverings for the head and shoulders so far described, there is no doubt that the single most popular garment is the *rebozo*; in some communities it has even replaced the *quechquémitl*. In regions where the *rebozo* has been adopted it serves a multitude of purposes and conforms to a variety of styles. After visiting Michoacán's markets, Lumholtz observed that 'the most attractive of all the wares displayed were the beautiful *rebozos* hung up on strings as on a clothes line'. Although written some eighty years ago, this remark still holds true for this and many other regions where weaving is still practised. Some distinctive examples have already been mentioned, although it seems likely that stereotyped factory shawls will eventually eclipse them. Unusual ways of wearing *rebozos* occur in some Zapotec communities where women arrange them like turbans, and in parts of Michoacán where they are narrowly folded during festivals and crossed about the wearer's torso. When used for bundle carrying or to support infants on the back, the *rebozo* is tied across the chest, and in large families it is not unusual to see small girls and even small boys cradling younger siblings in this manner. Modesty, a desire for privacy and the fear of *mal de ojo* ('evil eye') lead many women to veil their faces, yet there is also an art of flirtation, whereby the long fringed ends may be coquettishly twirled.

In the sculpture and codices of long ago women who were not of high rank were represented without shoes, and today the majority still go barefoot, particularly in the highlands of Chiapas and Oaxaca. Occasionally women may adopt home-made sandals like their menfolk, but few communities possess standardised footwear for women. One exception is Yalalag, where Zapotec women wear festival sandals of leather featuring bird and butterfly designs which are cut out to show coloured velvet beneath. According to Carlota Mapelli Mozzi, women refrain from everyday use lest gossiping villagers describe them as *callejeras* (fond of gadding about the streets). Formerly *ixtle* sandals were worn in the region, and the practice continues as mentioned in parts of Morelos. Factory footwear is catching on in some communities, however: in Ocumicho, for example, Tarascan women now wear heavy black shoes when participating in *fiestas*, and young Lacandón women have taken to buying sandals of coloured plastic.

Hair attracts a great deal of care. Washed as often as the water supply permits, it is also anointed in some villages with *mamey* oil. Before the widespread availability of plastic combs Indians relied on horn or wooden ones and on fibre brushes, while it is reported by Pennington that the Tarahumara still make use of pine cones or the bristly covering of a cactus fruit. Sometimes, as in Michoacán, juice from the *órgano* cactus is used to intensify blackness or to dye greying hair. The Cordrys have even recorded that in Tetelcingo, Morelos, Nahua women employ a green hair colourant which they extract from the leaves of a shrub.

Styles are varied and often elaborate – especially during festivals and ceremonies. Very rarely is the hair left loose or cut, although Huichol women do occasionally wear fringes. Braids are a favourite way of restraining the hair, and in some villages a single one is preferred. Most women use two, however: if braids hang down behind their ends may be joined, or they may be wrapped across the top of the head. Over recent decades Chinantec women from Usila have evolved a unique and exotic coiffure by twisting their braids into a tall cluster towards the front of the head. Women who do not plait their hair may choose instead to wind it across the top of the head in two rolls, or to shape it into a bun on the nape of the neck. The horn-like style in the Codex Florentino (see p. 72) seems to have disappeared, but the use of trimmings has not. Today these include brilliantly coloured rayon ribbons, hand-woven tapes in villages such as Venustiano Carranza, and woollen cords which are intertwined with the hair. Ornate cords, replete with vivid pom-poms and sections of beading, are made in San Pablito and attached to a single plait (see p. 64), while bridal cords from Pinotepa Nacional carry silken tassels which hang down on either side of the face. In Santa Catarina Estetla Mixtec women occasionally bind their plaits so tightly with braid that they stick out stiffly, and in Huazolotitlán hair is divided in two sections and wrapped over filling cords which today are made from wool, but which formerly were spun from combings of human hair. Also traditional are the narrow cotton headbands which are worn by Tarahumara women, and the colourfully feathered breasts of small birds which married Lacandón women tie on to the backs of their heads. Flowers are sometimes adopted during *fiestas* by Totonac and Yucatec women, but I have not been fortunate enough to see the sight described in 1924 by Thomas Gann, who spoke with praise of the gala attire of Maya women near Santa Cruz and noted 'a small coronet of fine beetles, resembling tiny electric lamps, in their magnificent hair'.

The pre-Conquest *rodete* (see illustration, p. 44) has endured in several communities. One of these is Yalalag, where Zapotec women wear a complicated festival head-dress which is fashioned from thick cables of black wool, and another is Cuetzalán. Here Nahua women construct majestic turbans from purple and green woollen skeins, which are sold in the Sunday market by vendors from Tlatlauqui. Piled high on the head, these cords are twisted into the hair and frequently topped with a *quechquémitl*. Vermilion or black wool is used in Mixistlán, Yacochi and Cotzocón by Mixe women, who either position the *rodete* on top of the head or wrap it with their hair, according to the custom of the village. This second method is similar to that employed by the Huastec who live near Tancanhuitz in San Luis Potosí. Woollen strands of many colours are placed like a circlet about the head, and the hair is crossed over and under it until both are secure. Investigation by the Cordrys has shown that in Tameletón Huastec women still construct their head-dresses with pliant lengths of vine and that Nahua women in Cuatlamayán retain a tubular structure which they make by binding

Zapotec woman of Yalalag, Oaxaca, *c.* 1890. Contemporary costume still comprises a two-web tasselled *huipil*, a wrap-around skirt and a *rodete*.

Nahua women from San Francisco Huehuetlán, Oaxaca, with *ikat*-dyed *rebozos*, and *huipiles* appliquéd with strips of ruched cloth. Necklaces are of red glass beads and seeds; earrings are imitation silver.

strips of cotton cloth or wool about a core of banana-tree bark. A further variation is to be found in Huistán, where Tzotzil women wrap red woven ribbons about their hair during festivals to form a crown. It is possible that these splendid head-dresses may have originated long ago to provide a base for transporting round-bottomed pots on the head, but today they are purely decorative.

In any modern market the most popular stall is often one which carries a supply of trinkets. Plastic slides and ornamental hair combs are worn in colourful array by Totonac and Tzeltal girls who live near Papantla and Ocosingo, but stall-holders also do a steady trade in showy earrings, gilt crosses and strings of plastic beads. This trend

is not new, for Lumholtz referred some eighty years ago to the spread of 'cheap tawdry jewellery', and changing fashions over the intervening decades have done much to alter Indian taste. Distinctive styles of adornment persist in many marginal communities, however: Tarahumara and Seri women continue to make necklaces from seeds, shells, pieces of reed and tiny balls of wood or clay, and to create ingenious earrings which sometimes incorporate buttons, mother-of-pearl pendants and bright fragments of plastic. Polished fish vertebrae, wooden carvings, small bones and toucan beaks are some of the embellishments traditionally favoured by Huave and Lacandón women.

Glass beads retain immense popularity, and have taken over in many cases from the seeds and other natural decorations just mentioned. Huichol women delight in threading tiny beads which are wound in five colourful coils about the neck, or in netting patterned bracelets, pectorals, rings and earrings which are tied through the earlobe with *ixtle*. Lacandón women and small girls also take great pride in displaying as many necklaces as possible, and these are hung with shiny safety-pins and coins – one woman even displays several Japanese yen and the key to her doorlock, which is the only one so far installed at Najá. Curiously beads have become the sole distinguishing feature for the identically dressed Nahua of Zitlala and Acatlán in Guerrero: whereas inhabitants of the first village favour a single string of red beads, those from the second prefer a single string of imitation yellow amber. Because of its ability to simulate rarer and more expensive substances, glass has similarly replaced coral and imported jet in many communities, and beads are often interspersed with coins and medallions. Never does modern glass match the splendour of the old trade beads, however. These reached some of the most remote corners of Oaxaca and date back in many instances to the sixteenth and seventeenth centuries. In San Pedro Quiatoni highly prized necklaces of Venetian glass have been passed down from generation to generation, while a few Mixe women in Mixistlán and Yacochi still wear twenty or more strands of beads which together weigh up to $3\frac{1}{2}$ lb (1.6 kg). These majestic necklaces include numerous white beads of opaque glass which may have come from China on the Manila galleons. Sadly younger women are losing interest in these heirlooms, many of which have already been sold off to private collectors and museums. The passage of time has not eroded the appeal of *papelillo*, however, which was introduced into Mexico at the close of the last century. Despite rising prices, Trique, Chinantec and Tarascan women continue to deck themselves resplendently with these brilliantly painted beads of paper-thin glass and to secure the various strands with colourful ribbons (see pp. 164, 176).

Fine ornaments of silver and gold are also worn in numerous communities. The early years of Conquest led to the disappearance of lost-wax techniques and representations of native gods; yet Indian metalsmiths received inspiration from European methods and from the range of medals, rosaries, crosses and reliquaries that symbolise the Catholic faith. Many such adornments, both Colonial and modern, are worn today in Oaxaca, and include the famous compound crosses of Yalalag. Filigree, which became a speciality in Yucatán, is still used to create earrings and long, lace-like rosaries. The introduction of coins also had a strong impact, and during the prosperous years that preceded the Revolution Nahua women in Amatlán de los Reyes wore a profusion of gold and silver coins with strings of coral. The custom persists on the Isthmus, where many Tehuanas still display their savings during festivals in the form of chokers, bracelets, rings, earrings and heavy coin necklaces of gold or dipped silver.

Necklace of red glass beads and silver ornaments, Oaxaca. Earrings: (*top row*) gold, Michoacán; (*2nd row*) diminutive painted gourds, Guerrero; painted wood, Michoacán; (*3rd row*) painted horn, Mexico; nickel, Mexico; (*bottom row*) silver, Tlatlauqui, Puebla.

In time of need these can be pawned or sold, and later retrieved or replaced. Although such reserves of wealth are rare in Indian Mexico, Zapotec women in the valley sometimes invest money by buying earrings of gold, pearls and precious stones, and I have seen tourists ask their owners the price, thinking them to be inexpensive trinkets, only to react with amazement when their true value is revealed.

In less acculturated areas village silversmiths continue to meet local demand with earrings and necklace-ornaments that suggest a more native tradition. In the highlands of Puebla the craftsmen of Tlatlauqui assemble elaborately jointed fish scale by scale so that they move in the style of pre-Conquest figures. Great skill is also demonstrated in Oaxaca, where Indian jewellery features turkeys, prancing horses, rabbits, diminutive suns and alligators devouring fish. As for the Mazahua, they favour heavy earrings incorporating doves and Moorish-style crescent moons inset with tiny stones and coloured glass. The early 1980s have seen a rapid rise in the price of silver and gold, however, and it seems unlikely that most Indian women will be able to afford these metals in the future. Already the Mazahua are relying increasingly on earrings of beaten tin, while the Otomí of Santiago Temoaya now buy nickel earrings which incorporate tiny ten-*centavo* coins.

Although many jewellery designs once possessed a magical significance, their value today is largely decorative. Throughout Mexico, however, strong belief exists in the power of amulets to ward off illness and misfortune, and to protect the wearer from *mal de ojo* ('evil eye'). Inexpensive Catholic medallions, sold outside churches on Saints' days, are worn with tufts of coloured cotton or wool, while the market stalls of herbalists and healers stock a supply of talismans which include the seed known as *ojo de venado* ('deer's eye'). The importance of coral is summed up by the popular saying *coral contra envidia y el mal* ('coral against envy and evil'), and its curative powers are widely acclaimed. According to a Zapotec informant, coral absorbs the wearer's illness and pales visibly in the process. In Chiapas amber amulets from Simojovel take the form of tiny hands, hearts, droplets and flower buds, and these may be tied about the necks and wrists of children. Protection is similarly sought in San Pablito, where Otomí children are given bead necklaces hung with tiny pockets containing aromatic herbs to combat *los malos aires*, or 'bad airs', which are thought to carry disease.

The religious importance of face painting has already been mentioned. Like their menfolk, Huichol women often adorn their cheeks ceremonially with symbols traced in yellow. Alternatively they may colour their cheeks red with a mixture of powder and grease. Petals from the sacred *totó* flower are sometimes stuck with saliva to the centre of each cheek, serving as in Lumholtz's time to express 'their wishes to the gods'. Facial decoration is also practised by conservative women in the Seri community of Punta Chueca. According to a report by W. J. McGee which was published in 1898, designs were beautifully executed and denoted membership of the various Seri clans. Present-day markings are greatly simplified, however. Applied to the cheeks and to the bridge of the nose, they are achieved with a combination of natural and commercial colourants.

Festivals predictably attract the finest display of jewellery and clothing that women can muster. Many ceremonial *huipiles* and head-dresses have already been described, and in some villages special *enredos* are also used. In San Pablito gala skirts are woven from white wool instead of cotton (see p. 165), while women in San Pedro Amuzgos who usually go skirtless don *añil*-dyed *enredos* under their long *huipiles* during *fiestas*. Costly items like the wedding *huipiles* of Zinacantán or the gala costumes of Tehuantepec may occasionally be hired. In some communities marriage contracts include a series of agreed gifts. In Tantoyuca, for instance, Huastec brides and grooms present each other with a set of clothes and are helped by their godparents to dress for the ceremony, while in Totonac areas of lowland Veracruz considerable outlay is demanded of the groom's parents. If sufficiently prosperous, they may be required to endow the bride with gold jewellery, organdy clothing, hair ornaments, shoes and even an umbrella. The costs involved in sponsoring a traditional wedding are such that, according to H. R. Harvey and Isabel Kelly, Totonac sons may be encouraged by their parents to elope with their brides instead.

High expenditure is also assumed by women dignitaries. Responsibilities are gladly borne, however, for service to the saints and the community is seen to confer great honour. In parts of lowland Mixteca ceremonial necklaces are sometimes worn, and garments too may be special. In San Pedro Jicayán the ceremonial *huipil* (see illustration, p. 215) is reserved not only for brides but also for the wife of the head man and is worn during the feasts over which she presides. Religious protocol ensures the survival of local costume in Tarascan villages such as Ocumicho, where women known as *guaris* participate in ceremonies and processions, and in Chiapas where dignitaries uphold numerous traditions. Tzotzil status is indicated by the use of black woollen *huipiles* in Zinacantán and by the adoption of ribbon necklaces in Chamula, while Tzeltal authorities in Tenejapa display a greater wealth of brocaded decoration on their gala *huipiles* than other women. Instances such as these not only confirm the enduring vitality of female costume but serve additionally to underline the sacred role which it retains in large areas of Indian Mexico.

Four-web bedspread woven on a backstrap loom by Otomí weaver Ana Cecilia Cruz Alberto of San Miguel Ameyalco, Mexico. European horses, churches and other colourful motifs are brocaded in acrylic on a white cotton ground. Such items, intended for sale in Mexico City, are more crudely woven than traditional *ayates*, but demand also stimulates inventiveness and helps perpetuate weaving skills. Museum of Mankind, London.

Conclusion

This book has concentrated largely on the technical and decorative aspects of Indian dress, and on the fusion of native and European traditions. Members of conservative communities still feel that their needs are best met by natural fibres which offer protection against the rigours of climate, by home-woven cloth which can combine durability with beauty, and by indigenous or adapted garments which offer versatility and elegance, while in less marginal societies countless women continue to embellish bought cloth with ingenuity and skill.

Mention has also been made of the social and ceremonial importance of clothing. Analyses of Mexican Indian cultures by anthropologists frequently stress the importance of community ties and contrast the collective identity shared by villagers with the individualism of *mestizo* neighbours. Further generalised comparison suggests that while *mestizos* tend to identify with the national culture the loyalty of Indians is often directed more immediately towards their own community and region, with costume serving as a bond and as a symbol of unity. 'We are Mexican, but first and foremost we are Lacandón', explained an inhabitant of Najá recently, 'and we don't want to cut our hair. Some say we are savages, but we don't want to change our hair or our dress.' Ricardo Pozas Arciniega, in his book *Chamula: un pueblo indio de los altos de Chiapas*, confirms the power of costume to distinguish members from different communities and notes that a man or woman who marries into another village is bound to reflect that change of allegiance in his or her dress. On a personal level costume is closely linked with social relations and protocol and separates the world of *fiestas* from the everyday world of work, but in a wider context it serves to symbolise a person's 'Indianness'. It implies that the wearer speaks an Indian language, lives in an Indian village, belongs to a traditionally structured society, and indicates his or her willingness to 'participate in rituals and religious ceremonies with total conviction and with a knowledge of their transcending importance'.

It is impossible in many Indian societies, even four and a half centuries after the Conquest, to separate the secular from the sacred, and some attempt should therefore be made to set costume in its spiritual context. We know from accounts by Durán and other chroniclers that idols were magnificently dressed in pre-Hispanic times, and it is interesting to note that in the Chiapas highlands, where villagers often prefer to manage their own churches without the help of a resident priest, saints are clothed with similar care and devotion to reflect the costume styles of the community. In Magdalenas and Santa Marta, for example, one of the sacred *cargos* (offices) is the weaving of *huipiles* for the Virgins, and once a year before the chief *fiesta* each garment is washed and the water drunk by the participants. In San Juan Chamula the patron saint wears the white head-cloth reserved for village dignitaries, while Santo Tomás of Oxchuc is dressed in a long shirt and carries a netted bag. Sometimes, as in San Pedro Chenalhó, images are deemed 'rich' if decked with several layers of clothing. According to Pozas Arciniega, loyalty to village costume is reinforced by allegiance to the saints. This is the case in Huistán, where men refuse to adopt conventional clothing; if asked by outsiders why they prefer their own costume, they reply 'Do you not see that this is how our *Santo Patrón* is dressed?'.

The Huichol also clothe many of their indigenous deities in their own likeness. Lumholtz, who was privileged to inspect a number of sacred figures, noted that Nakawe (Grandmother Growth) was dressed in a skirt of woven *ixtle* and two *quechquémitl*. Although terms such as 'prayer' and 'worship' do not exist in the Huichol language, the goodwill and protection of the gods are sought with festivals

Cross dressed in an embroidered *huipil* in the Maya village of Xocen, Yucatán.

and ceremonial offerings, and in the daily life of each individual. Dress is looked on as an expression of faith and features in a number of myths. According to one legend recorded by Robert M. Zingg, 'a fine Huichol man's costume is what first enabled the Sun Father to rise in the sky and shine', and he notes the Sun Father's injunction to the Huichol to keep a neat appearance. He who wears fine clothes will have cattle and cheese as well as *chiles* and *tortillas*, but he who dresses lazily will be reduced to eating wild roots and animals like a rat. Other legends chronicle the adventures of culture heroes who are protected against their enemies by their finery or vanquished for lack of it, and a further reference by Zingg shows that a shaman is helped in the power of his singing by his attire.

Although the costume symbolism of the Huichol could provide subject-matter for an entire book, a few instances will go some way towards demonstrating the mystical significance still retained by many garments, trimmings, colours and designs. Waist-sashes, which are identified with serpents because of their long, winding shape and because of the reptilian markings which they often display, serve as requests for rain and for the benefits which rain brings – namely good crops, health and a long life. Feathers are also greatly prized. Magical powers are attributed to birds as it is thought that they can see and hear everything during their flight above the Earth, and different birds are associated with different deities. The eagle belongs to Grandfather Fire, the turkey to Father Sun, and their plumes are eagerly sought for the hats of *peyote* pilgrims. Squirrels were the helpmates of Father Sun in the first times, so their tails are similarly valued by *peyoteros*. Because colours are also identified with specific deities, they must be carefully chosen during the making of offerings and the elaboration of garments. The five colours of maize are sacred, while blue and green are water colours. According to Lumholtz, all things including rain are seen in terms of colour, and Huichol perceptions are heightened and inspired by the divine and brilliantly coloured visions which come with *peyote*. Indeed these visions may partially explain Huichol enthusiasm for luminescent acrylic yarns, which are matched in startling and dazzling combinations in many contemporary weavings.

Designs, which serve as visual prayers, protect wearers from harm and carry many layers of meaning. Drawn from nature, they include antlered deer, scorpions, squirrels, vines, and squash-plants. Zig-zag lines that suggest lightning are associated with rain, together with double water-gourds, while the white *totó* flower that grows during the wet, maize-producing season is both a petition for and a symbol of maize. Another popular motif is the eagle. Thought to guard the young maize, it may be shown in profile with a single head or from the front with two heads to represent both profiles. In Lumholtz's view this double-headed design is native to the Huichol and not inspired by the Hapsburg eagle, although he does concede that the crown which appears frequently is borrowed, presumably from coins which circulated during the Colonial period.

Colours and design motifs also play a symbolic role in the Chiapas highlands, where they reflect the fusion of ancient Maya and Christian beliefs. Walter F. Morris, who has made a careful study of Tzotzil and Tzeltal costume, has identified approximately 1,500 weaving symbols. Used in different combinations in different villages, they perpetuate traditional agricultural and astronomical concepts, and conform to a strict mathematical aesthetic. An analysis by Marta Turok of the ceremonial *huipil* from Magdalenas underlines the importance of numerology. When brocading these richly patterned garments, weavers customarily construct eighteen lines of diamonds,

Illustrations by Carl Lumholtz from *Unknown Mexico*, 1902. *Top* Evolution of the Huichol *totó* design: all motifs are woven or embroidered, except the last which is beadwork and represents the flower in side view. *Bottom* Huichol man's woollen shirt, with embroidered designs of the *totó* flower.

intending nine to show behind and nine in front. Alternatively they may opt for twenty-six lines which divide into two groups of thirteen. These calculations relate to Maya cosmology, which supposes the sky to have thirteen levels and the underworld nine. As for the diamonds, they are flat representations of the Earth which is thought to be cube-shaped; their corners correspond to the four cardinal points, and also to the four corners of the sky and of the maize field. Completing the 'text' of the *huipil* are a number of plant elements signifying beans, maize and flowers, as well as a series of zoomorphic motifs. These are highly stylised to suggest bats, bees, spider monkeys and a host of other creatures, yet they carry names like *Santo* ('Saint'), *Gran Santo* ('Great Saint'), *Cabeza de Nuestro Señor Esquipulas Sobre la Santa Cruz* ('The Head of Our Lord of Esquipulas on the Holy Cross') and *Camino de la Serpiente* ('Path of the Snake'). With their several layers of meaning these symbols are almost certainly related to pre-Conquest deities, although today they serve as intermediaries between villagers and the Catholic hierarchy. As in the past, colours are identified with the cardinal directions. White, yellow, red and black are the colours of maize, and they are linked with the north, the south, the east and the west respectively, while green denotes vegetation and renewal.

Also important is the overall layout of patterning in many highland *huipiles*. Together motifs form a gigantic cross, which was a pre-Conquest as well as a Christian symbol. The wearer, who is in the centre of this cross, is thus surrounded by the levels of the universe, as well as by family symbols which are integrated, together with her personal 'signature', into the design. These are not matters which weavers will willingly discuss with outsiders, however, and symbols are, after all, an often subconscious expression of inherited beliefs which have been overlaid by Catholic teachings. Yet in all these communities where the textile arts remain central to religious life and thought the decorative value of garments and motifs is clearly incidental to their mystical purpose.

In less conservative regions, where the influence of missionaries has made greater inroads on native mythology, the symbolism of traditional designs has been largely forgotten. Step-frets, whirlpools, serpents and double-headed birds have been joined in many villages by elements deriving from Europe, the Near East, China and The Philippines. Yet even amidst relative acculturation villagers maintain a degree of reverence for textiles and for the motifs they carry. If asked to explain their allegiance to certain forms, women often reply '*es costumbre*' ('It is the custom'), but with this apparently simple answer they are proclaiming the spiritual importance of continuity. Designs, whatever their origin, have become hallowed by time and by local usage. Women who work hard to clothe themselves and their families take great pride in their skill, because they believe that they are contributing to the well-being of society and playing their part in ensuring divine harmony. It comes as no surprise, therefore, that women should so often wish to be buried in their finest costume and will refuse all offers from collectors. Just as a man's *sarape* may serve as his shroud, so a treasured *huipil* or *quechquémitl* may be destined for the grave, and in Cancuc, where corpses are buried inside the home and clad in several layers of clothing, mourners are said by Carlota Mapelli Mozzi to encourage the dead on the journey that awaits them by exclaimng '*Qué rico se va*' ('How richly he or she goes!').

In spite of tenacious retention of costume and other cultural values by many Indian groups, however, it would be short-sighted to overlook the various pressures for change which exist and which seem bound ultimately to erode their separate identity.

If life may be compared to a web of cloth on a loom, then it will be seen that each thread which is added or removed affects the whole. The availability of plastics, the introduction of new agricultural methods, the loss of a dance or the disappearance of a garment may seem insignificant when considered individually, but these are the causes and effects which chart the transition from an Indian to a *mestizo* way of life.

The often long periods spent working away from home have already been mentioned as a factor in the decline of contemporary male costume, while military service is another, but when young girls seek employment as servants in local towns or in Mexico City they too learn to look on village styles as 'uncivilised' and as a source of shame. Meanwhile, in the countryside a network of newly created roads is bringing hitherto isolated villages into increasing contact with the national culture. 'We felt foolish to be seen in our *calzones* when the road came, so we stopped wearing them', the Trique president of San Andrés Chicahuaxtla explained recently, and these sentiments could have been voiced in any number of other villages. Radio also aids in the acculturation process, for although many programmes are designed to help Indian listeners, the majority are aimed at a *mestizo* audience. While visiting Magdalenas I could not but reflect on the incongruity of the situation as I watched a weaver brocading cloth in front of her mountain hut while her radio combined advertisements with a dramatised serial about a fur-coated city heroine.

Missionary involvement is another significant factor. It would seem fair to say, for example, that Seri culture has changed more drastically over the last twenty years than in all the centuries following the Conquest. Since the arrival of North American Evangelists in the 1950s and the subsequent demise of shamanism, face painting has been strongly discouraged together with the use of jewellery. Evangelical Christianity has similarly replaced traditional Lacandón values in the southern community of Lacanjá, where men have begun to abandon their *huipiles* and flowing locks in favour of Western clothing and short haircuts. Resettlement, undertaken in the national interest, can also sever native traditions. In recent years the construction of a dam has entailed the relocation of several Mazatec communities, and the development of oil-wells seems destined to affect the Indian way of life in many regions.

One of the strongest forces of change, even in isolated villages, is formal schooling. It is hoped by successive governments that education will give children a grasp of the Spanish language, banish illiteracy, and ultimately draw Indian minorities into the national orbit. Culture clashes have resulted in some instances, however, and Robert Redfield's study of life in the Yucatec village of Chan Kom chronicles a controversy regarding costume which occurred in about 1940. According to him, it was announced by the schoolteacher's wife that all female pupils 'would be clothed in dresses and that their hair would be bobbed, to make them conform with the appearance of girls in civilized and cultivated communities'. Some parents co-operated, we are told, but many opposed the ruling and kept their daughters at home. Although contemporary educational policy frowns on extreme interference of this type, school uniforms have become compulsory in several regions. Near the town of Huejutla in Hidalgo, for example, Nahua school-children now wear sombre Western-style uniforms instead of the colourfully embroidered blouses and *manta* garments of their parents.

Fortunately there is a praiseworthy movement in many areas to train Indian teachers but progress is slow, and it has to be admitted that all too often there remains a lack of understanding between *mestizo* instructors and their charges. Teachers from towns are sometimes unsympathetic to Indian customs which they regard as proof of

Tzotzil weaver wearing a ceremonial *huipil* in Magdalenas, Chiapas. The loom symbolises the joining of the universe, with warp and weft representing underworld and sky. Brocaded motifs may be interpreted on many levels and include diamonds (termed 'the grand design'), flowers, stars and toads (see p. 161).

backwardness, and many continue, whether directly or unconsciously, to encourage their pupils to acculturate and to change their language and clothing. In the Otomí village of San Miguel Ameyalco, where wrap-around skirts and blouses have been discarded in recent years, a woman explained her own defection thus: 'In school we were more or less given the choice of being Indian or Mexican. It was explained that if I dressed like my mother I would remain Indian, so I chose to be Mexican and changed my dress.' Interestingly this woman admits proudly to being Otomí but interprets the term 'Indian' as an insult.

This inherent contradiction leads on to a much wider question – namely the self-image of Indian peoples. Villagers are highly sensitive not only to implied criticism by teachers but also to the attitudes of *mestizo* neighbours whose sense of superiority is barely veiled in many regions. It is not unusual in Chiapas, for example, to hear non-Indians refer to themselves as *gente de razón* ('people of reason'), and it is sad but hardly surprising to find that Indians in some areas prefer to avoid potential disdain or mockery by assuming a *mestizo* appearance when visiting large markets and towns. Costumes may be left at home, or covered over as in several Mazahua communities where men wear Western trousers over their *calzones* and bought shirts over embroidered ones. The following legend, recorded among the Cora by Lumholtz, recounts the adventures of the god Morning Star, yet it also takes dress as the symbol which precludes the acceptance of Indians into non-Indian society. According to Cora mythology, the god was befriended in spite of his poverty by his *mestizo* neighbours and invited to dine in their homes. While he dressed like them their hospitality remained exemplary, but on one occasion he appeared as an Indian boy. Because his hosts failed to recognise him, they treated him with brutality. He returned the following night wearing 'the clothing by which they knew him', riding a horse and displaying 'a nice blanket' and a *sombrero*. Again they greeted him with courtesy and offered him their food. He then abused the food and taxed his hosts with their violence, explaining: 'As you did not give me anything yesterday, I see that you do not want to give food to me, but to my clothes.'

Ironically, the sale of Indian garments and weavings continues to provide many *mestizo* traders with a useful source of income although, as Donald and Dorothy Cordry have commented, they are frequently unaware 'who had made or used' the articles offered for resale, or 'from what villages they came'. Since the creation in 1948 of the Instituto Nacional Indigenista much has been done to combat the exploitation of Indians by traders, but as in all countries the profit margin remains a constant theme of contention, with artisans complaining that they are underpaid for their efforts and shopkeepers complaining that it is the tourists who are to blame. There is truth in both claims, but the end result is a lowering of standards. If weavers are cajoled into accepting low rates of pay, they will cut corners in order to produce more. Meanwhile, on the purchasing end tourists remain largely uninformed about the degree of labour and skill required to elaborate fine textiles, and all too often opt for cheapness as an alternative to quality. Given the extraordinary richness of costume traditions in both Chiapas and Oaxaca, it seemed tragic on a recent visit to the capitals of both states to see 'craft' shops selling shirts made from printed flour bags and industrial floor cloths together with an array of cotton clothing imported from India.

As might be expected, constant contact with the national culture eventually undermines standards even within Indian cultures. Reliance on commercial materials, the gradual over-simplification of textile techniques and an acquired taste for pattern-book stereotypes are among the reasons already given for the decline which is occurring in many communities. As societies change and as the sacred importance of costume is lost, women adjust to Western notions of saving labour and money. Often a transitional phase ensues: women are not yet ready to adopt Western dress but they are unwilling or have forgotten how to achieve desired effects in the traditional way. Many Zoque women, for example, have ceased to embroider their blouses, which are themselves replacements for the *huipiles* of old. Instead they now sew printed ribbon along the neckline to simulate embroidery. A similar ruse is employed in parts of Yucatán, where *huipiles* intended for everyday wear and locally designated *de las flojas* ('for lazy women') display printed bands of cotton cloth. Totonac and Huichol usage of factory organdy and colourful kerchiefs further exemplify this trend, as does a curious garment which the Cordrys discovered near Pinotepa Nacional. Fashioned in emulation of the region's now extinct brocaded gala *huipiles*, it was discovered on examination to consist of a patterned lace curtain.

Eventually acculturation leads, as it already has in numerous villages, to the almost total abandonment of Indian costume. This trend frequently starts with young people who have learnt to reject traditional values, and is often fostered by parents who are anxious to give their children the chance to enter the *mestizo* world. According to Carlota Mapelli Mozzi, Nahua mothers are sometimes heard to say proudly '*esta niña nunca supo llevar refajo*' ('This girl never knew what it was to wear a wrap-around skirt'). More commonly, however, children rebel against their parents' wishes. In her book *Cambio de indumentaria* Susana Drucker describes costume changes in Jamiltepec and quotes the advice given to a Mixtec daughter by her mother, who tells her not to adopt the commercial cloth dress because it is expensive, short-wearing, not as pretty as traditional styles, and because it will put off prospective husbands and cause talk. She also warns her that 'the daughter who is accustomed to wear the dress soon does not want to talk to her mother'. Notwithstanding such advice, more and more young people are succumbing each year to the attractions of modern clothing. Young girls may describe old-style garments as '*de las abuelas*' ('fit for grannies'), while young men often eschew the sandals and *calzones* of past generations in favour of tennis shoes and jeans.

Sometimes costume is a symbol dividing the 'progressive' and 'non-progressive' members of a community. This occurs in the Zapotec village of Santiago Choapan where, according to Julio de la Fuente, a woman who has exchanged her *huipil* for a blouse is termed '*civilizada no India*' ('civilised not Indian'). Understandably villagers who retain traditional costume often resent the implied defection of neighbours, and Drucker tells us that in Jamiltepec those who adopt Western dress are known as '*revestidos*' ('people in disguise') or, to translate more literally from the Mixtec, as '*gente pintada o con mascara*' ('painted people or people wearing masks'). Interestingly, however, it is reported by Nancy Modiano that Tzeltal men in Oxchuc who have changed their dress do not accept the implication that in so doing they are embracing *mestizo* values; they claim that they seek on the contrary to become better and more progressive Indians.

As is shown by the points raised so far, costume is bound up with a range of social issues and gives cause for much controversy. Indian costume has never been static, but it would be sad if over the next few decades its long evolution should end with the uniformity of Western dress. A nylon blouse or a denim jacket could be thought poor substitutes for a magnificently woven *huipil* or a finely patterned *sarape*, and many might agree that 'civilisation' would be poorly served by the loss of textile skills that have endured for countless centuries since their origin in the New and Old Worlds. Two government organisations – El Fondo para el Fomento de las Artesanías and El Museo de Artes e Industrias Populares – are valuably committed to promoting crafts and to maintaining standards by encouraging artisans in their work, while the world-famous Museo Nacional de Antropología e Historia offers a splendid tribute to Mexico's living cultures. Displays of costume and other Indian arts have surely done much to combat the ignorance of foreigners and nationals alike with regard to Mexico's rich and varied heritage, yet it cannot be denied that long-term prospects for the survival of Indian costume are bleak. So long as conservative Indians continue to encounter prejudice in their daily lives from local non-Indians, their self-respect is threatened and their regard for traditional values undermined. It could, however, be argued that such a process only serves to accelerate an inevitable trend. No village, after all, would wish to be frozen in time, and contact with a wider world leads naturally to the desire for change. Nevertheless, it will seem a sad reflection on progress if today's many fine costumes survive only as exhibits in glass cases and as apparel for balls and parades, or if the contemporary skills inherited from the Aztec or the Maya are reduced to the scale of table-mats for visiting tourists. In the words of José Ortega y Gasset: '*Raro será el sitio donde el pueblo no sienta ya como disfraz su traje popular*' ('Rare will be the place where people do not already regard their traditional costume as fancy dress'). Perhaps the marvel is that in Mexico Indian costume has lasted as long as it has.

Trique children in San Andrés Chicahuaxtla, Oaxaca. Girls wear richly brocaded *huipiles* and necklaces of *papelillo* like their mothers (see p. 164), but the *calzón*, worn here for show, has recently been abandoned by male villagers.

Appendix 1 The backstrap loom

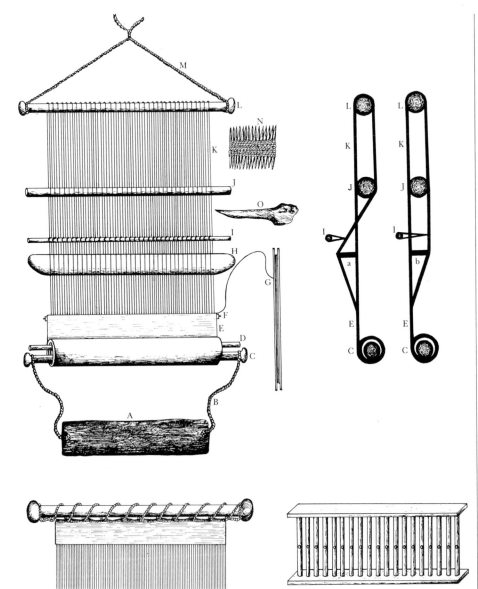

Far left Backstrap loom (*telar de cintura*), also known as a stick loom (*telar de otate*). Warp threads are wound directly round the loom bars to produce cloth with side selvages only.

A backstrap
B cord attaching backstrap to loom
C front loom bar
D rolling stick
E web of woven cloth
F tenter attached with thorns to underside of web
G weft thread wound on to shuttle stick, or bobbin
H batten
I heddle attached with thread to selected warps
J shed stick
K warp threads
L back loom bar
M cord attaching loom to tree or post
N comb
O bone pick

Left The principle of weaving: warp threads seen in side view forming (a) the shed, and (b) the countershed. These openings are enlarged by the batten, which also serves to beat down the weft.

Bottom left When warp threads are attached to the loom bars by cords, cloth with four selvages is produced. Weavers often initiate a weaving with a short section, or heading, at one end; the loom is then reversed so that the weaving may be continued from the opposite end.

Bottom right Rigid heddle, used instead of a stick heddle in some sash-weaving villages. Stiff twigs, drilled in the centre with small holes and fixed to an upper and lower bar of wood, serve to support the warp threads.

Appendix 2 Weaving techniques

Weaving is the interlacing of two sets of threads at right angles. Balanced cloth is created when the warp and the weft are equal in number and thickness. Warp- or weft-faced cloth occurs when the threads of one set are thicker or more numerous than those of the other set. (In the diagrams the warp is drawn vertically and the weft horizontally.)

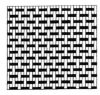

1 *Plain* (or *tabby*). Each weft thread passes over and under one warp thread.

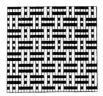

2 *Basket* (or *extended tabby*). Warp and weft threads move in equal groups of two or more.

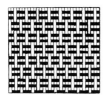

3 *Semi-basket.* One element is more numerous than the other. Here two weft threads cross one warp thread.

4 *Tapestry.* Widely spaced warp threads are covered by weft threads of different colours; these do not travel from selvage to selvage but move across selected areas only. With *kelim* junctures weft threads are turned back around warp threads, as here, creating vertical slits in the cloth. (This technique may also be used to create vertical neck openings.) Alternatively, weft threads may be turned round a common warp thread, or else linked together.

5 *End-to-end warp locking.* Short warp threads, generally of different colours, are linked together.

6 *Double weaving.* Two layers of differently coloured warp threads are periodically interchanged. One layer has two sheds operated by two heddles; the second has two sheds operated by one heddle and a shed stick. Pointed pattern sticks are also employed. Each warp thread is plain-woven with a weft thread of the same colour. Patterning is identical on both sides of the cloth, but the positions of ground and motifs are reversed (i.e. a red goat on a white ground becomes a white goat on a red ground).

7 *Gauze.* An open lace-like effect is produced when selected warp threads are crossed by hand and secured by the weft. There are many variations according to the complexity of manipulations. Weavers sometimes employ several heddles. Often gauze- and plain-weaving are combined, as here.

8 *Weft-wrap openwork.* One or more weft threads are wrapped round a group of warp threads to create openings in the cloth. Generally the technique is combined with plain-weaving, as here.

9 *Curved weaving. Quechquémitl*-weavers in parts of the Puebla highlands are able, by converting a group of warp threads to weft threads, to create cloth which is shaped at one corner of one end.

10 *Twill.* Diagonal lines are formed as warp threads are regularly positioned to the left or right of successive weft threads. When two warp threads pass over, then under, two weft threads, 2/2 twill is created, as here. Many variations are possible.

11 *Warp patterning.* Warp threads, manipulated by hand, are periodically made to cross varying numbers of weft threads to form raised patterning in the cloth.

12 *Brocade patterning.* Supplementary brocading threads are used to create super-structural patterning. They need not travel from selvage to selvage. Often brocading is combined with plain weaving, as here.

13 *Confite* (*confitillo*, looped weft, or pile weaving). Supplementary weft threads are looped with a pick to form raised super-structural patterning. Here the technique is combined with plain weaving.

Appendix 3 Embroidery stitches

Satin stitches, or flat stitches

1 *Satin.* Stitches may lie in any direction.
(a) With *reversible satin* thread travels back across the underside of cloth.
(b) *Surface satin* (*sham satin, laid satin*) is more economical as very little thread shows on the underside.

2 *Fishbone.* Two opposing rows of oblique satin stitches.

3 *Long and short.* Shading and filling device often used for variations of colour.

4 *Stem.* The needle is brought out to the left of stitches which proceed upwards. (When the needle is brought out to the right, the stitch is termed *outline*.)

5 *Back.* Each stitch touches the previous one.

6 *Running.* Stitch used for *pepenado*.

7 *Double running.* A second series of running stitches fills in the spaces between the first.

8 *Darning.* Ground threads are counted.

Looped stitches

9 *Chain.* Stitches form an interlocking line or filling; achieved by hand and sewing-machine.

10 *Blanket* (*open buttonhole*). Often used for edging cloth.

11 *Feather.* Line stitch worked by making a blanket stitch on either side of the line.

Crossed stitches

12 *Cross.* Ground threads are counted. Each cross may be completed individually in two movements. Alternatively, when large areas are worked, rows of single stitches may be worked diagonally from left to right and crossed on the return.

13 *Long-armed cross.* Worked from left to right to resemble a close plait. Each stitch must be completed before the next is begun.

14 *Herringbone.* Worked from left to right.

Knotted stitches

15 *French knots.* Thread is twisted twice round the needle before it is taken back through the cloth close to where it had emerged.

Couching
Technique open to many variations whereby delicate, metallic or thick threads are sewn on to the ground material with other threads. Couching stitches include chain, stem and feather.

16 *Plain couching.* Laid satin stitches kept in place with simple couching stitches.

Glossary

altiplano — High plateau of central Mexico.

amate — Bark paper (from the Náhuatl amatl).

añil — Indigo (Indigofera anil).

appliqué — Technique whereby shaped sections of cloth are stitched to a cloth background.

artisela — Artificial silk.

ayate — Square or rectangular carrying-cloth (from the Náhuatl ayatl).

batik — Method for resist-dyeing cloth: designs are created by applying a waxy substance to selected areas, rendering them impervious to dye.

calzón — In Spain a term for knee-length breeches, but in Mexico describing the trousers resembling long drawers which are widely worn by Indian men.

calzoncillo — Underpants, or long drawers.

calzonera — Over-trousers, usually with buttons down the sides.

caracol — See Purpura patula pansa.

Cenote — Sacred well at Chichén Itzá.

chamarro — Woollen top-garment, with or without sleeves, worn in the Chiapas highlands.

chaparreras — Open-sided leather leggings or over-trousers, abbreviated in the USA to chaps.

charro — In Spain the term denoted a peasant from the province of Salamanca, but in Mexico it is applied to horsemen; modern-day charros retain a showy style of dress.

chichicastle — Shrub supplying bast fibre (Urtica caracasana).

china poblana — Nineteenth-century female type with a distinctive and showy way of dressing.

cotón — Male shirt or tunic with sleeves.

coyuche — Natural brown cotton (Gossypium mexicanum; from the Náhuatl coyoichcatl).

Creole — Colonial and nineteenth-century term for someone of Spanish parentage born in Mexico; loosely applied also to people of mixed blood.

cuadrillé — Square-meshed factory cloth for embroidery.

enagua — Woman's skirt with waistband of European origin.

encomienda — System whereby Indians were entrusted after the Conquest to Spanish settlers, or encomenderos.

enredo — Wrap-around skirt of pre-Conquest origin with many alternative Spanish and Indian names.

fuchina — Commercial purple-coloured aniline dye.

gabán — Small sarape with head opening for men.

hacendado — Hacienda owner.

hacienda — Country estate.

henequén — Strictly sisal from Agave fourcroydes; loosely any agave fibre irrespective of species.

huipil — Woman's sleeveless tunic (from the Náhuatl huipilli). See p. 214 for constructions.

huipil de tapar — Head-dress worn by Zoque women in Chiapas.

huipil grande — Head-dress worn by Zapotec women in Tehuantepec and Juchitán, Oaxaca.

ikat — Method for tie-dyeing yarn.

ixtle — Fibre from several species of agave.

jorongo — Small sarape with head opening for men.

kelim joins — Vertical weft-joins in tapestry-woven cloth (See Appendix 2).

kelim slot neck opening — Vertical neck opening formed during weaving.

lechuguilla — Fibre from Agave lecheguilla.

macramé — Fringe or trimming of knotted thread.

maguey — Popular term for the Mexican agave which includes some 200 species.

mamey — Fruit from the tree Mammea americana.

manga — Cape; nineteenth-century examples were very ornate.

manta — Spanish term used after the Conquest to describe Indian mantles and webs of cloth; today it signifies unbleached cotton cloth, or calico.

mestizo — Mexican of mixed European and Indian descent.

negative design — Design represented by the ground material when surrounding areas have been filled in with embroidery or other means.

obraje — Privately owned textile factory where workers were often exploited.

ombré dyeing — Technique for producing shaded yarn.

paliacate — Bandanna handkerchief.

papelillo — Beads of paper-thin glass.

passementerie — Costume trimming, often of gold or silver lace.

peninsulares — Spaniards inhabiting Mexico but born in Spain.

pepenado — Running stitch on a flat or gathered ground.

percale — Commercial woven cotton fabric, often printed.

peyote — Halucinatory cactus (Lophophora williamsii), highly valued by the Huichol and gathered by peyoteros, or peyote pilgrims.

pita — Fibre from several species of agave and, in the past, yucca.

plangi — Method for patterning cloth by tie-dyeing.

posahuanco — Term for wrap-around skirt used in the Mixteca.

Purpura patula pansa — Shellfish dye.

quechquémitl — Woman's cape-like shoulder garment of pre-Conquest origin. See p. 212 for constructions.

quetzal — Bird with iridescent green plumage and long tail-feathers (from the Náhuatl quetzalli).

quetzaltalpiloni — Aztec hair ornament, showing status and military prowess, consisting of two quetzal-feather pom-poms on a ribbon.

randa — Decorative stitching used to join garment webs.

rebozo — Rectangular shawl.

retablo — Reredos, altarpiece.

rodete — Head-dress of cords.

sarape — Blanket, often with an opening for the head.

servilleta — Cloth, often used for ceremonial purposes or to cover food.

soyate — Flattened tube made from palm-leaf strands for use with cloth sashes.

Tacuate — Term applied to Mixtec Indians from the region of Santa María Zacatepec, Oaxaca.

tamal — Sweet or savoury food of ground maize (from the Náhuatl tamalli).

tilma — Man's rectangular cape of pre-Conquest origin (from the Náhuatl tilmatli).

tortilla — Flat cake of ground maize.

xicolli — Pre-Conquest sleeveless male garment variously described as a front-opening jacket and a closed tunic.

Bibliography

Abbreviations

ADV	Akademische Druck- und Verlagsanstalt
CIW	Carnegie Institution of Washington
HMAI	*Handbook of Middle American Indians*
INAH	Instituto Nacional de Antropología e Historia
INI	Instituto Nacional Indigenista
MNA	Museo Nacional de Antropología
MNAIP	Museo Nacional de Artes e Industrias Populares (INI)
PMAAE	Papers of the Peabody Museum of American Archaeology and Ethnology
SEP	Secretaría de Educación Pública
SI	Smithsonian Institution
SUP	Stanford University Press
UCP	University of California Press
UChP	University of Chicago Press
UNAM	Universidad Nacional Autónoma de México
UOP	University of Oklahoma Press
USGPO	US Government Printing Office
UTP	University of Texas Press

ANAWALT, PATRICIA RIEFF
'The *xicolli*: an analysis of a ritual garment', *Actas del 41 Congreso Internacional de Americanistas* 2: 223–35, México DF, 1976
'The Ethnic History of the Toltecs as Reflected in their Clothing', unpub. paper, 43 International Congress of Americanists, Vancouver, 1979
'Costume and Control: Aztec sumptuary laws', *Archaeology* 33 (1): 33–43, New York, 1980
Indian Clothing Before Cortés: Mesoamerican Costumes from the Codices, UOP, Norman, 1981

ANDERSON, RUTH MATILDA
Hispanic Costume 1480–1530, The Hispanic Society of America, New York, 1979

ANONYMOUS CONQUEROR
'Narrative of Some Things of New Spain ...', trans., notes Marshall H. Saville, *Documents and Narratives concerning the Discovery and Conquest of Latin America* (1), The Cortes Society, New York, 1917

BARBA DE PIÑA CHAN, BEATRIZ, and MARTÍNEZ DEL RÍO DE REDO, MARITA
Alhajas Mexicanas, Artes de México (165), México DF, 1973

BARTON, MARY
Impressions of Mexico with Brush and Pen, Methuen and Co. Ltd, London, 1911

BAZANT, JAN
'Evolución de la industria textil poblana 1544–1845', *Historia Mexicana* 13: 437–516, México DF, 1964

BEALS, RALPH LEON
The Contemporary Culture of the Cáhita Indians, SI, Bureau of American Ethnology, Bul. 142, USGPO, Washington, 1945

BENÍTEZ, FERNANDO
Los indios de México, 4 vols, Ediciones Era SA, México DF, 1970–2

BENNETT, WENDELL CLARK, and ZINGG, ROBERT MOWRY
The Tarahumara, an Indian Tribe of Northern Mexico, UChP, Chicago, 1935

BIRD, JUNIUS B.
'New World fabric production and the distribution of the backstrap loom', *Irene Emery Roundtable on Museum Textiles, 1977 proceedings ...*, 115–26, Textile Museum, Washington, 1979

BORAH, WOODROW
Silk Raising in Colonial Mexico, Ibero-Americana (20), UCP, Berkeley, 1943

BROCKLEHURST, THOMAS UNETT
Mexico To-day ..., John Murray, London, 1883

BROUDY, ERIC
The Book of Looms: a History of the Handloom from Ancient Times to the Present, Studio Vista, London, 1979

BRUCE, ROBERT D.
Lacandon Dream Symbolism, 2 vols, Ediciones Euroamericanas Klaus Thiele, México DF, 1975–9

BRUHN, WOLFGANG, and TILKE, MAX
A Pictorial History of Costume: a Survey of Costume of all Periods and Peoples ..., Praeger, New York, 1955

BULLOCK, WILLIAM
Six Months' Residence and Travels in Mexico, John Murray, London, 1824

BURGOA, FRAY FRANCISCO de
Geográfica descripción ... (1674), 2 vols, Archivo General de la Nación, Pubs 25–6, México DF, 1934

BURNHAM, DOROTHY K.
Warp and Weft: a Textile Terminology, Royal Ontario Museum, Toronto, 1980

CALDERÓN DE LA BARCA, FRANCES
Life in Mexico ... (1843), Dent and Sons, London, 1970

CANCIAN, FRANK
Economics and Prestige in a Maya Community: The Religious Cargo System in Zinacantan, SUP, Stanford, 1965

CARRILLO Y GARIEL, ABELARDO
Indumentaria colonial a través de la pintura, Ediciones de Arte 5, INAH, México DF, 1948
El Traje en la Nueva España, Dirección de Monumentos Coloniales, Pub. 7, México DF, 1959

CASTELLÓ YTURBIDE, TERESA, *et al.*
El Rebozo, Artes de México (142), México DF, 1971

CENSO GENERAL DE POBIACIÓN IX (unpub.)
Secretaría de Industria y Comercio, Dirección General de Estadística, México DF, 1970

CHRISTENSEN, BODIL
'Otomí Looms and *Quechquemitls* ...', *Notes on Middle American Archaeology and Ethnology* (78): 122–42, CIW, Division of Historical Research, Washington, 1947
'Los Otomíes del Estado de Puebla', *Huastecos, totonacos y sus vecinos*, 259–68, Revista Mexicana de Estudios Antropológicos 13, México DF, 1953

CLAVIJERO, FRANCISCO JAVIER
Historia antigua de México, 4 vols, Editorial Porrua, México DF, 1945

CODICES
Codex Dresden (Royal Library, Dresden), fac. edn, ADV, Graz, 1975
Codex Florentino see Sahagún, Fray Bernardino de
Codex Madrid, or *Tro-Cortesianus* (Museo de América, Madrid), fac. edn, ADV, Graz, 1967
Codex Mendoza (Bodleian Library, Oxford), fac. edn, 3 vols, ed. James Cooper Clark, Waterlow and Sons, London, 1938
Codex Zouche-Nuttall (British Museum, London), fac. edn, Dover Publications Inc., New York, 1975

COE, MICHAEL D.
Mexico, Thames and Hudson, London, 1962

COOK DE LEONARD, CARMEN
'Minor Arts of the Classic Period in Central Mexico', *HMAI* 10: 206–27, UTP, Austin, 1971

CORDRY, DONALD B., and DOROTHY M.
Costumes and Textiles of the Aztec Indians of the Cuetzalan Region, Puebla, Mexico, Southwest Museum Papers (14), Los Angeles, 1940
Costumes and Weaving of the Zoque Indians of Chiapas, Mexico, ibid. (15), Los Angeles, 1941
Mexican Indian Costumes, UTP, Austin, 1968

CORTÉS, HERNÁN
Hernán Cortés: Letters from Mexico, trans., ed. A.R. Pagden, Grossman, New York, 1971

COVARRUBIAS, MIGUEL
Mexico South: The Isthmus of Tehuantepec, Alfred A. Knopf, New York, 1946

DECAEN (ed., pub.)
México y sus alrededores: Colección de vistas, trajes y monumentos, México DF, 1855–6

DÍAZ BOLIO, JOSÉ
'La serpiente de cascabel en los huipiles de Yucatán', *La serpiente emplumada*, 312–18, Eje de Culturas, Mérida, 1964

DÍAZ DEL CASTILLO, BERNAL
The True History of the Conquest of New Spain, 5 vols, introd., trans. A.P. Maudslay, Hakluyt Society, London, 1908–16

DONKIN, R.A.
Spanish Red: an Ethnographical Study of Cochineal and the Opuntia Cactus, Transactions of the American Philosophical Society 67 (5), Philadelphia, 1977

DRUCKER, SUSANA
Cambio de indumentaria: la estructura social y el abandono de la vestimenta indígena en la villa de Santiago Jamiltepec, Colección de Antropología Social (3), INI, México DF, 1963

DUBY, GERTRUDE
Chiapas indígena, UNAM, México DF, 1961

DURÁN, FRAY DIEGO
Historia de las Indias de Nueva España ..., 2 vols, Editorial Porrua, México DF, 1967
Book of the Gods and Rites of the Ancient Calendar, eds, trans. D. Heyden and F. Horcacitas, UOP, Norman, 1971

EMERY, IRENE
The Primary Structures of Fabrics, The Textile Museum, Washington, 1966

ENCISO, JORGE
Designs Motifs of Ancient Mexico, Dover Publications Inc., New York, 1953
Designs from Pre-Columbian Mexico, ibid., 1971

FIELD, FREDERICK V.
Pre-Hispanic Mexican Stamp Designs, ibid., 1974

FUENTE, JULIO DE LA
'Los Zapotecos de Choapan, Oaxaca', *Anales del INAH* 2: 143–205, México DF, 1947
Yalalag: una villa zapoteca serrana, INAH, México DF, 1949
'Cambios de indumentaria en tres áreas biculturales', *Boletín Técnico* 1 (2) 3–21, INI, México DF, 1958

GAGE THOMAS
The English American: A New Survey of the

West Indies (1648), ed. A.P. Newton, George Routledge and Sons Ltd, London, 1928

Thomas Gage's Travels in the New World, ed. J.E.S. Thompson, UOP, Norman, 1969

GANN, THOMAS
In an Unknown Land, Duckworth and Co., London, 1924

GARCÍA CUBAS, ANTONIO
The Republic of Mexico in 1876, trans. G.F. Henderson, La Enseñanza Printing Office, México DF, 1876

GARCÍA VARGAS, MARÍA
'Técnicas textiles de San Bernardino Contla', *Boletín* 2: 79–100, Departamento de Investigación de las Tradiciones Populares, Dirección General de Arte Popular, SEP, México DF, 1975

GERHARD, PETER
'Shellfish Dye in America', *Actas y Memorias del 35 Congreso de Americanistas* 3: 177–91, INAH, México DF, 1964

GIBSON, CHARLES
Tlaxcala in the Sixteenth Century, Yale University Press, New Haven, 1952

GRIFFEN, WILLIAM B.
Culture Change and Shifting Population in Central Northern Mexico, Anthropological Papers (13), University of Arizona Press, Tucson, 1969

GUITERAS-HOLMES, CALIXTA
Perils of the Soul: The World View of a Tzotzil Indian, The Free Press of Glencoe Inc., New York, 1961

GUTIÉRREZ, TONATIÚH, and ELECTRA L. MOMPRADÉ
Indumentaria tradicional indígena, Historia General del Arte Mexicano V, Editorial Hermes SA, México DF, 1976

GUZMÁN, EULALIA
'Huipil y maxtlatl', *Esplendor del México Antiguo* 2: 957–82, Centro de Investigaciones Antropológicas de México, México DF, 1959

HARVEY, H.R., and KELLY, ISABEL
'The Totonac', *HMAI* 8: 638–81, UTP, Austin, 1969

HERNÁNDEZ, FRANCISCO
Obras completas; historia natural en la Nueva España, 3 vols, UNAM, México DF, 1959–60

HERRERA Y TORDESILLAS, ANTONIO DE
Historia general …, 4 vols, Madrid, 1601–15

HEYDEN, DORIS
Indumentaria antigua de Oaxaca, Colección Breve (10), MNA, México DF, 1972
'The *quechquemitl* as a symbol of power in the Mixtec codices', *Vicus Cuadernos …* 1: 5–24, México DF, 1977

JETER, JAMES, and JUELKE, PAULA MARIE
The Saltillo Sarape, exh. cat., Museum of Art, Santa Barbara, 1978

JOHNSON, IRMGARD WIETLANER
'El quechquemitl y el huipil', *Huastecos, totonacos y sus vecinos*, 241–57, 1953. *See* Christensen, Bodil
'Hilado y tejido'. *Esplendor del México antiguo* 1: 439–79, 1959. *See* Guzmán, Eulalia
'Textiles', *The Prehistory of the Tehuacan Valley* 2: 189–226, UTP, Austin, 1967
'Basketry and Textiles', *HMAI* 10: 297–321, UTP, Austin, 1971
'Vestido y adorno', *Lo efímero y lo eterno del arte popular mexicano* 1: 161–267, Fondo Editorial de la Plástica Mexicana, México DF, 1971
Design Motifs on Mexican Indian Textiles, 2 vols, ADV, Graz, 1976

Los textiles de la Cueva de la Candelaria, Coahuila, Colección Científica (51), INAH, México DF, 1977
'The ring-warp loom in Mexico', *Irene Emery Roundtable …*, 135–59, 1979. *See* Bird, J.B.

JOHNSON, IRMGARD WIETLANER, and FRANCO, JOSÉ LUIS
'Un huipil precolombino de Chilapa, Guerrero', *Revista Mexicana de Estudios Antropológicos* 11: 279–91, México DF, 1967

JOHNSON, JEAN B., *et al.*
'Industrias y tejidos de Tuxpan, Jalisco', *Anales del INAH* 14: 149–217, México DF, 1961

KAMPEN, MICHAEL EDWIN
The Sculptures of El Tajín, Veracruz, Mexico, University of Florida Press, Gainesville, 1972

KELLY, ISABEL, and PALERM, ANGEL
The Tajín Totonac, Part I, SI, Institute of Social Anthropology Pub. 13, USGPO, Washington, 1952

KEREMITSIS, DAWN
La industria textil mexicana en el siglo XIX, Sep-Setentas, México DF, 1973

LANDA, FRAY DIEGO DE
Relación de las cosas de Yucatán, trans., notes Alfred M. Tozzer, Papers PMAAE 18, Harvard University, Cambridge, Mass., 1941

LARSEN, JACK, *et al.*
The Dyer's Art: Ikat, Batik and Plangi, Van Nostrand Reinhold, New York, 1976

LECHUGA, RUTH D.
Una investigación entre los Otomíes de Querétaro sobre las técnicas del plangi, Cuadernos de Trabajo, MNAIP, México DF, 1978
Las técnicas textiles en el México indígena and *La indumentaria en el México indígena*, Fondo Nacional para el Fomento de las Artesanías, México DF, 1982
El traje indígena de México: su evolución desde la época prehispánica hasta la actualidad, Panorama Editorial SA, México DF, 1982

LINATI, CLAUDIO
Trajes civiles, militares y religiosos de México, Editorial Innovación SA, México DF, 1978

LUMHOLTZ, CARL
'Symbolism of the Huichol Indians', *Memoirs of the American Museum of Natural History* 3, Anthropology 2 (1): 1–228, New York, 1900
Unknown Mexico, 2 vols, Macmillan and Co., London, 1903
'Decorative Art of the Huichol Indians', *Memoirs of the American Museum of Natural History* 3, Anthropology 2 (3): 279–327, New York, 1904
New Trails in Mexico, T. Fisher Unwin, New York, 1912

McGEE, W.J.
The Seri Indians, Bureau of American Ethnology Annual Report 17 (1), USGPO, Washington, 1898

MacLEOD, MURDO J.
Spanish Central America: A Socioeconomic History, 1520–1720, UCP, Berkeley, 1973

MAHLER, JOY
'Garments and Textiles of the Maya Lowlands', *HMAI* 3: 581–93, UTP, Austin, 1965

MAPELLI MOZZI, CARLOTA, and CASTELLÓ YTURBIDE, TERESA
El traje indígena en México, 2 vols, INAH, México DF, 1965–8

MARÍN DE PAALEN, ISABEL
Etno-artesanías y arte popular, Historia

General del Arte Mexicano IV, Editorial Hermes SA, México DF, 1974

MASTACHE DE ESCOBAR, ALBA G.
Técnicas prehispánicas del tejido, Serie Investigaciones (20), INAH, México DF, 1971

MENA, RAMÓN
El Zarape, Anales del Museo de Arqueología, Historia y Etnografía 3, México DF, 1925

MENDEZ, SANTIAGO
'The Maya Indians of Yucatán in 1861', *Indian Notes and Monographs* 9: 143–95, ed. F.W. Hodge, Museum of the American Indian, Heye Foundation, New York, 1919–20

MODIANDO, NANCY
Indian Education in the Chiapas Highlands, Holt, Rinehart and Winston Inc., New York, 1973

MORLEY, SYLVANUS G.
The Ancient Maya, rev. George W. Brainerd, SUP, Stanford, 1956

MOTOLINÍA (FRAY TORIBIO DE BENAVENTE)
Memoriales …, ed. Luis García Pimentel, Documentos Históricos de México 1, México DF, 1903
Motolinia's History of the Indians of New Spain, trans., notes F.B. Steck, Academy of American Franciscan History, Washington, 1951

NEBEL, CARLOS
Voyage pittoresque et archéologique dans la partie la plus intéressante du Mexique, Paris, 1836

NUTTALL, ZELIA
'A Curious Survival in Mexico of the Use of the *Purpura* Shell-fish for Dyeing', *Putnam Anniversary Volume*, 368–84, New York, 1909

PASO Y TRONCOSO, FRANCISCO DEL (ed.)
Papeles de Nueva España, ser. 2, 6 vols, Geografía y Estadistica, Madrid, 1905–6

PENNINGTON, CAMPBELL W.
The Tepehuan of Chihuahua: Their Material Culture, University of Utah Press, Salt Lake City, 1969
The Tarahumar of Mexico: Their Environment and Material Culture, ibid., 1974

PENNINGTON, CAMPBELL W., and IRIGOYEN R., FRUCTUOSO
Unpublished letter, 1982

POZAS ARCINIEGA, RICARDO
Chamula: un pueblo indio de los altos de Chiapas, 2 vols, INI, México DF, 1977

RANDS, ROBERT L., and RANDS, BARBARA C.
'Pottery Figurines of the Maya Lowlands', *HMAI* 2: 535–60, UTP, Austin, 1965

REDFIELD, ROBERT
A Village that Chose Progress: Chan Kom Revisited, UChP, Chicago, 1962

ROTH, H. LING
Studies in Primitive Looms, Bankfield Museum Notes, Halifax, 1934

SAHAGÚN, FRAY BERNARDINO DE
Codex Florentino: General History of the Things of New Spain, ed., trans. Arthur J.O. Anderson and Charles E. Dibble, Monographs … (14) parts 2–13, University of Utah and School of American Research, Santa Fe, 1950–69

SARTORIUS, C.
Mexico and the Mexicans …, Trübner and Co., London, 1859

SOUSTELLE, JACQUES
Daily Life of the Aztecs on the Eve of the Spanish Conquest, Weidenfeld and Nicolson, London, 1963

SPINDEN, HERBERT J.
A Study of Maya Art …, Memoirs PMAAE 6, Harvard University, Cambridge, Mass., 1913

STAPLEY, MILDRED
Tejidos y bordados populares españoles, Editorial Voluntad SA, Madrid, 1924

STARR, FREDERICK
Indians of Southern Mexico: An Ethnographic Album, Chicago, 1899
'Notes upon the Ethnography of Southern Mexico', *Proceedings of the Davenport Academy of Natural Sciences* 8–9, Davenport, Iowa, 1900–2
In Indian Mexico, Forbes and Co., Chicago, 1908

START, LAURA E.
The McDougall Collection of Indian Textiles from Guatemala and Mexico, Occasional Papers on Technology 2, Pitt Rivers Museum, University of Oxford, Oxford, 1980

TAX, SOL, JIMÉNEZ MORENO, WIGBERTO, *et al.*
Heritage of Conquest, the Ethnology of Middle America, The Free Press, Glencoe, Ill., 1952

TOOR, FRANCES
A Treasury of Mexican Folkways, Crown Publishers, New York, 1976

TUROK, MARTA
'Diseño y simbolo en el huipil ceremonial de Magdalenas, Chiapas', *Boletín 3*, Departamento de Investigación de las Tradiciones Populares, Dirección General de Arte Popular, SEP, México DF, 1974

TYLOR, SIR EDWARD B.
Anahuac; or Mexico and the Mexicans, Ancient and Modern, Longman, Green, Longman and Roberts, London, 1861

VOGT, EVON Z., *et al.*
HMAI 7–8, *Ethnology* (1–2), vol. ed. Evon Z. Vogt, gen. ed. Robert Wauchope, UTP, Austin, 1969

WEIDITZ, CHRISTOPH
Das Trachtenbuch des Christoph Weiditz von seinen Reisen nach Spanien, 1529 …, ed. Dr T. Hampe, Berlin and Leipzig, 1927

ZINGG, ROBERT MOWRY
The Huichols: Primitive Artists, G.E. Stechert and Co., New York, 1938

Index

References in italic are to illustrations.